COUNTER INSURGENCY & QUEST FOR PEACE

A COMPARATIVE STUDY

COUNTER INSURGENCY & QUEST FOR PEACE

A COMPARATIVE STUDY

Colonel Anil Athale (Retd)

(Established 1870)

United Service Institution of India
New Delhi

Vij Books India Pvt Ltd
New Delhi, India

Published   by

Vij Books India Pvt Ltd
(Publishers, Distributors & Importers)
2/19, Ansari Road, Darya Ganj
New Delhi - 110002
Phones: 91-11-43596460, 91-11-47340674
Fax: 91-11-47340674
e-mail : vijbooks@rediffmail.com
web: www.vijbooks.com

Copyright © 2012, United Service Institution of India, New Delhi

ISBN: 978-93-81411-11-7

CONTENTS

ACKNOWLEDGEMENT

A work that spanned close to two and half decades naturally has many 'Godfathers' that helped me along the way. This project is seeing the light of the day thanks to the Centre for Armed Forces Historical Research (CAFHR) at the United Services Institute, New Delhi and its staff that honoured me with first the General Palit and later the Chhatrapati Shivaji fellowship, from 2006 to 2010. Maj. Gen SCN Jatar (Retd) through Smt Vimalabai Jatar Trust helped me to travel to South Africa for a crucial input in this work.

This work was ably guided by Lt Gen Ashok Joshi, and but for his sharp intellect and great inputs, this would have remained at best a collection of anecdotes. Maj. Gen. Keshav Pendse was equally generous with his help in writing the book. I owe a great intellectual debt to late Lt Gen Eric Vas, a long time friend and associate in our think tank INPAD (Initiative for Peace and Disarmament). He was my guru. The second guru, who sharpened my analytical ability is Dr Sri Nandan Prasad, the former head of War Studies Division, where I worked for four years from 1986-1990. I owe a huge debt of gratitude to all of them.

Thanks are due to the great institution, the Indian Army, to which I very proudly belong, for it hosted and protected me in my over 15 trips to Kashmir from 1991 to 1999. It is impossible to name the Generals and other officers and men who never let me feel unwanted despite my status as a retired officer. I specially remember the help and encouragement by the then Army Chief, late General BC Joshi. Thanks are due to Dr. SD Pradhan of the Joint Intelligence Committee (later deputy National Security Advisor) for the Sri Lanka project. Mr AE Furness of the British Foreign Office was instrumental in making my Northern Ireland trip happen. Professor Peter Vale of Rhodes University and Prof. Sandy Africa were of immense help in arranging meetings in South Africa as well as giving their valuable input. Prof Vale's able student Ms Estelle Prinsloo was a tremendous help during that trip.

The support of my family was crucial, as always and thanks are due to my wife, Ms Gouri Athale, Asst Editor the Economic Times for polishing my language and accomplished daughter, Ms Ira Prem for diligently going over the manuscript and editing it.

I beg forgiveness in case I have missed out on some names, and wish to assure that it was not due to ungratefulness but due to memory lapse.

- Author

Introduction

I am happy to present this work, which is the result of close to twenty four years of study of insurgency. In 2006, I approached Major General DK Palit, VrC, FRGS and a dozen of military histories in India with a proposal to do a comparative study of the Indian experience in counterinsurgency. General Palit and the Board of Trustees of Gen. Palit Military Studies Trust at the United Services Institute (USI), New Delhi, were kind enough to accept my proposal. After working for close to two years, I felt the need to expand the scope of the work and added insurgency studies outside India. The USI was again approached and I was awarded the Chhatrapati Shivaji Fellowship at the USI's Centre for Armed Forces Historical Research. The duration of this fellowship was two years, i.e. from 2008 to 2010.

I entered the field of counterinsurgency by accident. In 1988, as a Joint director in War Studies division of Ministry of Defence (New Delhi) I was working on the research project dealing with the 1962 Sino-Indian War under the leadership of Dr. Sri Nandan Prasad.[1] In 1988, the joint director working on insurgency project, Dr. SD Pradhan,[2] was drafted to join the Joint Intelligence Committee. Dr. Prasad asked me to take over the project dealing with the insurgency in Mizoram in addition to my other duties. I was happy to take on this added responsibility and completed the project by 1990. The 200 page book is however held in government records and is a classified document. At the end of 1989, I was sent to Sri Lanka to study the operations of the Indian Peace Keeping Forces.

[1] Dr. Sri Nandan Prasad is a former director national archives and co-author of a 16 volume history of Indian Armed Forces in Second World War. He was the director of the project to research and write the history of post independence conflicts fought by India.

[2] Dr SD Pradhan later went on to become the chairman of Joint Intelligence Committee.

In 1991, I took voluntary premature retirement to devote my time to full-time research in defence and strategic studies. In 1991, alarmed at the adverse media coverage of the Army's operations in Kashmir, I offered to write for the media to correct the distorted picture. For the next seven years I regularly visited Jammu and Kashmir to study and write on the situation there. My study was published in 1997 in book form.[3] One thing led to another and in 1993 the British government invited me to visit Northern Ireland (July 1993) and the Joint Intelligence Committee asked me to do a research project on Sri Lanka in 1996-97. In 1994, a noted Gandhian and industrialist, late Navalmal Firodiya, encouraged me to undertake socio-economic development work in Kashmir as an antidote to insurgency; thus was born Project Hope. All this while, I continued to give feedback to the Indian Army on Kashmir. In 2006, I led a team of 15 social activists and journalists to the Chhattisgarh state to study the Naxalite problem there.

I was always fascinated by the success of the anti-Apartheid struggle in South Africa. In 2008, thanks to help from Prof. Peter Vale (Rhodes University, SA) and Prof Sandy Africa (University of Pretoria), I visited South Africa to understand the story of anti-Apartheid struggle. The visit was facilitated by Smt Vimlabai Jathar Trust with a travel grant.

The present work therefore is a cumulative effort of the last twenty four years of study, fieldwork and thinking.

It would not be an exaggeration to say that insurgencies, or Little Wars are likely to be with us for a very, very long time. The reasons are many and range from the globalisation of rising expectations to demographic explosions. Paraphrasing a very seminal observation by General Palit on the 1973 Yom Kippur War, that tactics and strategy have been reduced to 'weapon dialectics'(the Arab and Israeli tactics and strategy were dictated by the range of anti aircraft missile shields), I would say that today, conflicts are again seeing a rise of ideology as a dominant force. Present day conflicts can well be understood as a dialectic between reason/peace vs. revolution/ violence. Increasingly the line between war, insurgency and terrorism is being blurred.

---

[3] Athale Anil Colonel, 'Let the Jhelum Smile Again', Aditya Prakashan, Mumbai, 1997.

I have had operational experience in field in the North East and Kashmir at micro level as Infantry Company Commander. The study of internal revolts or insurgencies and peace processes that include counterinsurgency or use of force, falls firmly in the domain of social sciences. But before we undertake the study proper, it is necessary to understand the nature of social sciences and problems that are inherent in the study of any social phenomenon. The social sciences use natural sciences as a paradigm and aspire to imitate them. Natural events occur automatically and follow natural laws. They are not goal oriented. The events and the inter-relationship between them are predictable. Social phenomena are on the other hand, goal directed. There exists a direct relationship between natural laws and natural events, while social events need a motive.

In addition, there are several facets of social sciences that need to be reiterated. Natural sciences tend to converge-physics with chemistry and with biology etc., while the study of social sciences has a tendency to become divergent- economics becoming independent of politics and so on. Social sciences also do not have the ability to isolate phenomena for a cause-effect study. In addition, in social sciences there is a marked relationship between various causes- economics impacting on social or political impacting both. There is a comparatively lower occurrence of such impacts in the natural sciences. In social sciences one cannot claim to be a detached observer but a part of the milieu and hence a participant. A degree of subjectivity is therefore inherent. In light of this it is indeed necessary to clearly and unambiguously state one's own moral compass and philosophical moorings.

Since social phenomena typically do not lend themselves to laboratory-level experimentation, repeatability and certainty of results, the best that a social scientist can look for and claim, is coherence. At a philosophical level we could well say that the very process of acquisition of knowledge is to see coherence- in nature or within the area of human behaviour, which is what social sciences are all about.

The tendency of social sciences to look for laws and rules is fraught with danger. As in any inexact science, this form of rigidity of method can lead to greater distortion rather than if one adhered to more modest claims of coherence. Economists and some behaviourists have put forward such claims. But real life experience tells us that the so-called laws and rules are more exceptions than a rules. Reasonableness, rationality and explanation, are the main criteria for this research. [4]

Study of insurgency/counter insurgency and related peace processes, has at its foundation the belief in the desirability of preservation of the state. According to Thomas Hobbes (Leviathan) some form of state has always existed in human history, whether it is a tribal chief, kingship, dictatorship or democracy.[5] In the current epoch of history of humankind, the state seems to be an enduring and useful institution next only to family (nuclear or otherwise). The very longevity of the existence of the state in human history shows its usefulness to humanity. Revolts against 'state' are thus a destabilising factor. But this brings in a factor of 'legitimacy' of the state.

The state faces challenges at two levels, individual and group. When an individual acts against the law, (that is based on the prevailing norms or social consensus) the state uses its coercive machinery of police forces and brings the culprit to book. Judiciary tries the case and awards punishment. This is an accepted norm and the state's use of force or violence against an individual is accepted. But for legitimacy, the judiciary must be independent and fair, something that is monitored by human rights groups all over the world. However there is a difficulty when a state, hiding behind the 'sovereignty' principle, enacts discriminatory laws. Unfortunately there is as yet no global consensus on this issue and an individual fighting or violating an unfair law can well be classed as a 'freedom fighter' and not a criminal.

When a group resorts to organised violence and challenges the state, it is termed as an insurgency. There is a common perception that 'one man's terrorist/insurgent is another man's freedom fighter'. This is moral relativism at its worst and has done greater damage to world peace than even nuclear weapons. If a state is 'legitimate' then an armed challenge to it is illegitimate. The twin bedrocks of a state's legitimacy are democracy, that guarantees individuals their fundamental rights and freedoms and the federal principle

---

[4] Kaplan A, "The Conduct of an Enquiry', Sachin Pub. Jaipur (India), 1980
[5] Hobbes, Thomas, 'Leviathan', EP Dutton &Co, New York 1950.

that grants to groups/tribes/sects/faiths, the right for cultural expression and freedom to practice their faith, use their language and lead a collective life of their choice. When a state meets these two basic criteria, it has unmatched legitimacy and the use of force to overthrow it is insurgency/terrorism. The world is witness to the bloodbath that Europe went through in the last three centuries by application of the 'nation state' principle- even the two World Wars of the 20th century were essentially an intra-Europe affair.[6] The anarchy and bloodletting that the world saw in former Yugoslavia in the 1990s are examples of the absurdity of the 'nation state' principle. Ultimately world organisations had to intervene in former Yugoslavia to stem the rot.[7] Based on these two basic facts, the study that follows takes a position-though unstated, that stability of a state is a desirable goal and all insurgents/terrorists who use violence are NOT freedom fighters. Only those who are under the rule of illegitimate states- those that do not give fundamental rights or violate the federal principle, need be seen as freedom fighters.

The later part of the 20th century saw a process of globalisation that was often described in economic terms, but was a much more comprehensive process. The centrifugal forces of globalisation include the information revolution (instant and easy access), international trade, wide travel links due to the communication revolution, weapons with global effects and reach and issues like climate change that do not respect political boundaries.

The antithesis of these centrifugal force of globalisation viz. centripetal forces, have arisen essentially due to the fear of loss of identity that itself is rooted in the fear of change. The centripetal forces then congregate around issues of ethnicity, religion, language or history and begin to challenge the state from a secessionist platform.

The information revolution through satellite television and internet access at affordable prices has literally brought the world to our homes. This has given rise to revolts in the poorer parts of a state. These can be described

---

[6] Waltz, Kenneth, 'Man, the State & War', Columbia University, New York 1954.

[7] Magas, Branka, 'The Destruction of Yugoslavia: Tracking the Break-up 1980–1992', Verso, Great Britain, 1993. Woodward, Susan, L. 'Balkan Tragedy: Chaos & Dissolution after the Cold War', the Brookings Institution Press, Virginia, USA, 1995.

as 'aspiration'-induced rather than grievance based. Although insurgents take care to cloak their motives in suitable terms to claim victimhood, many Communist inspired revolts in less-developed parts of India use 'jealousy' as a spring board to resort to violence against the state. Underdevelopment or poverty has many reasons, ranging from lack of education, hard work and social cohesion. But the insurgents claim poverty to be a result of the rapacious policies of an unfair state and demand secession or attempt to overthrow the existing government.

Regional economic disparity is a major cause of internal violence. For instance, there is stark difference in economic prosperity between provinces on the Pacific seaboard and internal China. But in the case of China, the government and the Party ensure that no organisation other than 'state approved' ones are permitted, hence this may not happen. Stray instances of individual acts of terror have been reported. At what stage the cumulative effect of these isolated acts would lead to challenge of regime change is a matter of speculation. The jury is still out on the internal stability of China.[8]

The information revolution has also given birth to the 'Islamist revolt' that began with the 9/11 attack on the US and is continuing in Iraq, Pakistan, Afghanistan, Somalia, Thailand, Philippines and Nigeria. Where the Islamists are dispersed or are in tiny numbers, this has taken the route of terror campaigns in much of Europe and in India. The roots of this global revolt by some Islamists against the world order lay in the contradiction between the theologically ordained superiority of Islam as a religion and way of life vis-a-vis its presently hopeless power position in the world.[9] The memories of Islam's past glories and its present dismal state, attract individuals under militant banners worldwide. The present turmoil in the world variously called the war against terrorism, can be called a global protest movement by Muslims against their present low power status.

---

[8] *The Guardian* UK, 6 July 2009. Ethnic violence in China leaves 140 dead. Uighur protests over workers' deaths turn violent as mobs burn buses and attack Han residents in the western province. *The New York Times*, 15 July 2009. At a Factory, the spark for China's violence.

[9] The OIC or Organisation of Islamic Countries has been ineffective in stopping the invasions of its member states. Majority of the Islamic countries also stand at the bottom of the pyramid in terms of economic, social and educational indicators.

Macro-level understanding of the various issues in counter insurgency is essential, as, far too many studies on this subject, especially by military men, are more devoted to mechanics of counterinsurgency operations. This is like concentrating on the tactics, at the expense of strategic and policy areas. If there is a lack of understanding or flaw in strategy/policy then no amount of tactical brilliance can succeed. In fact a wrong strategy followed by brilliant tactics can actually bring about a greater disaster. To cite an example from Second World War, though not a counterinsurgency operation, the German attempt to conquer Russia is a good illustration. German neglect and mistakes in war strategy and policy led to defeat, despite their brilliant tactical conduct. Given the area and resources of Russia, the destruction of the Russian armed forces as a prelude to absorption of its territory was unattainable.[10] It is this that led to the ultimate debacle of the Third Reich. Similar neglect of overall strategy/policy has been a graveyard of military leaders and thinkers. The number of successful counterinsurgency campaigns can be counted on the fingers tips of one hand.

While military men (and a few women!) have been guilty of obsession with the tactical, social scientists and conflict resolution practitioners have ignored or wished away the necessity/importance of use of force. Peace process, in a holistic view, consists of the social/economic/political/psychological measures along with the military dimension. This study will encompass all these dimensions to paint a coherent picture and to avoid the pitfall of selective consideration of reality.

A word about the undeniable link between insurgency and terrorism is appropriate at this juncture. Ever since the September 11, 2001 attack on the US by terrorists of Al Qaeda, the world has been engulfed in a 'war on terror'. Often the words, terrorists and insurgents are used interchangeably. This is true to some extent, in that all terrorists are 'insurgents' since they intend to use force to overthrow the existing order. In the case of Islamist terrorists- their goal is to overthrow the world order and establish in its place an Islamic Caliphate. But the crucial difference between the two is that while the insurgents essentially target the counter-insurgent forces or

---

[10] Hart Liddell, 'History of the Second World War', Cassell, London 1970. p.709.

the functionaries of the state, the terrorists have no such compunctions and are ready to target unrelated people and objects, for destruction. The terrorists are in that sense closer to the 19th century anarchists.[11] However there are also commonalities. Terrorists, like insurgents, thrive on grievances and depend on the support of the people. Both groups operate secret cells and use the tactics of guerrilla warfare. Consequently, there is much that is in common between counter-insurgency and counter-terrorism. Our study is therefore of relevance to the present scenario since both insurgency and terrorism are major global concerns of the 21st century.

The layout of the book has been dictated by the difficulty in tracing the exact source of some pieces of information and thoughts. The format has been adopted to give some references in the body, with detailed biographical information in the end, categorised by subject. Though not very elegant, it is hoped that this will serve the interests of an informed reader, keen on further study.

A final word on the role of force is appropriate here. Counterinsurgency has a bad odour of violence. Civil society and many human rights groups look askance at use of force and violence that it engenders. But here is a soldier's dilemma- if a soldier does not use force in a combat situation, he has every chance of getting killed himself. While the force used by the soldier is roundly condemned, the insurgent gets away, literally, with murder. A soldier is not a murderer in uniform. Killing an unarmed person is as abhorrent to him as to any one else, but in an insurgency where the rules of war apply, and not those of the constitutional law, an unarmed citizen is often killed in cross-fire or by mistake. To hold only the soldier accountable is not just. Use of force against a violent, ideology driven insurgent is as necessary now as it was during the Second World War against Germany, driven by Nazi ideology. Realism dictates that force used at the right time and in right quantity may well obviate greater violence at a later date. Greater chance of success in achieving peace is the moral justification for

---

[11] Terrorism per se is not a new phenomenon for the world. Violence targeted at the non combatants and civilians has been used to create fear in the minds of people in the past as well. What is new is the fact that in a globalised world, the effect is widespread and opportunities are greater.

counterinsurgency as compared with the purist peace approach that opposes any use of force.

This is not a work that intends to go into micro level details and indulge in tree counting. The aim is to see the forests, rivers and hills. As a junior army officer I often wondered as to how a senior commander who visited a battalion for a brief period made a judgement on the efficiency level. After close to two and half decades of being in this business of studying insurgency, I now understand it. Experience teaches you to look at the exactly right place to find the weak spots and major trends. One can call it developing and eye or nose for the truth…

The approach of this book is historical analysis, though for ongoing insurgencies such as in Kashmir or Naxalism, the book may border on comments on current events. History is an 'exemplar' and if used as a tool of analysis of events, trends and personalities, gives us a coherent picture of reality. This does not mean that there is any kind of historical determinism or history repeats itself *mantra.* The biggest advantage of this approach is that it allows for hidden relationships between factors, even if the researcher has failed to spot them. If Marx could conjure up an entire universe based on economic determinism, using historical analysis is far closer to the real world.

Section 1 - Issues in Focus

Definitions, Logical Formulations and Methodology

The statement that man is a social animal is well known. It should be noted that man is also a violent animal! Before there is a charge of 'gender discrimination', let me hasten to add that when I use the term 'man', I am including women too. In India the symbol of strength is a female Goddess- *Durga* and retributive justice is meted out by *Kali*. There has never been a period in recorded and ancient history when in some corner or the other of this planet Earth, human beings were not slaughtering their own species.[1]

Conflicts and peace studies form part of Political Science. But Political Science, a discipline within the Social Sciences, is still at a pre-paradigmatic stage. There are differences on basic definitions, boundaries and accepted premises.[2] There is an endless debate between 'Realists' and 'Idealists'. Thomas Kuhn asserts that there is a major difference between Social and Natural Sciences.[3] While controversies over fundamental issues are endemic in the Social Sciences, in the case of Natural Sciences, at any given time, there are clear and universally accepted scientific laws, postulates or

---

[1]Conflict and violence is hard wired into humans according to some biologists. While there is no conclusive evidence of the biological origin of the human conflict, it is nevertheless a pointer inthat direction. Barash David P. 'Sociobiology and Behavior', Elsevier Pub. New York, 1982, pp 367-387. *American Political Science Review*, Vol. 79, No. 2, June 1985, Washington DC, Madson D. Biochemical Property relative to Power seeking in Humans, pp 448-457.

[2] Kaplan, A. 'The Conduct of Enquiry', Sachin Pub. Jaipur, India, 1980, pp. 118-119. At the broadest, politics is defined as authoritative allocation of values. A simpler and preferred definition is 'it is a science of governance internally and relations between the states externally.' Dahl, Robert S. 'Modern Political Analysis,' Prentice Hall Pub. New Delhi, July 1978.

[3] Kuhn, Thomas S. 'The Structure of Scientific Revolution', University of Chicago Press, Chicago, USA, 1970. p. viii.

achievements and discoveries of a fundamental nature. These form the basis of further problem-solving and scientific progress - from Newtonian laws of motion to Einstein's theory of relativity or Quantum theory. Social Scientists on the other hand are divided into 'Schools' –Realists, Idealists, Behaviourists, System Theorists' et al.[4] It is therefore necessary in any social science research project to clearly define the terms and boundaries at the very outset.

In addition to the problems posed by the under-development of Political Science as a discipline, study of insurgency and related peace processes, suffer from the multiplicity of meanings in popular as well as serious literature, on the subject. In popular mind, *Guerrilla Warfare* is confused with insurgency. The term Guerrilla war, means 'little war'. The word is of Spanish origin and was first used to describe the activities of Partisan fighters in the 'Peninsular War' (1807-1814). After the French invasion of Spain and Portugal by Napoleon, a popular revolt against the French rule took the shape of harassing attacks against the French lines of communication and isolated detachments. Spanish and Portuguese citizens fought alongside British regular forces. The terrible bloodletting suffered by the French in the war, specially the Partisan actions, is regarded as a major cause of the ultimate defeat of Napoleon. Partisan warfare is necessarily an adjunct of the fighting of the main force. Even at a later date, during the First and Second World Wars, such operations were carried out behind the enemy lines and were of some significance in the ultimate analysis. But 'Partisan Warfare' is different from insurgency war as understood in the present era. All this makes it mandatory to layout the road map and clarify meanings of various terms, right at the outset.[5]

Conflict and violence is the permanent state of human society. Violence and conflicts can be at many levels, such as violence between individuals, crowds or formally organised tribes that are labelled, nation states. At the level of individuals, it is labelled 'crime'. When between two 'crowds', it is

[4] Hass, Michael & Kariel, Henry S (Ed), 'Approaches to Political Science', Chandler Pub, Scranton USA,1970. p. 4

[5] Paret, Peter (Ed), 'Makers of Modern Strategy', Princeton University Press, 1986

called a riot, and slaughter between organised groups/tribes is even glorified as war.[6] When there is a violent conflict within a group, a state or tribe/ society, it is generally referred to as an insurgency or rebellion. If a successful outcome is reached, it is then legitimised as a 'revolution' or 'freedom struggle'. Success has a tendency to change perception. This brings in the issue of right or wrong and legitimacy, an issue that will be dealt with later, in some detail.

Causes of violence amongst cavemen could be the coveting of women, another's cave, land, gold or other precious materials, revenge, jealousy, sport or seeking excitement out of boredom that afflicts affluent societies. These were the motivations generally ascribed to cavemen! But if we strip off the veneer of propaganda and spin, there is realisation that nothing much has changed even in the 21st century of the Christian era. Crimes, rebellions/ insurgencies and wars still continue and the motivations are much the same. The two major wars of the 21st century i.e. the American attack on Iraq and Afghanistan were for resources (oil) and revenge (for the attack on 9/11 on the US), respectively.

Fighting and killing in groups, called soldiering, is the world's oldest profession with the second oldest giving it a close run. In the entire human history, peace has been sporadic and in short supply. This gets reflected in the most common greeting between two humans- 'peace be with you' or variations of it. All religions of the world stress on peace. Paradoxically, despite all religions' exhortation for peace, the birth of the concept of religion added a new dimension to human conflicts- the "My God/religion is better than yours" syndrome. The conflict over religion got accentuated when followers of some religions propagated the notion that only theirs was the true religion and their Prophet was the last true Prophet. To the followers of these creeds, history and human evolution ended with their holy book. All that mankind was then expected to do was to interpret and re-interpret the sole holy book and implement its teachings. In reality, this was an attempt to camouflage imperial ambitions and the lust for temporal power under the cloak of pious religious idiom.

---

[6] Waltz, Kenneth N. 'Man, the State and War,' Columbia University, New York, 1954.

During a considerable period of human history, almost up to the 18th century, a major driving force for conflicts was religion. Jomini, the French military historian of Napoleonic era, devoted a separate chapter to what he called 'Wars of opinion'[7] He identified religion as the earliest form of ideology for war:

'Religion can be a powerful ally, for it excites ardour of the people and also creates a party.'

Even in the 20th century, two major conflicts in Asia, the Korean War and Vietnam War had subtle undertones of religious conflict. In Korea as well as Vietnam, the regimes supported by the Christian West, initially were dominated by their co-religionists. But such is the dominance of the West in the field of research that this issue is seldom mentioned and has never been seriously investigated.[8]

In the latter half of the 20th century, world politics was dominated by the 'Cold War', a power struggle between the Communist Bloc and the Capitalist bloc. This struggle was carried out under the shadow of a nuclear stalemate between the two bloc leaders, the United States of America and the USSR (the erstwhile Union of Soviet Socialist Republics or Soviet Union for short). The fear of a nuclear war leading to the destruction of the Earth dampened the direct confrontation between the two sides. Instead, the armed

---

[7] Howard, Michael, 'Studies in War and Peace', Maurice Temple Smith, London, 1970. Chapter titled 'Clauswitz and Jomini'

[8] West, Morris, 'The Ambassador', Dell Pub. New York, 1965, pp. 44-49.

Fisher, James T, 'Dr. America: The Lives of Thomas A. Dooley, 1927-1961', University of Massachusetts Press, 1997.

Dr. Tom Dooley attained iconic status not only among American Catholics, but wider society as well. He was also an instrument in the hands of the (so-called) Vietnam Lobby, a group of Public Relations executives, former Socialists turned anti- Communist, shadowy military figures and CIA operatives. These folks, none of whom were Catholic, ardently desired a Catholic figure who might be a bridge between American non-sectarian anti-communism and the fiercely Catholic leader in South Vietnam, Ngo Dinh Diem.

When North Korea was occupied by the USSR in 1946, most of Pyongyang's 300,000 Christians fled to the Allied controlled Republic of Korea (ROK). The Leninist People's Democratic republic of Korea (PDRK) brutally oppressed many religious believers from the Buddhist, Confucianist and Shamanist religions as well. Christianity is frequently credited with fomenting a strident Korean nationalism among the citizens of the ROK. Christian nationalism provided a persuasive influence on the ROK's embryonic democracy and intimidated the regime in Pyongyang.

part of the power struggle was carried out through the medium of guerrilla wars. It was a tool used by the 'weaker' Communist bloc to change the global power balance under the shadow of the threat of nuclear destruction. Open confrontation carried the risk of escalation and the communist powers were at a disadvantage in the field of technologies of conventional weapons. At the other end, at the level of combat, insurgents and counter insurgents per force had to forgo use of weapons of mass destruction. Thus, the communists successfully managed to dictate the terms of engagements. Captain B. H. Liddell Hart in his foreword to the book on Mao's thoughts on guerrilla war says,

"Campaigns of this kind, (revolutionary wars) are more likely to continue because they fit the condition of modern age, while at the same time (are) well suited to take advantage of social discontent, racial ferment and nationalistic fervour."[9]

Liddell Hart's observation appears to be relevant for the 21st century as well. The 'Cold War' confrontation ended in the last decade of the 20th century with the dissolution of the Soviet Union. World trade, travel and technological changes (especially in the information technology) have brought in 'Globalisation' of world economy, politics and culture. Many of these forces were in existence even in the last few decades of the 20th century, but the Cold War had acted as a brake. The end of the Cold War accelerated this process.

The interconnectedness of the world has created an environment akin to the Cold War era's Balance of Terror, wherein direct conflicts between states have become a rarity. International organisations and a consensus on treating the 'State' as a unit for stability of the world order have further reinforced this thinking since 9/11.[10] This trend is likely to last for a long

---

[9] Griffith Brigadier General Samuel B. (Trans.), 'Guerrilla Warfare By Mao Tse Tung and Che Guevara', Cassel & Co. Ltd, London, 1962. p. xii, quoting from foreward by Capt. B. H. Liddell Hart.

[10] On September 11, 2001, a group of terrorists belonging to Al Qaeda hijacked several commercial planes and attacked twin towers in New York and Pentagon in Washington DC. It was the first direct attack on the mainland of the US in over 100 years and led to the start of the 'War on Terrorism'.

time until mankind progresses to the creation of a world government with teeth to mediate between warring states and with the power to intervene between states. But globalisation as a process has NOT addressed many of the underlying causes of conflict. Hence in the medium to long term future, conflicts within states or insurgencies are also likely to continue and may become the major challenge confronting mankind.

Modern technology is a double edged weapon. While it has solved many a problem of mankind, it has also empowered individuals as well as small groups with enormous capacity for destruction. Threats of 'Global Terrorism' are a by-product of the process of globalisation and technological changes. Terrorism and insurgency are terms used interchangeably- this issue will be dealt with in greater detail later.

The ideology of nationalism originated in Europe and gave birth to the concept of the nation state. 'We versus They', became a powerful impulse for conflicts. In the past, 'Wars of National Self Determination' had acquired a legitimacy and popular sanction in the wake of the Great War. In much of the world, at the dawn of 21st century; the clock seemed to have turned full circle and secession, based on the nation-state principle, no longer enjoyed the sanction and support of the powerful. Fear of global anarchy and need to proceed with economic globalisation were powerful impulses for this change.

The 'state' exists with all its coercive power as the mediating agent between competing interests of individuals as well as groups, forming parts of a society in a given geographic area. Seen in this light, whether in primitive tribal societies, or in monarchies of the past or modern democracies, the state in some form or the other always existed. It is an *a priori* requirement for human existence. Thomas Hobbes, the 16th century English philosopher remarked that in the absence of a state, it would be war of everyone against everyone and Man's life, nasty brutish and short.[11] The primary role of a state is to maintain rule of law internally and peace and security externally. It is universally recognized that that the state has the right to use the necessary force to achieve it. Without this essential function being efficiently carried

---

[11] Hobbes Thomas, 'Leviathan', EP Dutton & Co, New York, 1950, p.105.

out the state cannot justify its existence. Civil society cannot function without the rule of law enforced by the state. Economic progress, civilisational goals, culture; nay life itself is not possible in the conditions of internal turbulence and external insecurity.

Insurgency or revolutionary warfare is defined as an act of using force to overthrow the established system and replace it with a 'just' order that makes claims on legitimacy and propriety. Revolutionary war or insurgency is thus very closely linked with the political aim and presupposes an ideology distinct from the one followed by the existing government and the state or at least such an impression is successfully created. Insurgents use tactics of Guerrilla warfare characterised by hit and run attacks, ambushes, sabotage and attacks on the supply lines of regular forces. However at the ultimate stage, the Guerrillas resemble a 'state' and could and do adopt the tactics of open confrontation. Mao conceived this form of struggle as passing through several phases, merging into each other. [12]

The first phase is of organisation, consolidation and preservation. In this phase, a regional base is selected in a difficult and isolated area where volunteers are trained and indoctrinated. These trained cadres then spread out to persuade and convince a large number of inhabitants in the surrounding area, of the justice of the 'cause'. This, in effect, weaves a web of sympathisers around the base, as a protective cover. The mass of sympathisers is a reservoir for a supply of fresh recruits, food and other essentials and to act as the eyes and ears of the revolutionaries. Armed action in this phase is sporadic and the main emphasis is on organisation. In order to build a cadre of committed supporters, Mao also laid great stress on 'constructive action'.

In the second phase, the emphasis shifts to military action. The guerrillas organise themselves in small hard-hitting bands and carry out ambushes and sabotage. Elimination of reactionary elements and collaborators is undertaken. The primary purpose of these military actions is to procure arms and ammunition and expand the 'liberated areas'. The insurgents also

---

[12] Griffith Brigadier General, op cit.Dutt Dev (Ed), 'Mao Tse Tung ,ON WAR', The English Book Depot, Dehradun,1966

gain battle experience and valuable publicity.

After successful completion of the second phase and when the Guerrillas have obtained sufficient strength, the revolutionaries are organised in orthodox units and resort to open fights and are ready to give a decisive blow. This phase can be a protracted one, interspersed by series of negotiations. These three phases are not watertight compartments and merge into each other. The revolutionaries can also shift from the third phase (decisive action) back to first phase of lying dormant, should the situation so dictate.

Even regular forces have been known to use these tactics to supplement conventional warfare on one or more fronts. The 'Partisan Warfare' in the rear of occupying German troops in Russia during the Second World War and Brigadier Wingate's Chindit operations in Burma during the same war, are some examples. Thus it is necessary to make a clear distinction between Guerrilla warfare and Insurgency. While all Insurgents are Guerrilla fighters, all Guerrilla wars cannot be classified as insurgencies. Insurgencies are armed revolts carried out with the support of the masses against the state and its armed forces. It is a problem of 'internal security' rather than 'external aggression.' In a world state system with 'municipal laws' and anarchy as far as use of force to achieve objectives is concerned, 'insurgency' in one country invariably attracts external support from across the international boundaries. Insurgents in that case then act as a 'fifth column' in a role reversal.

A further confusion has arisen due to frequent use of the word 'terrorists' in case of insurgents fighting an urban Guerrilla war. Guerrilla tactics in urban settings involve 'collateral' damage and casualties and therefore it is easy to stick this label. But a clear distinction needs to be made in case of urban insurgents who could and do cause damage to persons/property in the vicinity of, say, a vehicle ambush and 'Terrorists' who on the other hand target unrelated (or at the most with very tenuous links) persons, property or installations. The terrorists are in that sense like the 19th century 'Anarchists' or the thugs, zealots and assassins of a bygone era. They have always existed in human history. Modern means of destruction and global mobility have added to their potency. The instant and worldwide media coverage have further ensured that their impact is multiplied manifold. The terrorists could also be insurgents with similar aims; the difference is in tactics, not objectives.

Insurgency is defined as a violent challenge to the state's exercise of monopoly on use of force and threatens its very existence. The insurgents hope to establish a new order and a government that accords with their revolutionary thesis. The challenge could be to capture state power in the entire geographic area under its control or only in parts of it. In case of the latter, it could be classified as a secessionist insurgency. The challenge is thus at two levels, a physical challenge and an ideological one! The insurgents thus question the very legitimacy of the state that has structures like the police and judiciary that uses 'adequate' force against its own citizens.

There is a cliché 'One man's insurgent is another's freedom fighter', making it difficult to distinguish between a freedom struggle and an insurgency. Here the pitfall lies in the fact that the discourse on this is coloured by the currently dominant views in the West. The classic example is the two decade long Vietnam War (1956 to 1976) fought by the Americans in South Vietnam. While the Americans called it an insurgency, for the bulk of the Vietnamese, it was a freedom struggle against a foreign power and part of the anti-colonial movement. The case of Afghanistan is even more illustrative. The fight against the Russian intervention from 1979 to 1988 was classed as *freedom struggle* of the Afghans (the good *Jihad*) and was supported by the West. Fast-forward to circa 2001, and intervention by the Americans and NATO forces plunged Afghanistan into a *Second Jihad* (this time, a Bad Jihad). The Afghans fighting the American supported government are termed *Insurgents* or worse (religious fanatics/ fundamentalists etc). Does this mean that the term insurgency and freedom struggle are *relative and interchangeable?*

As one recalls childhood memories, one realises how our generation was fed on a diet of *Cow-boy Westerns* by Hollywood.[13] One recalls with horror that the massacre of native Americans (then characterised as Red

---

[13] Aleiss, Angela, 'Making of the White Man's Indian: Native Americans and Hollywood movies.' Praeger Pub, New York, 2005.

Indians) was presented as chivalrous and was applauded as entertainment-a kind of repeat of what the Romans did to the *Christians* by feeding them to lions! The point to note is that domination of the media space by the powerful tends to distort the moral compass of a generation. In India, a generation of Indians was so dazzled by the British Empire that they swallowed hook, line and sinker, the imperialist version of Indian history. Indians who fought the British were regularly (and even today) described as the 'enemy'. It is necessary to be aware of these distortions while dealing with and defining revolts and insurgencies lest one sounds like the erstwhile Anglophile WOGs (Westernised Oriental Gentlemen) of colonial India.

But here we come up with another one of the problem of a researcher. Notwithstanding the caveat stated earlier that insurgencies are essentially an internal security challenge, it is obvious that in almost all the insurgencies there is an element of external support and interference. In fact many a time the two are seamlessly woven into each other. Thus the Vietnam War at once was a freedom struggle by the Vietnamese against the American neo-colonialism; it also was a proxy war by the erstwhile Soviet Union and China to extend their sphere of influence in South East Asia at the expense of the Americans. The Americans fighting in Vietnam on the other hand used the slogan of *Defence of the free world*; while the primary motivation was the fear of *Domino effect* on South East Asia. In Afghanistan, the *Jihad I* was similarly a proxy American war against the Soviet Union, a part of global power struggle between the two. In Kashmir, since 1989 India is facing an insurgency and a proxy war by Pakistan that wants to annex that area. The conclusion one can draw from the above discussion is that there is no *pure* insurgency and the internal and external dimension are intertwined. But in spite of this ambiguity, counter-guerrilla warfare and counter-insurgency are as different as chalk and cheese. Essentially, the differentiation is based on the degree of external dimension in the conflict. Where the external force is predominant, one would class it as counter-guerrilla war and not counter-insurgency. This is a serious and important issue and needs some deliberation.

The ideological confusion in the use of the terms counter-insurgency and counter- guerrilla war, is a product of the fact that in terms of *technique* of fighting, both are indeed similar. At the risk of oversimplification, these forms of warfare are dominated by infantry tactics such as ambushes and raids and the guerrillas/insurgents deliberately obscure the difference between an ordinary citizen and a guerrilla fighter.

But partly this clubbing together of counter-guerrilla warfare and counterinsurgency is also a deliberate ploy by the external power that intervenes militarily in another country. Since wars of domination or those fought for geopolitical purposes are both unfashionable and unpopular, these interventions are falsely described as *counter-insurgency* while installing a puppet government as an ideological fig leaf. For instance, the Americans intervened in Vietnam in 1960s due to the fear of spread of Communism in the entire SE Asia- the so-called *Domino Theory.* The Soviet Union, similarly intervened in Afghanistan in 1979, to take advantage of the revolution in Iran and strengthen its position in the Middle East. The Americans went into Afghanistan in 2001 to root out Al Qaeda and punish the Taliban for supporting it. India sent in troops to Sri Lanka in 1987 to safeguard the Tamils and also to look after its strategic interests in Trincomalee port. In all these cases, the intervening power feigned that it was fighting the guerrillas to establish democracy, for nation building or for defending freedom! It is interesting to speculate whether the intervening powers would have still intervened if say the Vietnamese Communists had broken with the Russians/ Chinese and assured the Americans that they were not interested in spreading Communism? (As indeed is the case in the year 2011 and the same Communist Vietnam is an ally of the US) If the Taliban would have handed over Osama Bin Laden to the Americans in 2001, would the Americans have remained in Afghanistan to *usher in democracy?* Similarly would Indians have intervened in Sri Lanka if that country would have promised that it would not bring in influences inimical to India?

Counter-guerrilla warfare and counter-insurgency thus differ in terms of ultimate objectives. In counter-guerrilla warfare, the principles of war are applicable and resorting to counter-guerrilla operations is NOT due to choice but compulsions dictated by the adversaries and international or/and domestic opinion. In a counter-guerrilla war there is a very clear us *versus* them divide, while in counter-insurgency the situation is much more ambiguous.

In secessionist insurgencies that enjoy wide support, a similar us *versus* them divide exists. The insurgents do perceive themselves as freedom fighters as in Nagaland, Mizoram or in parts of Kashmir. But the state that counters this revolt is still bound by limits imposed by counterinsurgency and does not have the aim of destruction of the *enemy*. Thus while for one side it is total war being fought with guerrilla tactics for the other it is a limited conflict and counter-insurgency that aims at change of behaviour in order to win hearts and minds.

In all cases, it is the *legitimacy* of the ultimate aims that defines whether an operation is counter-guerrilla war or counter-insurgency.

It Would be Fair to Therefore Define Insurgency as

'An armed challenge to an established state by a group with some popular support and possible external help. Its aim could be to overthrow the regime and take over the state and establish a new order and a state of its own choosing, or, to secede and form a new state.'

Insurgencies can be further classed into *Ideological* and *Realist/ Materialist*.[14] The goals and nature of insurgencies often change, but all insurgents, irrespective of real motives, claim to be idealists.

Religion at one time represented the totality of doctrines in human life, covering social, political and spiritual aspects. Insurgencies with roots in a religion can exploit the vast reservoir of historical and mythical sources of motivation and strength. Religion as an ideology is indeed formidable, since it is an ideology that is prevalent all over the world and its influence begins in childhood. It is not an acquired ideology, but one is born into it. It is a part of one's upbringing and not a 'free choice'. Religion defines not just relationship between man and God but also man and man. While it may be of little significance in day to day life, its role in forming attitudes, shaping behaviour and mindsets is important, even in industrialised and modern societies. In case of close-knit rural communities, its role is significant.

---

[14] International Journal of Middle East Studies (2003), vol. 35 No.:3, Hechter Tirza, 'Historical Traumas, Ideological conflicts and Mythologising'

It is tempting to club Communist-led insurgencies based on theories of class warfare and focussed on *material goals* as 'realist' conflicts. But on the other hand Communists themselves claim that it is an ideological conflict like the ones based on religion or ethnicity.

Communism, in a sense, is akin to religion, with its own holy book (Das Capital), the Holy Trinity (Marx, Engels and Lenin) and the Holy Land, the erstwhile USSR (now China).[15] But essentially, at the level of followers, it was about securing economic rewards and therefore a 'realist' conflict with material goals. At a deeper level, many insurgencies of ethno/religious nature cloaked themselves in Communist rhetoric in order to secure the support of the erstwhile USSR. It is this socio-economic core of the Communist insurgencies that led to the prominence of socio-economic counter measures to deal with it. There is a vast body of Communist literature on tactics and organisation of resistance which insurgents of all hues used and continue to use, to the hilt.

Most insurgencies are multi-dimensional: economic, political, social and psychological conflicts in a dynamic *inter se* relationship and variable salience. Insurgencies manifest themselves as guerrilla war supplemented or supplanted by acts of terrorism. Terrorism could be a tactic or the main strategy. While superficially a conflict may appear to be a religious one, an in-depth analysis may show that it is rooted in socio-economic problems.

Conflict itself is a dynamic interaction between violence and counter violence. The creation of durable peace is the systemic model to affect mass behavioural change: to shift the conflict from violence to debate or bargaining; from conflict to competition, co-existence and finally co-operation. This is similar to many other intra-society disputes but the main difference is that coercion or use of force has a legitimate role.

All conflicts have unique features due to cultural, racial or historical differences. Yet there are commonalities, universally present, like the basic human emotions of fear, greed, the desire for a good life and factors like the

---

[15] Engles Frederick,'The Role of Force in History,'Anamika Prakashan, NOIDA, 1987. Fuer Lewis S (Ed), 'Marx and Engels- Basic Writings on Politics', Anchor Books, New York,1959.

urge for survival and the preservation of an identity. Deep- rooted and serious conflicts are the ones that have persisted for a long time and affect a large section of humanity (deep-rooted refers both to the cause and the longevity of conflict). Conflict over some tangible interest like territory, economic gain or some other material object, can be resolved through bargaining. But when the conflict is value - and need- based, that is related to the defence of a religion, culture, identity or a claim for equality of treatment, these reflect demands that are not divisible. Thus the 'realist' conflict is seldom deep-rooted while the religious or ideological one is. If the conflict is over an object, due to rage or for revenge - in principle at least, there are many means available for resolution. Where the conflict is merely a means determined by a ' superior purpose' there is no reason to either restrict it or even avoid it. In this situation violence itself becomes the purpose. Ideological conflicts have a tendency to move towards the mythical 'total war' and present the greatest danger, since the use of weapons of mass destruction fits in with this conception.

As seen earlier, the insurgents who wish to overthrow the existing regime or secede, use the argument of 'Justice' or claim their struggle to be a means to bring in a 'Just Order'. No term in Political Science is loaded with more meaning and interpretations than this. The issue of relative 'legitimacy' of the state and the insurgent's actions is crucial and provides ethical foundations for either the insurgency or counter- insurgency efforts. For it must be clearly understood that in a situation where a group is using violence against the state, it is *ipso facto* also challenging the legitimacy of the monopoly of the state to use force. The issue of legitimacy is not simply a moral or an ideological factor but has a direct effect on the effectiveness of the force so used. This is specially the case as counter-insurgencies aim at change of heart and not breaking of heads.

The protracted nature of the conflict and domination of the human element, go on to reinforce the importance of legitimacy. When the insurgency is widespread and enjoys greater support within the state, it begins to be referred to as a 'Civil War' with both the insurgents and counter-insurgents acting like a state in being. The difference between the insurgents and counter insurgents tend to disappear and the conflict begins to resemble an inter-state war. In Sri Lanka, the LTTE (Liberation Tigers of Tamil Elam) had reached this stage until May 2009.

A viable and attractive cause could transform individual frustrations and group problems into an internal revolt. Yet the struggle for the hearts and minds of the people is not like a 'love triangle' wherein insurgents and counter-insurgents are both like two suitors wooing one girl. It is also a struggle between the heart and mind. In the Indian experience in the North East it has been seen that continuous deprivation of basic necessities to rebels and making them available to the loyal population made the choice stark for most people. Eventually mundane concerns of living, raising family etc (mind), scored over the lofty but unattainable goal of independence or a proletarian revolution (heart).

The use of force to keep internal peace and therefore a counter to insurgency is inherent to the very concept of the state. Internally the state has the monopoly of power and has to meet challenges from individuals or groups, who for variety of reasons may wish to use force to achieve personal or group economic /political /social objectives. In a democratic setup such as the one in India, the Constitution provides scope for and lays down the rules within which this can be legitimately achieved. The use of force or coercion by either individuals or groups is a challenge to the state and if it has to survive, it has to meet this challenge. This could be achieved through peaceful means but if that fails, the state has no option but to use force, else the very foundation of civic society will collapse.

Relevance of the Indian Experience

India, the world's second most populous country with over a billion people, is diverse on an unimaginable scale. It has all the world's religions, 17 major languages and diverse races. It has an unbroken record of inclusive tradition going back three millennia. There has never been mass violence or a history of extinct races. The massive bloodletting witnessed in 1947 before and after break-up of India and in 1971 in what is now Bangladesh, are the two exceptions. But these bouts of violence occurred because the secession that took place in 1947 was essentially based on the notion of rejecting everything that the sub-continent stood for.[16] There has been a constant effort to deny the past and even wipe it clean from public space; the starkest example of this was the destruction of the Bamiyan Buddhas,[17] statues in Afghanistan. These statues were part of Afghan heritage and pre-dated the birth of Islam

India became a full-fledged democracy at its birth in 1947. It has been tackling insurgencies and secessionist movements in the predominantly tribal dominated North-East, Muslim-dominated Kashmir and Communist insurgencies in Telangana, Bengal, Chhattisgarh/Jharkhand/Orissa/Andhra states. India intervened in the secessionist movement in neighbouring Sri Lanka and has gathered unmatched experience in this kind of warfare. The country dealt with these revolts in the context of a democratic structure, the rule of law and concern for human rights, making the Indian experience useful beyond its borders.

Insurgency in India can only be understood against the backdrop of the current stage of political evolution. Development is commonly thought in economic terms alone. There are instances where economic development has been independent of political development as in the former Soviet Union or currently in the People's Republic of China. Examples such as oil-rich states in the Middle East come to mind, as these countries, though wealthy, are under-developed, politically. But theory has it that political development is impossible without a degree of economic development and vice versa. Economic development of a self-sustaining nature is impossible without political changes – this is the lesson of the collapse of Communism in Europe and may yet prove true in China. The concept of development is thus related to both economic and political development.

---

[16] Shah, Mohammed (Ed), 'The Aligarh Movement : Basic Documents 1864-1898', New Delhi Prakashan , New Delhi, 1978 Vol. III , pp 1069-1072. Chaudhry, Muhammad Ali, ' The Emergence of Pakistan', Columbia University Press, New York, 1967.

[17] In March 2001, the Taliban regime of Afghanistan, with the help of Pakistani engineers, blasted the 2nd century statues of Buddha.

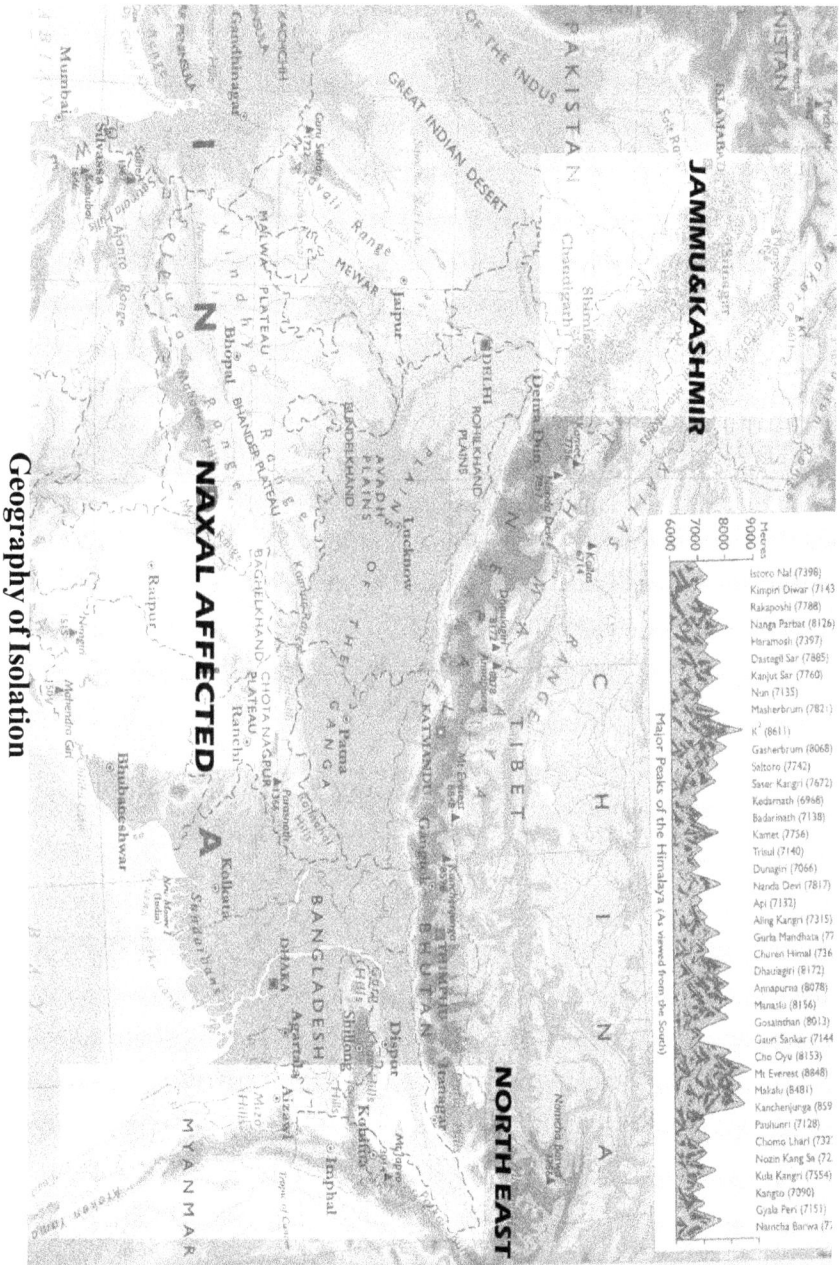

Social Order Versus Political Order

Much of the confusion and criticism of the role of the state in an insurgency situation in India, stems from the difference between a sociological and political perspective. Sociologists seek primacy to social organisations in maintenance of peace while political scientists believe that to be a function of a state.

In addition, during its long history, India managed to maintain internal peace through social order. Notwithstanding the rigidity and injustice, it gave political stability and created a virtual self- governing society on matters of personal law, family and social peace. The remarkable and long lasting internal peace in India can be directly attributed to the social order and cast a long shadow on Indian thinking. The mechanism worked because it was self regulatory and force had no role. In turn, even the invaders ranging from the early Muslims like the Arabs, Afghans, Persians and Mughals to the British, did nothing to either disturb or modify the society. Rural India where 80% of the people lived, was left alone. The British made it explicit by concentrating on law and order only. The society was more or less left alone except for some social reforms such as sati and child infanticide. Even these changes were made by the British in co-operation with the Indians.

After independence, when India accepted the Western model of development and 'progress', all that changed. The state began taking on an activist role in society on the basis of borrowed ideas-'liberal' from the democracies and 'coercive' from the former Soviet Union. State by its nature is an agency to use force. Hitherto force was used to maintain status quo while now it was used for variety of objectives. Politics or science of governance is often referred to as "Danda-niti" and the Hindi word for government is 'Shasan', the other meaning of which is coercive correction.[18] Once the task of keeping order moves away from society to the state, several other differences also crop up. Political power or capturing the state is now seen as the most important societal goal. This gives rise to

---

[18] Kautilya, Samasastry Dr. R (Trans) , 'Arthashastra', Wesleyan Press, Mysore, India, 1923.

ethnic groups and factions who all vie for political power. If there is a failure to form genuine coalition of interests or run a proper federal system, then the state is engulfed by violence both on the periphery as a secessionist attempt and in the heartland as a violent struggle for power.

A sociologist's perspective on the issue of use of force gives primacy to civil society in maintaining peace. According to some views, there are also economic, administrative, legal and political perspectives. But administrative or legal are methods or means to maintain peace. The economic perspective is that of Political Economy, as there is now a clear view that there is nothing such as a 'pure' economic viewpoint. Essentially there are only two major perspectives that is, political and social. In the political perspective, it is the state that is primary and its use of force to achieve state's aims, including keeping peace, is traditionally regarded as legitimate both internally and internationally. In a sociologist's view, order is maintained by civil society. Force or violence when used, signifies the breakdown of order. Violent social upheavals or revolutions are not normal but abnormal social phenomena. On the other hand in the political perspective, the use of force or violence is the norm and is a legitimate part of politics. It is this that separates politics from sociology in the ultimate analysis.

Nature of Insurgency and the Legitimacy Factor

Fundamentally, the issue of right and wrong and questions on human existence, such as "Who am I?" or "What am I?" have been thought by human beings over several millennia. The issue of questions on the reason or rationale for human existence gave way to philosophical speculation and enrichment of the spiritual life of man. But the notion of right and wrong: behaviour, thoughts, goals, aspirations and even sex, has given rise to countless conflicts that divided mankind and is at the root of violence in the world. Many of these notions, thoughts and mores are transitory and vary over the ages, across regions and between groups. To illustrate, slavery, marrying a sister or a widowed mother, killing non-believers, untouchability, dictatorship of the proletariat and associated Socialism/Communism were all concepts and acts regarded as 'right' and the acts, thoughts and organisations promoting these were "legitimate' for an individual, group, society, nation and the world

29

at that point in time. In a different context in time and space, many of these actions would be regarded as horrific and criminal. Thus there is no universal consensus at any given time on the issue of what is 'legitimate'.

In a world consisting of politically, economically, socially and strategically isolated regions, these differing concepts of 'legitimacy' were a matter of academic curiosity for 'National Geographic'-like organisations. But in a 'globalised' world, the differing concepts of 'legitimacy' lie at the root of much of the violence and insecurity in the world.

It is the complexity, dynamic nature and diversity that give rise to the consideration of 'legitimacy' as an important factor while dealing with internal conflicts. This is less of an issue in inter-state conflicts since prevailing notions of 'legitimacy' give a state's fight for 'national interest' moral sanction. The emotion of 'my country always right' is fairly deeply ingrained in the human psyche. The United Nations has well-defined rules for such use of force and fairly clear consensus on the issue of force in self defence by a state.

The issue of self-belief in legitimacy is not merely a philosophical concern but has operational significance in countering an insurgency. Wearing down the enemy and lowering his morale are concepts that are common to all forms of warfare. In the classical concept, destruction of armed power leads to collapse of the enemy's morale and eventual victory. But in an insurgency, the order gets reversed- it is the loss of morale that leads to the defeat of enemy's armed forces and victory.

Traditional societies when confronted with new/alien norms, legislation and economic relations, often react to these changes in a violent manner. Many a revolt can be understood as a resistance to change. Violent internal conflicts are a part of 'developmental processes'. Political development is signified by the effectiveness of the government and ineffectiveness signifies underdevelopment, as evidenced by violence and instability. Political institutions in a developed country mediate between competing groups and individuals, and maintain peace. This is the main function of these institutions. In a developed country, these institutions are characterised by adaptability, autonomy subordination, complexity and coherence in disunity.[19]

A large proportion of the population of the developing world depends upon agriculture for subsistence although industrialisation and modernisation proceed apace. Industrialisation brings in its wake, Western values. This change can often generate alienation and loss of norms due to the conflict between the old indigenous and new value systems. Historically, this has been accompanied by violence. In addition, within many countries, societies in different regions are in different stages of modernisation. In addition, there are racial, linguistic and religious differences. All these factors make the resistance to modernisation and the associated violence turn into secessionism. The spread of education, information and literacy generate additional pressures due to heightened awareness, leading to heightened expectations.

The Indian civilisation is remarkable in having the acceptance of pluralism as a core value. This has led to a state founded on universal principles, with a system that grants every citizen fundamental rights without discrimination. The State automatically enjoys a legitimacy that is not available to racist, theocratic or ideology-based dictatorships. The core values of the state have to be such as to appeal to not only the majority but also to the smallest minority groups. Universal Humanism has to be the basis of these core values. The legitimacy of a state is not based on a legally accepted Constitution or core values alone. It must also be based on the 'reality' of the behaviour of its agencies and administrative practices.

There are several aspects of legitimacy, all equally important. First of all is the factor of morality. In a contest between the state and a group using violence to overthrow it, either in the entire country or in parts of it, moral and ethical issues cannot be ignored. The second aspect of legitimacy is systemic. The systems of the state have to be both fair and democratic in order for it to have legitimacy. This is different from rhetoric and is an issue of management and checks and balances. The third aspect deals with the quantum and quality of force being used. In order to have legitimacy, force cannot be excessive and/or indiscriminate. And the final issue is about the

---

[19] Dahl, Robert S. 'Modern Political Analysis,' Prentice Hall Pub. New Delhi, July 1978.

perception of people about the comparative legitimacy of an insurgent group and the state. It is this contest that will largely influence the final outcome of the struggle. Mass media plays a major role in shaping these perceptions and can be a critical component of the struggle between an insurgent and the state.

A state founded on universal principles has a strong sense of legitimacy. On this basis it claims the right to use force, based on the internationally accepted norms and principles that emerged in 17th century Europe. Force may be used against local majorities, intent on separation or against recalcitrant groups bent upon imposing a particularistic ideology which may have majority support in a given geographical area. This is the very precondition for existence of pluralistic societies, that are the reality of the twenty-first century.

Counter insurgency has been the graveyard of many military thinkers and practitioners.[20] The main reason being that unlike military problems that have clear cut objectives, known premises and clear methodology, insurgency is like an *Amoeba that changes shape, size and reproduces itself.* The military analyst uses deductive logic to simplify a complex problem. 'Get to the meat', 'Cut out the flab', are some common military terms. No wonder the militaristic approach and reductionist deductive logic miss the target and end up creating a greater mess than what existed before the action. Insurgencies are not simple military problems yielding to 'yes-no' logic and solutions. In addition, there is no clear-cut division between tactical, strategic and policy levels. The conflict process is diffused, with crucial decision-making often devolving to the lower echelons of command. Both these factors make it desirable or even mandatory that there should be an 'understanding' of all these throughout the chain of command, from the top of the Government, downwards. Success of counterinsurgency depends upon political and military judgement, from the platoon level upwards. A well-informed subordinate is less likely to take an action that may well end up having adverse strategic or policy implications. It is proposed to promote

---

[20] T.E. Lawrence, also famous as Lawrence of Arabia, led an Arab revolt against the Turks during the First World War (1914-1919). In his book 'Seven Pillars of Wisdom' he compares the Turkish military response to Arab insurgency as attempt at "eating soup with knife".

'understanding' of the insurgency at the level of policy makers and implementers in order to help and supplement the evolution of policy, doctrines, strategy and tactics.

The Chinese revolution that culminated in 1950, the resultant Communist take over of China, and the successful Cuban revolution, added to the commonly-held perception of the virtual invincibility of this technique of waging war. In the decade of 1970s, as the Vietnamese guerrillas scored a spectacular military victory over the mighty United States, insurgency or revolutionary war acquired a great mystique. The Afro-Asian countries lacking industrial muscle saw in this method, an instrument to fight the industrialised nations of the West. As the 20th century was drawing to a close, the broad process of globalisation made open confrontations between nations, a rarity. Yet in many parts of the world, guerrilla wars continued. Many serious analysts of military affairs believe that this is likely to be the shape of most conflicts in the 21st century as well.

Holistic Approach to Peace Process

The "Peace Studies Approach" emphasises persuasion, negotiation, socio-economic measures and winning over the people and excludes coercion. In the case of counter insurgency, the emphasis shifts to the use of force to create conditions to implement the peace agenda. This differs from the Peace Approach in that the use of coercion is an integral part of the process. Critics often dub classical counter insurgency as aiming at preservation of the status quo, or the imposition of a status quo ante. This puts it in an ideologically weaker position while dealing with an insurgency which promises change/revolution/utopia. A revolt seeks to attain 'ideological' and non-material goals such as the preservation of identity, or ushering in the Kingdom of one's preferred God. Countering it, involves enforcing values and ideals, maintaining peace and a system of just governance. Durable peace, conceptually defined as a situation in which an individual and society can fulfil their aspirations, is only possible if the counter insurgent brings about a 'regime change' in the thinking and behaviour of the target region, nation or group by putting forth and enforcing alternative visions and ideals.

The Peace process, seen in these terms is not merely negotiation, bargaining and debate on socio economic measures, but also involves coercion and the use of force. It is the totality and the combined effect of these measures that result in the establishment of peace. As noted earlier, the aim of counter-insurgency as well as the peace process is to transform a conflictual relationship into a co-operative relationship. In view of the interconnectedness of the two, it is axiomatic to study all of these together.

The one thought that must be uppermost while dealing with the issues of insurgency is that there *is no silver bullet solution!*

Methodology

Keeping in mind that effective communication of one's research outcome is an important consideration, it is proposed to adopt the comparative case studies route as the research methodology.[21] It is accepted that there are idiosyncrasies of particular cases, and case studies cannot establish the proposition. Still, case studies are important as they can help in production of a hypothesis about recurring patterns. If co-relational studies satisfactorily establish a pattern, for instance between religious ideology and violence, then case studies would provide valuable inputs to find answers to the critical questions such as the causal relationship between these two variables. Deviant case analyses here can provide an understanding of those instances that do not fit in the general pattern of association.

The case studies approach should not be confused with 'Historical Determinism'. Case studies are undoubtedly history but do not subscribe to the axiom viz. history repeats itself or 'lessons of history' and 'learning from the past,' which are milder variations of the same. Instead, the comparison of multiple case studies as an approach resembles the clinical methodology of treating a disease. A disease, whose origin is not clearly known, although the symptoms are! Medical sciences collect case histories of likely causes, various symptoms and reactions to various treatments. At the end of it all, medical scientists attempt to establish preventive measures,

---

[21] Hass, Michael op cit, Russet Bruce M, Ch. 14, 'International Behaviour Research: Case Studies and Cumulation', pp. 427-430.

identify the best treatment and ultimately cure the patient. Comparative case studies in social sciences are akin to this successful practice in the medical profession.

It is proposed to take up the case studies of several insurgencies, counter insurgencies and peace processes. The various case studies chosen have different geographical, racial, political and economic contexts. It is hoped thereby to avoid the pitfall of narrow focus and attempt universality of relevance.

The comparative case study method will seek to promote understanding about questions such as: Is it possible to identify certain principles of counter-insurgency? What role does "Legitimacy" play? Here, the concept of legitimacy encompasses both means and ends. What kind of force produces the desired results? Maximum (shock and awe), adequate or minimum? Is massive force counter-productive since its indiscriminate nature prolongs the life of an insurgency by creating a new motivation for 'revenge'? Does the sequential approach work better than a multi-pronged one?

Perceptions of leaders as well as cadres, of insurgents as well as counter insurgents on issue of effectiveness of various measures, economic, political, military will be a major input. In addition, an attempt will be made to identify 'turning points', if any, of the conflict and study them in depth.

Thomas C. Schelling mentions in his work on the 'Strategy of Conflict',[22] that much of the research in the strategic field is akin to a man searching for a needle only under a lamp post! Here, the selection of case studies has been done keeping in view the availability and access to information. The case studies selected, differ widely in terms of socio-economic and ideological contexts. The North Eastern revolts by Naga and Mizo tribes had an element typical to primitive tribes living in a harsh, mountainous terrain. Right till the 1950s, some Naga tribes were head hunters. Throughout the nearly two-decade old violent conflict, the tribal's maintained a steady code of honour in selection of their targets. At times, the conflict almost came to resemble a competitive sports event! Many parts of the world, particularly Afghanistan,

---

[22] Schelling, Thomas S, "Strategy of Conflict', Harvard University, Cambridge (Mass) , 1981.

resemble the conditions of North East. In the Kashmir conflict, on the other hand, there have been no 'rules of the game' and violence is ruthless, even women and children are not spared. The religious idiom is used both as justification of violence and as a motivating force. Establishment of the rule of *Sharia* (the Islamic Law) has often been invoked as the goal of the insurgents. In Sri Lanka, the issue of identity as Tamils, essentially a linguistic/cultural/racial/historical concept, has predominated and religion has taken a backseat. The Tamil rebels are also the virtual pioneers of suicide attacks in the modern era. One President, two defence ministers and one ex-Prime Minister have fallen victims. In one particularly effective attack the entire Defence Ministry building was destroyed by a Tamil suicide bomber.[23] A study of the Tamil insurgency will throw some light on the motivations, modes and psychology of this deadly modern scourge. The author has also been involved in studying the insurgency in Northern Ireland and the Naxalite movement in Chhattisgarh. Wherever useful, the events/trends and outcomes there are used to supplement or supplant the conclusions.

The end of the Apartheid regime in South Africa and victory of the African National Congress could be classed as one of the defining moments of the 20th century. As an ideology, the South African racism appeared well entrenched. The South African state also seemed strong and secure. But the impossible happened, the insurgents won and there was a regime change. What was the combination of factors that led to the demise of the powerful racist ideology? An in depth study of the closing days of the Apartheid regime gives valuable insights into tackling ideology based conflicts.

In classical Clausewitzian formulation,[24] insurgency technique relies on 'resistance' over long period and wide spaces, to ultimately through a process of accumulation, overcome the adversary. Counter to this, is to limit the space and attempt to lower the intensity of 'friction' and also reduce the timeframe. There appears to be some evidence, from preliminary studies, that insurgencies do have a 'shelf life'. In this sense it is also a contest in stamina. The book examines this issue in detail.

---

[23] 16 Nov 1992. In a LTTE suicide attack the defence ministry building was destroyed and a deputy defence minister as well as an Admiral died in the attack.

[24] Howard Michael op cit.

Conclusion

The basic approach of this study is based on realism. Human conflict is a reality and has to be dealt with. There is a thin line between 'realism' on the one hand and cynicism and pessimism on the other. A middle path between a priori conflict resolution and conflict glorification is sought to be followed. Banishing human conflict is a utopian goal. Sages, prophets and religions have been propagating it for over a millennium, without success. Conflict control/management is therefore a rational and reasonable goal. Though not morally elegant, its justification and morality rests on greater chances of its success versus the Utopian goal of abolition of conflict.

Human conflict is possibly hard wired into mankind.[25] A state or a coercive organisation that keeps peace between human beings has existed since time immemorial. In the context of an integrating world economy, there is a consensus to treat the 'state' as a unit. The politico-economic environment in the 21st Century has rendered the inter-state conflict a rarity while intra-state violent conflict has taken centre stage. Increasingly, the conflict has assumed the shape of guerrilla wars and terrorism. The underlying causes of these conflicts are not easy to identify, let alone eradicate. The conflicts could be over material issues or ideology. The process of globalisation has created a situation in which the 'little wars' have a global fall-out. A comparative case studies methodology is employed to promote wider and deeper understanding of the phenomenon and to tackle the issue and usher in peace.

As a first step, the study looks at how it all began. The understanding of 'how' is expected to answer why it all began. This knowledge is important since it helps to establish clear boundary conditions and identify tipping points, factors and processes that could even help prevent an outbreak or at least give an early warning.

---

[25] The 'Power Drive' inherent to a man is linked to his hormones and libido. Henry Kissinger had an interesting observation when he asserted that 'Power is the ultimate aphrodisiac', indirectly linking power and basic human need for sex.

Section 2 - Beginnings

The North Eastern India

On 1st March 1966, at 02. 30 AM, with clock work precision, Mizo rebels attacked 30 towns and military posts in all the districts of Mizoram. Operation Jericho was a complete and total surprise. The next day India woke up to the screaming news headlines, "Revolt in Mizoram". In the initial attack, the rebels captured the towns of Lunglei and Champai. Both these places were manned by company-strength paramilitary Assam Rifles. In the capital Aizwal, the rebels had only partial success. The troops there continued their tenuous hold on the fortress-like Treasury building, located on a ridge in the centre of town. At 27 posts in all, the rebels attack was successfully resisted. An estimated 8,000 rebels took part in this operation. The security personnel, mainly from the Para-Military Assam Rifles, numbered around 2,000.

The tongue shaped province of Mizoram is located between Burma (Myanmar) on the east and south and Bangladesh (erstwhile East Pakistan) to the west. It measures 240 kms north -south and 70 -100 km east-west. The total area is 21,000 sq. km and the population according to the 1991 census was 500,000. In 1966, at the beginning of the insurgency it was estimated at around 200,000. Located between 22 and 24 degrees North latitude, Mizoram is a hilly country with the average height of the hills ranging from 800 - 1000 meters above mean sea level. Six hill ranges run north to south separated by fast-flowing rivers. The hills have a compressed clay or sand stone composition and are prone to frequent landslides. A full 62 % of the area is covered with thick bamboo jungles. Villages are located on hilltops and were connected by footpaths only. Average annual rain fall is between 211 and 355 cm. The only dry months are October and January to May. The population density is 30 per sq. km. In 1966, the only connection with the rest of the country was a single jeep-able track from Aizwal to Silchar in the plains.

The population is divided into five main and eleven minor tribes. Lushai is the main tribe. Tribal differences exist but are not very pronounced. Mizo folklore traces the origin of the Mizo people to the Mekong delta in Indo-China. There was a steady movement since the 10th century, of sub-tribes moving in and colonising the area. The last to enter were the Lushais , who came in via the Chindwin river valley of Burma. The villages were ruled by a village council presided over by a hereditary chief. Their main economic activity was shifting agriculture, using the slash, burn and sow technique. Principal crops grown were rice, gram and mustard. Mizos were Nature worshipers before their conversion to Christianity in the 19th century.

In 1959, the area was subjected to 'Mautam' famine (every 59 years large-scale bamboo flowering occurs and this leads to an extraordinary increase in rodent population, which is a virtual rat invasion). The Government of Assam was slow to react. A retired Sergeant of the Indian Army, Lal Denga organised volunteers to carry out famine relief work under the banner of the Mizo Famine Front . This soon turned into the Mizo National Front (MNF) and demanded an independent state of Mizoram. The neighbouring East Pakistani Government encouraged Lal Denga and many Mizos crossed over to receive arms training there. The immediate provocation was the provincial Government's move to induct an additional battalion in Mizoram in view of the tension and secession openly being preached by the MNF. Talking to this author in 1988, Lal Denga, then the Chief Minister of Mizoram, dramatised the whole episode. He claimed that until the last minute he tried to avoid conflict and even made a last ditch effort by trying to talk to the Governor of Assam. His request was to stop the additional battalion from coming into Mizoram. It seems that this was an after thought. The co-ordinated attack on 1st March must have required extensive preparations and detailed planning that had no connection with the move of additional troops. Given the lack of radio communications with the rebels, it is unlikely that at that late hour Lal Denga could have put the genie back into the bottle.

What makes the Mizo revolt interesting is also the topsy-turvy sequence! An open confrontation and armed assault on the state is generally the final stage of an insurgency, not the first. The shock of it all was even greater as

Mizoram had a reputation of being a peaceful area. The image of 'Gay Lushai' was firmly etched in the armed forces as many had served in that area during the Burma Campaign of Second World War and had fond memories of happy-go-lucky Mizos wielding nothing more lethal than a guitar.

Of course there were long-term causes and grievances. In 1947, after India attained independence, all the tribal areas in the North East, including Mizoram, became part of the newly created province of Assam. The capital, Shillong, was located 500 kms away and had very little control over the far-flung areas. By virtue of their numbers, the administration was dominated by the plains' Assamese. World over, the dislike of plainsmen by hill people is a fact of life. Mizo people's demand for a separate province was turned down. Instead the tribal areas were given a district council set-up with limited administrative powers. Forest lands, in effect most of the area, were kept out of the jurisdiction of the district councils thus making them an ineffective body. No sooner was the province of Assam formed, than the provincial govt imposed the Assamese language on the unwilling tribals. The administration was dominated by the plains Assamese and the tribal aspirations for self-rule remained unfulfilled.

The Central Government, under Nehru adopted a policy of gradualism in terms of integration of the tribals with the mainstream. The Inner Line restrictions were kept intact. Dr. Verrier Elvin, a former missionary who had settled in tribal land, was the guiding spirit behind these moves. The Indian Government also gave protection to tribal laws and customs by inserting a provision in the Indian Constitution that gave it protection and also a veto to tribals on the matter of which of the Union laws were to be applicable in tribal land. These were eminently sensible measures and should have taken care of the tribals' fears as well as aspirations. But it was the integration of these areas with the province of Assam that reduced the effectiveness of these well-meaning steps.

The political ambition of Lal Denga, a commoner, also played a role. The District Council set-up was dominated by the hereditary elite. There is some truth in Lal Denga's later assertion that all that he aspired for was a statehood and power to the 'people'.[1]

In direct contrast to this lightning-like revolt in Mizoram, was the slow build-up of anger and violence in Nagaland. Though the insurgency in Nagaland, the oldest in the North Eastern India, served as an inspiration and 'example' to the neighbouring Mizos, the beginnings of the trouble in Nagaland followed a very different trajectory.

The Nagaland state in extreme North-Eastern India, is bordered on the west and north by Assam state, on the east by Myanmar (formerly known as Burma), on the north by Arunachal Pradesh state, and on the south by Manipur state. Nagaland is one of India's smallest states, with a total area of 16,579 sq km. The Naga Hills run through this small state, which has Saramati as its highest peak, at a height of 12,600 ft. The main rivers that flow through Nagaland are Dhansiri, Doyang, Dikhu and Jhanji. The terrain is mountainous, thickly wooded, and cut by deep river valleys. There is a wide variety of plant and animal life. Nagaland has a monsoon climate with generally high humidity and receives an average rainfall of 1800 and 2500 mm a year. The population of Nagaland is entirely tribal. The Nagas belong to the Indo-Mongoloid family. The fourteen major Naga tribes are the Angami, Ao, Chakhesang, Chang, Khemungan, Konyak, Lotha, Phom, Pochury, Rengma, Sangtam, Sema, Yimchunger and Zeliang.

The Naga Hills and Tuensang district, as the area was called then, lay in the grey area where the British did not extend their administration. In 1929 the Simon Commission visited India to discuss the issue of self-government. The Commission also visited Kohima and here the Nagas presented a memorandum claiming that they were NOT Indians and wished to be treated as an independent state. Thus the roots of Naga separatism appeared to go deep. But the Naga argument that they were 'independent' of India and had no connection with it, was not borne out by history.

In the 13th century, King Sukhapa of Shan State (in present day Myanmar) invaded the area and subjugated the Nagas. The Shan rule was brutal and the Nagas suffered privations. In the 14th century, the Ahom Kings of Assam defeated the Shan Chief and brought the Nagas under their

---

[1] Mizoram insurgency and counter insurgency data in a graphic form is depicted in Appendix B..

influence. Initially the Nagas welcomed the Ahom rule and often paid tributes to them. Later there were frequent clashes between the Ahoms and Nagas and in 1620, King Gadadhar Singh took harsh action and forced the Naga chiefs to come to his capital and pay taxes. In early 19th century the British occupied Assam and the Naga areas were annexed The British however left the Nagas alone and had a policy of minimum interference. This changed in 1851 when in the wake of Naga attacks on the plains, the British took strong retaliatory action. In 1877, the Naga Hills district was created with its administrative headquarters at Kohima. The Nagas welcomed British rule as it stabilised the area and brought an end to inter-tribal warfare. Nagas, though referred to as a common group, were actually divided into several tribes including the Angami, Ao, Sema, Konyak, Thankhuls and several other small tribes. Each tribe had its own language and communication between tribes was impossible.

There was constant pressure from Christian missionaries to be permitted to carry out their activities in these areas. The British were alarmed at the activities of Hindu missionaries in neighbouring Manipur, hence changed their policy and permitted the spread of Christianity in tribal areas. Sir Dalton, Commissioner of Chota Nagpur (with a significant population of tribals) wrote that the wild tribes have no religion. "They want religion and were they Christians, they would be a great asset in times of trouble with the vast non-Christian population. " It cannot be doubted that the large population of Christian hills men between Assam and Burma (now Myanmar) will be a valuable asset to the (British) state". Sir Johnston, Commissioner of Manipur, strongly echoed his views and advocated the induction of clergymen from the Church of England.

The words of Sir Dalton were to prove prophetic. In 1944-45, Japan invaded Burma and reached the gates of India. The British 14th Army suffered a humiliating defeat. For a moment it seemed that the Japanese would reach Calcutta and shake up the British Empire in India. But in the epic battle of Kohima in March 1944, the Japanese advance was checked. The Nagas played a stellar role in these battles as guides, porters and spies to help the British defeat the Japanese. A monument was erected in Kohima to honour two Nagas who, disguised as mess waiters, stole the Japanese plans of advance! The Nagas got training in guerrilla war and were hailed as saviours by the British. The end of the war saw huge caches of arms and ammunition abandoned in the jungles. Thus here was a tailor-made situation for insurgency-well trained guerrilla fighters, plenty of arms and ammunition, heightened self-esteem as victors over the Japanese, a sense of separateness due to geography, British policy and nudging from the missionaries. At the time of independence in 1947 there was also a genuine apprehension about the fate of 'Christian Nagas' in a predominantly Hindu India. All that a separatist insurgency needed was charismatic leadership. This void was filled by Zaputo Angami Phizo, an active and educated Naga who had been assiduously building his contacts across the tribal divide. The Naga Club at Kohima was founded in 1918 and was a regular meeting place for the Naga intellectuals. This formed the nucleus of leadership of the insurgency when it broke out in the late 1950s.

Right from the beginning, the Naga movement was a purely political one in the sense that the Nagas did not put forward any economic demands nor claim economic grievances. The starting point of the Naga argument was that they were not Indians, were never part of India nor ruled by the Indians. They only had some relationship with the British and now that the British were leaving, like India, Nagas should get their independence.

Mr. Y. D. Gundevia, an officer of the Indian Foreign Service who dealt with the Naga problem sums up the Naga attitude as, "Naga movement is a political one with suspicion and fear as a superstructure and an unworthy feeling of racial separation and superiority as the basis."

So convinced were the Nagas of the justness of their cause that they expected the Indian leadership to accept their demands. The Naga National Council (NNC) made several attempts to meet the national leadership in Delhi. But beset as it was with a far bigger challenge of refugees from Pakistan, the Kashmir war and communal rioting all over India, the Nagas did not receive a favourable response. The Governor of Assam, Sir Akbar Hydari was asked to deal with the issue. Hydari, a civil servant with vast experience and knowledge of the North East, devised a nine- point plan. The salient points of this were the control over the natural resources and land was handed over to the Nagas and their tribal customs were given a legal protection. The agreement had a 10-year life within which the two sides were expected to work out a permanent arrangement. While the talks between the two sides went on, the Nagas collected signatures on a petition demanding independence and sent it to the President in August 1951.

It is difficult to pin point the event that led to the break between India and the Nagas but the refusal of the President to meet a Naga delegation in December 1953 could be one. Even earlier, irrespective of the Naga impasse, the Constitution making exercise went on with full steam and a General Election was announced in 1952 and held all over the country. The NNC announced a boycott of elections. The boycott was 100 % successful and there were no candidates and no voters in the entire Nagaland. Phizo staged his own elections and referendum and formed a Naga national government. Frustrated with the lack of response to their demands from Delhi, the Nagas launched a Civil Disobedience movement in 1953. While the Nagas continued preparations for an eventual armed clash with India, the movement was peaceful right till 1956.

The Naga leadership made several attempts to meet the Prime Minister Nehru, but failed. An incident that particularly shocked Nehru took place in May 1953. Aware of the Naga population in Burma (the Hemi Nagas) Nehru was keen to involve Burma in the pacification of the frontier areas. Nehru and Burmese Prime Minister U Nu paid a joint visit to Kohima in May 1953. A public meeting was organised where the two leaders were to address. But just as the meeting started, the entire lot of Nagas present got up and walked out! It was an insult such as Nehru had never expected! A furious Nehru vowed that he would never visit Nagaland, a vow that he kept till his death in 1964. Nehru was not an ordinary politician. He had a virtually absolute sway over the nation and a break between him and the Naga leadership had tragic consequences for the people of Nagaland.

The Government and the Nagas differed on the interpretation of Hydari's nine point plan. The Nagas expected that the arrangement was purely temporary and for ten years only after which they expected the

Indians to grant them independence! As the ten year period got over, the Nagas started an armed struggle and established their own rule over most of the area. In reaction, India sent in the Assam Rifles as well as a division of the regular army to re-take the area from the Nagas and establish control up to the Burmese border. A full-blown guerrilla war began that has still not completely ended.

Sri Lanka

Men make their own history, but they do not make it as they please; they do not make it under self-selected circumstances, but under circumstances existing already, given and transmitted from the past. The tradition of all dead generations weighs like a nightmare on the brains of the living.

-Karl Marx

Next is the mother of all old conflicts-the Sri Lankan Tamil revolt. Steeped in history, the two sides to the conflict, the Sinhalese and Tamils trace the origin of their dispute to 145 BC. 145 was the year King Dutthagamini, grandson of Devanampiyya Tissa, the first Buddhist King of Lanka met Tamil king Elara in a battle. In order to avoid unnecessary bloodshed, the two Kings decided to settle the issue by fighting a duel. In this duel, King Elara was killed. The 6th century Buddhist text *Mahavamsa* has glorified this event as the victory of Sinhalese over Tamil and Buddhism over Hinduism. Nearly two thousand years after the event, the reverberations of that event continue to echo in the jungles of Sri Lanka as the Sinhalese and Tamils fight it out.

Sri Lanka is an island nation that lies south of the Indian Peninsula. Home to around 20 million people (2001 estimates), it is tiny by Asian standards. The two main communities in Lanka are the Sinhala, around 78 percent and Tamil speaking people around 16% along with Moors, Burghers, Kaffirs, Malays and the indigenous Vedda people, who form the rest.

In the West, there is a tendency to view Asian history as a mere chronicle of events with no relevance to the present. In the current epoch of mankind where the West is predominant, history as a guide to

Tamil dominated areas

Scale 1:4 000 000

Statute Miles
0 10 20 30 40 50 100 160

0 20 40 60 80 100 160
Kilometres

Towns over 500 000
50 000

Longitude East of Greenwich

Conic Projection

INDIAN

GULF OF MANNAR

PALK STRAIT

PALK BAY

MADURAI

TRAVANCORE

TRIVANDRUM

KANNIYAKUMARI

Cape Comorin

TIRUNELVELI

RAMANATHAPURAM

NORTHERN PROVINCE

NORTH CENTRAL PROVINCE

NORTH WESTERN PROVINCE

WESTERN PROVINCE

CENTRAL PROVINCE

EASTERN PROVINCE

UVA PROVINCE

SABARAGAMUWA PROVINCE

SOUTHERN PROVINCE

SRI LANKA

COLOMBO

Negombo

Galle

ARABIAN SEA

understanding is generally neither accepted in academic circles nor is it considered 'respectable'. In countries of the Orient, history is seen as a continuous flow and therefore very much 'live'. In the Orient, and specially in the Indian subcontinent, of which Sri Lanka forms an inseparable cultural and political part, the tradition of 'oral history' has survived for thousands of years. This oral tradition adds another dimension to the importance of history and its place in shaping the perceptions of people.

The oral tradition has had two major effects. The obvious one is that as long as people survived, their history survived. Thus no amount of 'book burning', of which there was not much in Sri Lanka till recent times when the Sri Lankan army burnt the Jaffna library, could destroy the collective memory as long as the people survived. On the other hand, oral history, unlike the written one, is much more flexible and can be modified continuously to suit the needs of the present. In this form the oral tradition prevalent, makes history much more relevant to the present and the future. The oral tradition also ensures participation by the masses, crossing the barriers of literacy and education.

History is thus not a mere chronicle for the people but an 'exemplar' in day-to-day life. Any understanding of the problems faced by Sri Lanka has to begin at the beginning of history. Sri Lanka has, besides the oral tradition, also an extensive written history in Pali, Sinhala and Tamil. While the first two were contributions of mainly Buddhist monks, the later was based on court records of various dynasties of South India, notably the Chola and Pandya. The histories thus reflect not only the struggle for power within Sri Lanka but also the larger struggle waged by Buddhism against resurgent Hinduism in India. On such intermixing of religion and politics is based the record of Sri Lankan past that continues to influence the present.

The perception about the ancient history of Sri Lanka is divided along the religious line. The Buddhists laid claims that the Sinhalese from North India were the first immigrants to the island from India. The facts of geography and archaeology which are to the contrary, however, prove that civilisation indeed existed in Sri Lanka even before the arrival of Sri Vijaya. But the myth of Sinhalese being the original inhabitants has struck deep roots and in popular mind, Tamils in Sri Lanka are equated with invaders and usurpers. The deliberate twist added to the history as propagated by the Mahavamsa (a chronicle written by Buddhist monks) was deeply influenced by the struggle then on in India between Buddhism and Hinduism. The Buddhist monks of the 5th - 6th century were naturally obsessed with the preservation of their creed, at least in the island nation. The establishment of Mahavihara as the headquarters of the Thervad sect in third century BC institutionalised Buddhism and is possibly the world's oldest 'church'. The planting of Bodhi tree and at a later stage bringing of the tooth relic of Buddha to Anuradhapura established independence of the Sri Lankan Buddhist tradition from its Indian roots. *Over many centuries this has become the most powerful historical myth of Sri Lanka and the Sinhalese concept of being a chosen race as guardians of Buddhism, and Sri Lanka as the Dhamma dwipa has created an intimate connection between land, race, faith and language.*

The Portuguese were the first European power to reach Sri Lanka, followed by the Dutch and then even the French. However, except for introduction of Christianity and a few scattered forts, there is very little influence that has survived.

The British who had established themselves in neighbouring India, defeated the king of Kandy in 1815 and Sri Lanka or Ceylon as it was then referred to, became a colony of the British crown. The British incursions in Lanka started much earlier and were a result of their activities in South India with Madras as their base. The British presence in Sri Lanka was intimately connected with the Madras Presidency in the initial stages. Lanka became a Crown colony in 1802 but the Governor of Lanka was never a free agent and was influenced by the Madras Presidency, Governor General in India and the Indian military. The meagre military force in Lanka mainly consisted of Indian regiments recruited in Madras and early British rulers had a tendency to rely on Tamils for running the administration and revenue services.

The Buddhist Kingdom at Kandy had survived all these years but as the British eyed the highlands for establishing tea and coffee plantations, attempts began to be made to subdue and overthrow the last surviving independent King in Lanka. Jaffna Tamils, the age-old rivals of the Sinhalese sided with the British in this struggle. During the first Kandyan war, while the British pretended to negotiate, they secretly connived with the Tamils and put Muthuswamy, a Jaffna Tamil on the Kandyan throne. The British attempt failed and the entire expedition was wiped out and Muthuswamy executed on 24th June 1803. The Kandyan resistance did not last beyond 1815 and thereafter the entire island came under the British rule.

The one lasting impact of the British rule was the establishment of tea and coffee plantations in the mountains of Sri Lanka's wet zone. Right up to the First World War, the planters lobby was all-powerful and all the policies of the colonial rulers were tailored to suit their business.

The planters found the Kandyan Sinhala difficult workers and unsuited for plantation work. On the other hand, famine conditions and relative poverty in Madras province made available a large pool of workers at lower rates. In the later part of the 19th century, the British carried Indian labour to all corners of their empire. The plantation communities in Fiji, Mauritius, the West Indies and Malaya-Singapore, are the relics of the 'Plantation Raj' of that period. The first large scale induction of Tamil labour in Sri Lanka took place in 1828 and thus was introduced, another element of the racial conflict in Sri Lanka.

There was a major difference in the plantation labour in Sri Lanka and other places. Over a period of time, the indentured labour in places as far off as South America or even Malaya, lost all touch with the mother country and developed as independent communities. On the other hand, the Tamil labour in Sri Lanka never got 'Lankanised' and continued to maintain very close relationships with their families in India. Most of the labourers continued to repatriate their earnings to India and many returned to their homes at the end of their working life. The plantation Tamils can more rightly be compared with 'guest workers' from Turkey in Germany or the Algerians in France.

Sri Lanka has very little industry and plantations and offered the main job opportunities. As these jobs were taken up by the immigrant labourers, it bred resentment amongst the Sinhalese.

The British rulers showed marked preference towards the Tamils in the matters of other employments as well. This was partly out of the policy of divide and rule and also because the Tamils were the first to take to English education and were therefore preferred over the Sinhalese. The money lenders and big businesses was cornered by Chettiyars, the traditional business community of Tamil Nadu. With their extensive links and network in India, the export and import trade was largely monopolised by them.

The Moors or descendants of Arab traders were another community that prospered under the British. These people, Muslim by faith spoke mainly, the Tamil language. Taken together, the picture of British Sri Lanka was that of domination by Tamils in all walks of life.

Buddhism was the state religion in Sri Lanka. The advent of Europeans and the decline of Sinhalese political power led to the loss of patronage for the Mahavihara and other monks. The latter part of 16th and 17th century saw a rapid decline of Buddhism in Sri Lanka. Things reached such a pass that new monks could no longer be ordained in Sri Lanka. Kittisiri Rajsingha, the King of Kandy province (1756- 1779) sent a mission to Thailand and Burma to seek Buddhist elders and re-establish higher ordination in Lanka. Two more groups went to Burma. Three distinct Buddhist schools were set up in the 19th century.

The activities of Christian missionaries generated tremendous resentment. In the time honoured tradition of the Indian sub-continent, the two sides decided to resolve the differences through a public debate. From 1865 to 1873, a total of five debates between the Buddhists and Christians took place. In the final debate at Panadura in 1873, the Buddhist scholar Migettavatte Gunanada, a skilled debater, triumphed. An American theosophist, Colonel H S Olcott, heard of these debates and arrived in Sri Lanka in 1875. He converted to Buddhism and made Sri Lanka his home. The presence of Westerners openly championing the Buddhist cause had deep psychological effect on the Sinhalese and gave a boost to the Buddhist revival. In 1862, the Society for Propagation of Buddhism was established near Colombo.

The main threat perceived was from the activities of Christian missionaries who had moved into the field of education in a big way. Beginning in the last quarter of the 19th century, Buddhists became active in the field of education. Piyaratanatissa of Dodanduwa established two major institutes of Buddhist learning. In time the Vidyodaya Oriental college at Colombo (1872) and Vidyalankara College at Kalaniya became the centres of Buddhist learning and provided the nucleus to spread education amongst the Sinhalese.

Olcott and the Theosophical society established by him at Colombo, had soon over 350 Buddhist educational institutions established all over Lanka. Buddhist studies received a shot in the arm when a Sinhala Scholar, H. Suanagala translated the 'Mahavamsa" from Pali into Sinhala. The text that dealt with the 2500 year old history was available now to the people in their own language of daily use. This easy availability of various texts and high literacy made sure that the Sinhalese became conscious of their Buddhist heritage and also of the special place of Lanka in the history of the world. Spread of education and revival of Buddhism were the precursors to the rise of political nationalism of the Sinhalese.

Sri Lanka was often described as an 'ideal' colony by the British, except for the revolt of 1848 in Kandy province that was caused by unjust taxes and high-handed behaviour of the local administrators. Knowing the Buddhist way of life that does not accept killing, the British even imposed a tax on villagers for not killing stray dogs! Unrest was sparked by such behaviour, but it will not be an exaggeration to say that there was no 'freedom' movement in Sri Lanka as seen in India.

Communal tensions in the multi ethnic society often led to violence. In 1883 on an Easter Sunday, Catholics rioted against the Buddhists in Colombo. In 1915 again there were serious riots in many small towns of Sri Lanka over the issue of passing of Buddhist processions in front of the mosques. The Muslims objected to it but the courts ruled in the favour of Buddhists and under the influence of their hard-line leaders from India, the minority Muslims went on a rampage. The violence was only controlled after martial law was imposed. The Martial Law lasted for three months and the situation was brought under control.

Twenty years before the Buddhist revival, a parallel movement of Hindu revival began in the Tamil-dominated North and East. Arumuga Navalar was the most influential leader of this awakening. Navalar, a man of many part and talents re- established the Saivite doctrine and the Tamils were even more resistant to the efforts of the Christian missionaries' conversion activity. In 1849-50, Navalar established Saivite schools in every village in Jaffna. The Saivite schools emphasised modern learning and English education was part of their curriculum, unlike the Buddhists, who rejected English. This was to have a far-reaching effect as the Tamils soon became dominant in most government jobs. The advantage of English education makes Tamils even today more advanced than their Sinhalese counterparts.

It is the emphasis on English education that Navalar laid, that made all the difference. However unlike the Buddhist revival, the Hindu revival did not lead to any political organisation, as the main purpose was social and not political. However, orthodox Saivism did not respond to the Western challenge on egalitarianism and the caste system remained virtually unchanged. The Sinhalese on the other hand were more united politically as they did not have the rigidity of the caste system, to contend with.

Political developments in Lanka were slow to come. An organisation, the Ceylon National Congress came up as a representative body of Lankans to help the British administration. In its early stages, in 1921, two prominent Tamil leaders, Arunachalam and Ponnambalam, withdrew from the parent body and formed a separate organisation called the Tamil Mahajan Sabha and demanded special representation for Tamils and separate electorates.

Lanka was granted a limited representative government in 1924, much on the lines of the one granted later to India in 1935. Except for defence, external relations and some other matters, Lankans had the right to self rule. In 1931, a new Constitution came into being that widened the voting base. The only party to demand this was the Labour party that mainly represented plantation labour of Tamil origin. Ceylon National Congress did not become a political party and continued as an elite club. Politics in Lanka continued to be run by a few influential families with interests in graphite mines and trade.

The first full fledged political party was formed by Leftists in 1933-34 with Trotskyite ideology and a base in the ex-servicemen, de-mobilised after the First World War. Lanka Sama Samaj Party, devoted to socialism and having all sections represented, came into being in 1935. However the main strength of the leftist/socialists remained in the dock workers and plantation workers and there was very little support in the rural hinterland of Sri Lanka. At the time of independence in 1948, there was thus a virtual political vacuum. Potentially, the Buddhist revival movement and the 'Temperance' movement had the ability to mobilise the Sinhalese over the issue of religion and language.

The Sinhalese looked at independence as an opportunity to revive the spirit of the ancient Kingdom of the Sinhalese. Most people had only a hazy idea of what they wanted but revivalism had strong emotional overtones.

The two main communities living in Lanka had a consciousness of an identity, distinctiveness of culture, race, beliefs and institutions. But despite the history of constant warfare of nearly thousand years, there was peace as the forests that had come up over the ruins of the ancient Sinhalese civilisation acted as a physical barrier that isolated Tamil and Sinhalese peasantry. In the post -independence era, massive developmental works were undertaken and the barrier began crumbling, bringing the two hostile communities in contact again.

But the middle classes were not isolated and the first Tamil Sinhala clash was between these two contenders for power. The largest 'industry' in Lanka was the public service. With very little industrial growth and obvious limits to jobs in the government, fierce competition developed. The Sinhalese inability to compete with Tamils in the job market and in professions was the direct result of lack and neglect of English education. However in the popular mind, the easiest explanation offered was that the Tamils were cunningly packing the civil service with their own kind. A variation of the sons of the soil and quota system theories, so familiar to Indians, developed amongst the Sinhalese and the situation was ripe to be exploited by a politician. Sri Lanka found that man in SWRD Bandarnaike, an Oxford-educated aristocrat who sensed the Sinhalese mood and exploited it to the fullest. The educational activities of the Buddhists had spread literacy and Sri Lanka had very few illiterates. The educational system however concentrated mainly on the humanities and skill generation and science and technology were neglected. Thus the educated unemployed millions in Sri Lanka were a source of potential trouble and not a resource for national development. A similar phenomenon is observed in some other countries, where the spread of literacy has only engendered conflicts due to heightened expectations.

The beginning of the Lankan conflict was over language. In 1955 the United Front Government under Bandarnaike removed English as the official language and decided to replace it with Sinhalese progressively. At this move the Tamil demanded equal status to their language. The language row coincided with the similar problem in India. In some measure the Lankan Tamils' militancy was a reflection of similar sentiments in India. But unlike India where the issue was ultimately resolved through much good sense and the three language formulae, Lanka and its politics over language followed a very different path. The United Front government had to resign as it lost parliamentary majority and fresh elections took place in 1956. Bandarnaike and his newly formed Sri Lanka Freedom Party (SLFP) fought the elections on the issue of making Sinhalese the only official language. The Federal Party representing Tamils in North and East opposed this move and threatened a 'civil disobedience' movement over the issue. The Federal Party won all the seats in the Tamil-dominated areas and the divide over the language issue was reflected in the new Parliament.

In March 1957, at the annual conference of the Sri Lanka Freedom Party, the Tamil people's demand for equality of status for Tamil with Sinhala was turned down. But the conference decided to clearly define the term 'reasonable use of Tamil'.

The Federal Party that represented Jaffna Tamils was highly agitated against the move to make Sinhala the 'only' official language of Ceylon. It was interpreted not merely as a move to deny the rightful place to Tamil language but also a device to deny Government jobs to Tamils and treat them as second class citizens. The Tamils regarded this as a direct attack on their 'identity ' and not just language. The Federal party also received its inspiration from India where a similar attempt at imposition of Hindi language was being opposed in Tamil Nadu. The Dravidian movement in Tamil Nadu led by Dravida Kazhagam and its breakaway Dravida Munnetra Kazhagam , had a distinct secessionist flavour and a demand for an independent Dravidistan was the goal of these two parties. The Federal Party in Ceylon was comparatively moderate in its demands and only wanted a federal setup with equal status for Tamil in the Northern and Eastern provinces. A comparison of the politics of the Indian and Lankan Tamil parties shows that it was the former that was more militant and also separatist. Forty years later it seems impossible to believe, since Indian Tamils are today well-integrated in the Indian mainstream, while Sri Lanka fought a savage civil war. The reason for this contrast is the sage policy followed by India, where linguistic and racial diversity is respected, while in Lanka an attempt was made at one language, one race domination.

Bandarnaike-Chelvanaykam (B-C) Agreement of 1957

Bandarnaike and Federal Party leader S.J. V. Chelvanayakam met in Colombo in July and held discussions to find a way out of the language controversy. On 25th July 1957, at a joint press conference, the two leaders announced their agreement on the status of Tamil language as well as regional autonomy for the Tamil predominant North and East. The Federal Party cancelled its programme of civil disobedience that was scheduled to begin in August. The agreement was based on the four points elaborated by Bandarnaike,

(a) Tamils will have the right to be educated in their mother tongue.

(b) Tamil people will have the right to correspond with the Government in Tamil and receive a reply in Tamil.

(c) Tamil will be given recognition as a medium for Civil Services Examination.

(d) Regional authorities will have the right to transact their business in the language of the majority.

It was a reasonable compromise and showed clearly that Bandarnaike was no Sinhala chauvinist. Bandarnaike attempted to carry his party and the Sinhala public opinion with him by justifying the B-C Agreement as the classic Buddhist 'middle path' or madiyama prathipadawa. But his political opponents, mainly the United Nationalist Party of Dudley Senanayke, seized this opportunity to wrest political initiative. The B-C pact was dubbed as a 'sell-out' and invitation to partition of Lanka.

In the face of mounting opposition, Bandarnaike did not implement the major provisions of the B-C pact for nearly a year. Doubts began to be raised in Tamil North and East about the intentions of the Government. In a diversionary move, Bandarnaike's Government passed a law that all vehicles must have the ' Sri' sign in Sinhalese language. In Jaffna areas Tamil mobs went on a rampage and began tarring all Sinhala signs. The reaction was swift- a similar campaign of tarring all Tamil signs, in Colombo, began. The next stage of conflict was reached when Tamil-run shops in Sinhala-dominated areas were boycotted. All this vandalism was permitted by the Government of Bandarnaike and the police were instructed not to interfere. Slow erosion of law and order began in 1957 and was to lead to major violence the next year.

As yet another diversion from the failure to resolve the language issue, Bandarnaike raised the problem of plantation workers. A scheme to grant them residential permits and identity cards instead of citizenship was launched. But all this was to no avail and tension began building up in Colombo and many urban areas. Bandarnaike had come to power on the strength of the support extended to him by the Buddhist clergy. Nearly 1200 monks had campaigned for him. The monks and their Sinhala supporters now demanded their pound of flesh and Bandarnaike was powerless to stop the slide of the country into a civil strife.

Another grievance was added in a long list when, in April 1958, riots broke out over the issue of the settlement of 400 Tamils who were earlier working at the dockyard in Trincomalee. The Sinhalese in East Padavia, opposed it tooth and nail. The whole island had become a tinderbox due to the language agitation and any cause was seized upon by anti-social elements, to begin riots. The Government's approach of turning a blind eye to the violation of laws had come home to roost.

The final break between the Tamil and Sinhala communities came on the fateful day of 9th April 1958. On that day a 200-strong delegation marched to the Prime Minister's residence, demanding the abrogation of the B-C pact and a ban on the Federal Party. The agitators consisted of many Buddhists monks- the PM's special constituency. On that day, after a brief cabinet meeting, in a broadcast to the nation at 4.15 P.M., Bandarnaike announced the ending of the B-C pact. He put the entire blame for this on the Federal Party leadership and the anti - Sinhalese campaign as symbolised by the tarring of the 'Sri' on vehicle number plates in Jaffna. The very next day, the Federal Party gave a call to the Tamils to launch a civil disobedience movement.

Initially the news of disturbances came from the South and other Sinhalese dominated parts of Ceylon. Jaffna was relatively quiet. The Federal Party had planned a national convention at Vayunia on 25th May 1958 to take stock of the situation and chart its future course. The delegates going to this meet were attacked en-route. The police, apparently under Government. instructions, remained passive. Despite this, the convention did take place and the party decided to launch a non-violent movement against the Language Act any time before August 20.

On 26th May 1958, the Prime Minister, in an appeal to the nation, broadcast over the radio put the entire blame for the violence on the Federal Party and the Tamils. He singled out the killing of a local politician in Batticaloa, Mr. D A Seneviratne, a Sinhalese, to illustrate his point. The anti-Tamil violence that had been going on since 22nd May was completely glossed over. The PM's broadcast had a disastrous effect. Instead of bringing peace to the trouble torn island, the speech further stoked the fires of communal violence.

Rumour ruled the passions, as happens in such a situation. News of a particularly vicious killing of a Sinhalese woman school teacher of Panadura spread like wild fire and was a signal for the Sinhalese mobs to go on the rampage. Emergency was declared and the Governor General assumed all powers. Civil liberties were suspended and the Army and Navy were given orders to shoot at sight. The Federal Party and a newly formed Sinhalese extremist group, the Janata Vimukti Perumana (JVP), were banned. Till 28ᵗʰ May, Jaffna was relatively quiet. But as the news of killings of Tamils poured in, the Tamils retaliated. They turned their ire against the Buddhist vihara at Nagadipa. On 30ᵗʰ May, Tamil mobs destroyed the Dagoba and the Buddhist idol was desecrated and thrown into the sea. This idol was gifted by the Burmese Government in 1956, in commemoration of the 2500ᵗʰ anniversary of Buddha's *mahanirvana (death)*.

Meanwhile refugees continued to pour into the camps set up in Colombo. In order to protect Tamils from the fury of the rampaging mobs, these were handed over to the army. The armed forces performed creditably and were impartial in dealing with the Sinhalese and Tamils. On 3ʳᵈ June, in a well-executed and secret operation, six ships carrying 4,500 refugees left Colombo for Jaffna. Simultaneously, nearly 2,000 Sinhalese were evacuated from Jaffna. Ships of three nations, UK, France and Japan, participated in this task. This exchange of population was an important landmark in the unfortunate history of post-independence Ceylon and marked the de-facto partition of the country.

The emergency lasted nearly one year till March 1959. One remarkable facet of the 1958 riots was that the plantation Tamils remained aloof from these happenings and were left alone by the Sinhalese as well. While this turmoil was on, the Government received a judicial setback when on 19ᵗʰ May the judicial review committee of the Privy Council in London dismissed the Government's appeal against a Supreme Court judgment, that had struck down the refusal of the Government to grant citizenship to plantation labourers. This was a major blow to the Government's prestige and was to eventually lead to Ceylon giving up the British Dominion status and opting to become a Republic with the new name of Sri Lanka.

Along with the battle between Duttagamini and Elara of 145 BC, the Chola invasion and the subsequent shift of the Lankan capital from Anuradhpura and the defeat of the Kandyan King by the British in 1815, the language riots of 1958 marked a major turning point in the long history of

Lanka.

Outwardly language was the cause of dispute, but in reality the causes of the conflagration went much deeper. The primary motive behind making Sinhala the state language was to give advantage to the Sinhalese over Tamils in civil service jobs, till then disproportionately in the favour of the Tamils. Almost at the same time across the Palk straits similar confrontation was taking place over making Hindi the State language. In India the dispute was resolved through the three language formulae, Hindi the national language, English the link language and any of the seventeen Indian languages as the mother tongue.

The maximum blame for the events of 1958 is commonly placed on the vacillation and weakness of Bandarnaike. But that is not strictly true. The Federal party representing Jaffna Tamils (in reality Jaffna as well as Eastern province Tamils), overdid the protesting by demanding an equal status for Tamil. The demand was not for just equal status for the people but also for the language and culture. Tamils thus staked equal claims on Sri Lanka, a claim unlikely to be acceptable to the majority of the Sinhalese. Once the language dispute thus got transformed into the struggle for supremacy, old antagonisms and a repeat of history of the past wars was only a matter of time. In this miscalculation, the Tamils played into the hands of the Buddhist clergy who had become active in politics, not on the language issue but essentially to advance their agenda of making Lanka a Dhammadwipa and Dhamma shasana, in short a theocratic Buddhist state. It is doubtful if Bandarnaike or any other leader would have been able to withstand the pressure of the Mahavihara and the lobby of the monks. Bandarnaike's tragic assassination was to prove the point.

The move to exchange population was ill-conceived as it only meant that the Government itself accepted the division of the country into Tamil-dominant and Sinhala-dominant parts. In the later stage, in the new Constitution when the purpose of the Sri Lankan state, (as Ceylon was to be re-named later,) was clearly stated as 'to protect Buddhist faith', in all but name, Sri Lanka became a theocratic state losing its legitimacy in the eyes of religious minorities.

There is inevitability about the events of 1958, almost like a Greek tragedy. This was due to the fact that there was no anti-colonial struggle in Sri Lanka. Thus there was no mass mobilisation as had occurred in many countries of the third world including India. Instead the only mass movement was 'the temperance movement' with its heavy emphasis on Buddhism. Secular politics did not develop in Sri Lanka. This was not apparent for the first few years after independence as political power was in the hands of elites schooled in the British tradition who fashioned a Westminster-type Constitution and Parliamentary democracy. The coming to power of the SLFP was the first democratic expression of free will. Bandaranaike, an Oxford-educated Sinhalese, found himself in a cruel dilemma and was obviously not a leader who could swim against the current. By the time he saw the danger in the course that he was following, it was too late. It appears that Bandarnaike was well aware of the lurking danger of the Sinhala backlash and attempted to divert attention by taking a series of measures against illegal immigration from South India and also the favourite 'whipping boy' of the Lankan politicians - the plantation workers of Indian origin. In January 1959, their special representation in terms of four seats in the parliament was abolished. Bandarnaike also offered inducements for plantation labourers to leave Sri Lanka voluntarily. At the same time a special organization was set up with its headquarters in Jaffna, to detect and prevent illegal immigration from South India. Unfortunately these diversionary tactics had little impact on Sinhala public opinion.

Sinhala public opinion was increasingly restive over the delay in implementing the Sinhala-only policy. Bandarnaike was attacked on 25th September 1959 by a Sinhalese extremist. He died the next day. Bandarnaike thus became the victim of his own rhetoric. After this event, the process of Sinhalisation of Sri Lanka was carried on with greater vigour by his wife, Mrs. Sirimavo Bandarnaike, who became the Prime Minister after her husband's assassination.

Mrs. Sirimavo Bandaranaike vigorously followed the Sinhala-only policy and on 29th Dec 1960, the Parliament passed the bill making Sinhala the official language, replacing English. The act came into force on New Year's Day in 1961. No sooner had the Act been passed, than disturbances began in the Tamil-dominated North and East. To quell the disturbance, troops were airlifted to Jaffna area on 1st March. In the last week of March, talks were held between the Federal Party and Government to resolve the row. On 5th April the talks ended in failure. On 14th April, the veteran Tamil leader of the Federal party, Mr. Chelvanayakam launched a civil disobedience movement. On 14th April he inaugurated a parallel postal service with himself acting as the post master. The Federal Party also announced its intention to start its own police force soon. This open challenge to state authority brought a swift response and Emergency was declared on 17th April 1961. Ms Sirimavo was careful to declare that the emergency regulations applied only to the disturbed provinces. Under the Constitution, the measure was put forward for the approval of the Ceylonese Parliament. In the absence of the Federal Party members, all behind bars, the measure was passed. In July 1961, in an attempt to break the impasse, the Government appointed a committee of civil servants, three Sinhalese and three Tamils, to examine the language issue in depth. The committee came up with the recommendations that in the Northern and Eastern provinces, Tamil should be used as the language of the administration and correspondence with the Central Government in Tamil language will be acceptable. The unrest in the Tamil areas subsided as the Tamils were willing to give a chance to the new regulations.

In December 1965, the language policy giving due status to Tamil, was implemented by a Government order. The Buddhist clergy opposed the new language policy. Even the plantation Tamils joined in, as the use of Tamil was permitted only in the Northern and Eastern provinces thus depriving them of the same rights, as they lived outside these provinces.

Mrs. Bandarnaike of the SLFP, now in opposition, joined with the Marxists and launched an agitation against the Government's concessions to Tamils. To counter this move, the UNP organised its own 'nationalist' movement in the Sinhala-dominated Deep South to counter the moves of SLFP. Sri Lanka went through another bout of emergency as the armed forces were called in to deal with the general strike. But the language issue and Tamil separatism remained in check for the next five years as the Federal Party was part of the ruling coalition and for the first time, assurances to the Tamils were being implemented. The Lankan judiciary played a significant and positive role in the language dispute. In May 1964, a district judge ruled that Tamil civil servants who had failed to learn Sinhalese would still have the right to receive their annual increments.

Under relentless pressure from the SLFP and the Buddhist lobby, the UNP Government of Prime Minister Dudley Senanayake gave in to the demands of language chauvinists. On 23rd September 1968 it dismissed from service nearly one thousand Tamil civil servants for failing to learn Sinhalese language. The Federal Party representing Jaffna Tamils ended its four-year association with the UNP and withdrew its support to the Government over the dismissal issue. The decision was taken unanimously at the Federal Party's annual convention in April 1969. With this break, the brief period of peace between the Tamils and Sinhalese was about to end. The internal political dynamics of Lanka and the impending general elections had much to do with this toughening of UNP's stand on the Tamil issue. The work to grant Indian and Lankan citizenship to the plantation Tamils proceeded at leisurely pace. Under the terms of the agreement 300,000 persons were to be granted Lankan citizenship while 525,000 were to be granted Indian citizenship and repatriated to India. Till September 1968 ,only 84 persons were granted Lankan citizenship under the accord. On 23rd September 1968, prominent non-political Tamils attempted to forge a united front of all Tamils in Sri Lanka by bringing together the Federal Party and Ceylon Workers Congress. Nothing much came out of this move. The lack of unity between the Lankan Tamils and plantation Tamils has been and remains an enduring part of Lankan politics.

In keeping with the trend of Lankan politics, in the elections held in 1970, the SLFP led by Mrs. Sirimavo Bandarnaike came back to power with overwhelming majority. The SLFP had fought the elections on the platform of making Ceylon a Republic and giving it a new Constitution. The party promised a unitary form of government with a mixed system of proportional representation and direct election as well as an executive President to be directly elected by the whole country. This was to replace the old Westminster type democracy that Ceylon had had since independence.

The Federal party representing Tamil interests, opposed this move. On 28th June 1971, the Federal Party announced its decision to boycott the Constituent Assembly proceedings as it saw this move as a device to increase the Sinhalese domination at the cost of Tamils.

In April 1971, the extreme Marxist and Sinhala chauvinist organisation, the Janata Vimukti Premanna, launched an armed insurrection. Essentially it was a group of unemployed Sinhala youth venting its frustration. The Bandarnaike Government sought and obtained help from many countries including India, to deal with this rebellion. The JVP was however not crushed and was to re-surface at a later date.

Brushing aside the Tamil objections and on the support of her parliamentary majority, Ms. Bandarnaike ushered in the new Republican Constitution on 22nd May 1972. Ceylon now became the Democratic Socialist Republic of Sri Lanka. The Constitutional changes were seen as a move to make the Tamils, second class citizens. All the Tamil parties came together to form the Tamil United Front. This had representatives of both the Jaffna Tamils as well as the plantation workers. The Tamils of Lanka organised strikes and began preparations for 'direct action'. The situation was again reminiscent of the happenings of 1958. Mr. Chelvanayagam resigned his Kankesanturai seat and challenged the SLFP to defeat him, to prove that the Tamils supported new Constitution. The veteran Tamil leader won a thumping majority in the re-election. This was possibly the last attempt of the Tamils to solve their problems democratically and within the Constitutional framework. But the younger elements were restive and rejected the path of moderation as being ineffective. An 18 year old lad, V. Prabhakaran formed the militant organization of Tamil Tigers to carry out the struggle for an independent state of Tamil Eelam.

In 1971, the SLFP govt. of Mrs. Sirimavo Bandaranaike implemented a new policy called 'standarisation' in civil services and medical and technical educational opportunities. The ostensible reason for this was the Sinhalese lack of success in these fields and Tamils representation far in excess of their percentage (around 20 percent) of population. This was a policy of discrimination in favour of the majority of Sinhalese.

According to the 1969 figures, the Tamils had a share of 50 % seats in medicine and 48 % in engineering. After the 'standardisation', by 1977 their share dropped to 28 % in medicine and 19 % in engineering. Bright Tamil students thus felt deprived of educational opportunity leading to frustration and swelling of the ranks of extremists who demanded a separate state as the only remedy for Tamils. The openly discriminatory nature of these measures alienated the Tamil youth that increasingly gravitated towards the militant Tamil Tigers. The situation had come to such a pass that by 1980, Sinhalese who constituted 70 % of the Lankan population held 85 % of the govt. jobs and 82 % of the technical and managerial positions.

The discrimination against the Tamils in the civil services, was even more blatant. In 1970, Tamils formed only 5 % of the civil services. In 1977, not a single Tamil gained entry to the civil services. The armed forces also soon became exclusively Sinhalese as also did the police forces. The entire Government apparatus thus became alienated from the Tamils.

On 26th April 1977, Mr. S.V.J. Chelvenayagam, the 81 year old veteran Tamil leader died. With his death passed away the last moderate voice in Lankan Tamil politics. Mr. Chelvanayagam was an influential leader interested in preserving unity of Lanka and ensuring a place of honour for Tamils in a united Sri Lanka. He was the last important political figure to hold these views.

The SLFP Government on the other hand took recourse to increasingly repressive measures to deal with the Tamils. Its policies were based on reducing the majority of Tamils in the Northern and Eastern provinces through settling Sinhalese in these areas. To support these measures, the army was increasingly used as the Tamils resisted this attempt. The Jaffna area was under more or less continuous emergency. Even a gathering like the World Tamil Congress held in Jaffna was attacked and broken up by the high-handed police. As a result, the Jaffna Tamils gained the sympathies and support of the Tamil community, world wide.

The Tamils' fears about the Sinhala domination, expressed since 1957, seemed to have come true. As the repression against the Jaffna Tamils began, there was an outcry in the Indian state of Tamil Nadu. Tamils in both countries, not only shared a common language and culture, but had also maintained an intimate relationship including marriages, the most celebrated cases being the wedding of Vijay Amritraj, India's ace tennis player and now a media celebrity, to a girl from Jaffna and that of Sri Lankan ace cricketer Muttiah Muralidharan with a girl from Chennai. Jaffna University, one of the oldest in the subcontinent also housed rare Tamil manuscripts till its destruction at the hands of Sri Lankan Army, in 1983.

As a result of lack of opportunities at home, a large number of highly qualified Tamils from Sri Lanka began to migrate to the West where many countries granted them refugee status. Being highly educated and skilled, the expatriate Tamils have done well abroad especially in the US, UK, Germany and in South East Asian countries like Singapore and Malaysia. This web of the Tamil community world wide, continued to support the Sri Lankan Tamils with money as well as arms. Help also poured in across the Palk straits, where a sympathetic state Government turned a Nelson's eye to smuggling of arms and explosives.

The origins of militant groups are usually not easily traceable as most of the original leaders are no longer on the scene. The beginning of the Tamil militancy however can be traced to the year 1970 when Mr. Satyaseelan assisted by Tissa Weerasingham and Thangadorai established the Tamil Youth Front (Tamil Manavi Peravi). The 1971 insurrection by the JVP youth showed the Tamils the path to violence. But what really made militancy popular was the 'standardisation' policy implemented by the government of Mrs. Sirimavo Bandarnaike that discriminated against the Tamils in the matter of employment as well as admissions to the professional courses of higher learning. The increased unemployment that this measure generated amongst the Tamil youth gave the militants willing and dedicated recruits.

After the first anti-Tamil riots of 1956, clashes between the Sinhalese and the Tamils had been a regular feature of the Sri Lankan history. Riots occurred in 1958, 1961, 1974, 1977, 1979, 1981 and 1983. One common feature of all the riots till 1972 was that the Tamil violence was mainly reactive and unorganised. Riots invariably started in the Sinhala-dominated

South with the Buddhist clergy or extreme right Sinhala parties like JVP in the forefront. Mainstream parties like UNP or SLFP remained in the background, giving tacit support. Even in 1956, the government under late SWRD Bandaranaike had adopted a blatantly partisan stance favouring the Sinhalese. This became even more pronounced in the 1970s because of the policy of Sinhalese only and 'standardisation',[2]. The Government of Sri Lanka and its organs like police and the army came to be totally Sinhala-dominated. The focus of Tamil violence thus shifted from being anti-Sinhala to anti-Government. The distinction between Sinhala chauvinism and Government agencies became increasingly blurred. The Tamils now perceived the Sri Lankan state itself as the enemy, out to destroy them. Pitted against state power, Tamils soon felt the need to have a military arm of their own. While the Sri Lankan government or the world regarded these as terrorist groups, in the eyes of Tamils, this was seen as the sword arm of the as yet unborn state of Elam. This perception in the minds of majority of the Tamils in Sri Lanka gave a tremendous sense of legitimacy to the militant groups; the pre-eminent amongst them was the Tamil Tigers.

In 1975, V. Prabhakaran broke away from the Tamil Youth Front and along with Chetti Thanabalasingham formed the Tamil New Tigers (TNT). It is believed that Thanabalasingham was later assassinated on the orders of Prabhakaran, who then became the supreme leader of TNT, soon to be renamed Liberation Tigers of Tamil Eelam (LTTE). Prabhakaran belonged to the fishing community of Velvethiturai. Most of the recruits to the LTTE also belonged to this area and formed a strong core of support that owed personal loyalty to him. Initially Uma Maheshwaran, a surveyor by training and profession joined him, only to break away later. Siva Kumaran, Charles Anthony, Rajan Mahendran alias Mahattaya (deputy to Prabhakaran), Krishna Kumar alias Kittu, Kannan alias Gunda, Kalapathi alias Kala and Sathasivan Selvanayagam alias Sellakili, these seven most important leaders of LTTE formed the Praetorian Guard. Interestingly all of them were

---

[2] In 1971, a system of standardisation of marks was introduced for admissions to the universities, obviously directed against Tamil-medium students. K.M. de Silva describes it as follows: 'The qualifying mark for admission to the medical faculties was 250 (out of 400) for Tamil students, whereas it was only 229 for the Sinhalese.

involved in the first major violent action carried out by the LTTE – the assassination of the moderate Jaffna Mayor Alfred Duraiappah.

In 1972, in the very presence of the grand old man of Jaffna Tamils, S.J.V. Chelvanayakam, Mr. Kasi Ananthan, a Tiger sympathiser publicly stated,

" Mr. Duraiappah (the Jaffna Mayor) is an enemy of the Tamil nation. He does not deserve a natural death nor does he deserve to die in an accident. Tamil people, specially the youth must decide how the traitor must die..."

Three years later he was assassinated by the LTTE. Mr. Chelvanayakam, the old fox, denied ever having endorsed the violence and pleaded that he was hard of hearing due to old age. It is more likely that exasperated with the Sinhalese backsliding on agreements, the moderate political leadership of the Federal Party came to the conclusion that the only method left for the Tamils to survive was to engage in a violent conflict. It appears that the Tamil Tigers thus have always had backing from the Federal Party and its later incarnation Tamil United Liberation Front (TULF). This modus is not unique to Jaffna and is to be found in all such conflicts where the militant outfits have an over ground presence through the "moderates". The examples of Sinn Fein for the Irish Republican Army (IRA), Assam Gana Sangram Parishad for ULFA or Hurriyat Conference for multitude of militant outfits in Kashmir, come to mind. The major implication of this conclusion is that the Tamil Tigers were not some desperadoes fighting in isolation but had the full moral , material and intellectual backing of the Sri Lankan Tamil community numbering over five million. They also had the tacit sympathy, if not active support, of sections of the nearly 55 million Tamils in India; especially when Lankan Tamils were faced with extinction due to the actions of Sri Lankan armed forces.

The roots of the Sri Lankan conflict lay in historical memories and a threat to identity. The Sinhalese obsession with a unitary form of government, denial of federal structure and the narrow political interests also played a role. The final spark was the patently discriminatory employment policies that sought to reduce the Tamil people's dominance in the educational field. All these factors were exploited by the Buddhist clergy who dreamt of a

'Dhamma Dwipa' or Sri Lanka as the bastion of Buddhism. It was a case of multiple causes coming together in an unholy alliance to make the 'Serendipity Island', a hell on earth.

Jammu and Kashmir

The dispute over Jammu and Kashmir (J&K) is one of the oldest, unresolved, post Second World War international conflicts. India and Pakistan have fought two wars and two major actions over it.[3] But the insurgency in Kashmir is a relatively new phenomenon. It dates back to the decade of 1980s. Kashmir typifies the difficulty in demarcating conflicts as internal and external. The two elements are closely intertwined, and in a sense, feed on each other. It is true that the 'Kashmir dispute' predates the Kashmir insurgency. Pakistan describes it as 'unfinished business of partition' (of India in 1947 when Muslim majority provinces seceded). Howsoever irksome, the background to this dispute forms an essential part of understanding the insurgency.

Pakistan claims that as a Muslim majority area, Kashmir should rightfully have formed a part of Pakistan at the time of independence in 1947. Merging Kashmir with Pakistan is an obsession and a core value for that country. Pakistan points out that under the instrument of accession and also the proposals of the Commission of the UN Security Council dated 13th August 1948, India had agreed to decide the future of Jammu and Kashmir according to the wishes of the people. However, the truce agreement was never implemented as Pakistan did not agree to withdraw its forces from the territory captured. India argued that the ruler of the state accepted the merger into India under the terms of the Act of British Parliament. Sheikh Abdullah, the popular leader and his party the National Conference also supported this move. According to the Indians, the duly elected Constituent Assembly of the state merged the state with India in 1957 and the issue of ascertaining the wishes of people was no longer valid.

---

[3] The first Kashmir war was fought in 1947-48, almost immediately after independence. The second Kashmir war took place in 1965. Since that time there have been major clashes over Siachen area in the late 1980s and a major incursion in Kargil area in 1999.

The problem of Jammu and Kashmir is at once internal, regional and international. None of these factors operate in a water- tight compartment and often interact with each other. This has made the issue complex and has been responsible for lack of progress towards a solution.

Sheikh Abdullah and later his son Dr. Farooq, remained undisputed leaders in Kashmir right till the 1980s. But as soon as the Sheikh's party, the National Conference tasted power and their rule saw widespread corruption and inefficiency, the support evaporated. On 13th October 1983, a cricket match between India and West Indies was used by the fundamentalists as a platform to humiliate the Indian team and cock a snook at India. The Indian sportsmen were assaulted and booed, slogans in support of Pakistan were raised and the match was disrupted when it was thought that India was likely to win. All this took place in the presence of the Chief Minister Farooq Abdullah. As separatist violence in neighbouring Punjab reached a crescendo, the pro- Pakistani elements became even bolder and began attacking security forces vehicles. Even earlier, in July 1980, two incidents took place that were indicative of the future. In Srinagar, a military vehicle met with a minor accident with a small taxi (a three wheeler, popularly known as rickshaw). Immediately a mob went on a rampage and attacked several Government vehicles and burnt shops belonging to Hindus. In an even more serious incident, a team of 70 Income Tax officials who had arrived in Srinagar to investigate tax evasion by carpet exporters was attacked by a mob led by Dr. Farooq Abdullah himself. In both these incidents, the local police not only did not take any action, but sided with the miscreants.

In 1989, Sheikh Abdullah's birth anniversary was observed as a black day and his grave in Srinagar had to be put under massive security to save it from the wrath of people who intended to vandalise it.

The 1980s was an exceptionally violent decade in India. The violence in Punjab by Sikh extremists reached a peak in 1986-87. In 1987, India also got involved in Sri Lanka's ethnic conflict. In Kashmir, Farooq Abdullah had lost all credibility in the eyes of Kashmiris after his alliance with the Congress party. On 7th November 1986, Rajiv Gandhi, the Prime Minister of India, emulating his mother, signed an accord with Farooq and installed him as the

Chief Minister of Jammu and Kashmir. In the March 1987 elections, the alliance of National Conference and Congress won 2/3rds majority. There were allegations of wide spread irregularities in the election and Muslim United Front, a conglomerate of pro-Pakistan and fundamentalist Muslim parties claimed that they were cheated of certain electoral victory. Civil disturbances in Kashmir valley became a daily affair. Large scale smuggling of arms and ammunition began from Pakistan. The fall of the Berlin wall and the liberation of Eastern European countries from Soviet domination resonated in Kashmir. The situation was ideal for Pakistan to launch yet another attempt to annex Kashmir.

The foundation of unrest based on a militant Islam was laid during the ineffectual rule of Farooq Abdullah in the eighties. The spread of Madarssas or Islamic schools run by fanatical Jamaat cadres, was a new development. In addition, foreign funds from Iran and Saudi Arabia were permitted to flood Kashmir. Many international conferences of pan-Islamic organisations were held in Kashmir during this period. These gatherings received official patronage and support. None of these were purely religious gatherings and became a forum for attacking secular ideology and spreading intolerance. The people of Kashmir gave up their traditional attire for an imitation of the Afghan dress of loose salwar kameez. Women began wearing scarves to cover their heads and the Burkha (a black garment covering the entire body of the woman) made its first appearance. The slogan for 'Nizam E Mustafa' or rule of Sharia was also raised repeatedly from various public platforms.

It is believed that the plan to begin unrest in Kashmir was ready in Pakistan as early as 1980. However the massive presence of the Soviet army in Afghanistan and the popularity of Sheikh Abdullah in J&K forced Pakistan's military dictator Zia Ul Haq, to bide his time. The beginning of the Russian withdrawal from Afghanistan and the death of Sheikh Abdulla followed by the misrule, allowed Farook Abdulla's administration to prepare the ground for the launch of Operation Topac.

Pakistan had learnt a lesson from its failure in taking Kashmir in 1947 and 1965. Zia Ul Haq believed that for the insurgency in Kashmir to be successful, it had to be based on a bulk of fighting to be done by the Kashmiris themselves. The first phase involved arms training of Kashmiri youth in various camps, set up in parts of occupied Kashmir. The Inter Services Intelligence Agency (ISI) was given sole charge of this operation. Unemployed youth from urban areas were lured into these camps and the first batch was ready in 1982 after training for 3 months. As the state of J&K was plunged into political turmoil, more and more batches went to Pakistan and by 1987, there were close to ten thousand trained Kashmiris in the Srinagar valley.

All this time the pro-Pakistani elements were systematically inducted into the government. Thus it came to a pass that in 1987, arms and ammunition smuggled across the border were carried in police and forest department vehicles on the Indian side of the Line of Control (LOC) that demarcates the border between Indian and Pakistani held Kashmir. The modus-operandi was similar to the one successfully followed in Afghanistan. Armed youth were given a liberal supply of AK-47 or Kalashnikov assault rifles, machine-guns, rocket launchers and explosives. The emphasis was on the supply of modern heavy-volume fully- automatic weapons. In most cases these weapons were superior to the semi-automatic rifles and machine-guns of 1960s vintage that were available with the Indian Army. The move was a deliberate tactic to boost the morale of Kashmiri militants, otherwise not known for warlike qualities

The fight in Kashmir was given a religious colour, as a war between infidel and Islam. The Jamaat E Islami played a major role in this ideological orientation. At this time, the process of 'Islamisation' was on in Pakistan as well. It is around this time that the demand for 'Nizam E Mustafa' or rule according to Quran, made its first appearance in Kashmir. In all the earlier unrests, the common slogan used to be demand for 'Plebiscite'.

The year 1987 saw frequent demonstrations in Srinagar. Most marches were peaceful and would end up presenting a petition to UN representatives. The ineffectual Farooq administration often clamped curfew and orders prohibiting assembly of more than five people. These were routinely violated and an atmosphere of anarchy began to spread. The demonstrations were followed by general strikes on the flimsiest of excuses. The tourist trade was the first casualty of the civic unrest. The main organisations at the forefront were the Jammu Kashmir Liberation Front (JKLF) that demanded an independent Kashmir and Jamaat E Islami that wanted the state to merge with Pakistan.

All this while, a stream of young men began travelling to Pakistan to receive arms training. The smuggling of arms across the LOC also continued unabated. A very large quantity of arms and ammunition was brought in and kept hidden in the countryside and inside cities. Groundwork for eventual armed struggle was being carefully laid inside Kashmir. The Farooq Abdulla administration turned a blind eye to these happenings.

Kashmir valley had nearly a 200,000 strong Hindu community of Kashmiri Brahmins commonly referred to as Pandits. Intimidation of Hindus began in right earnest. Many Pandits began moving their families outside the Valley.

The year 1989 saw Farooq's administration at its nadir. On 14th August 1989, the pro- Pakistani elements in Srinagar carried out a march past in the national stadium in Srinagar, complete with a 21 gun salute and hoisted a Pakistani flag. The next day, 15th August was observed as a black day and day of mourning. Earlier, on 29th July 1989, Islamic activists threw acid on the faces of two Muslim women for their crime of not wearing a 'burqa' or a veil. On 21st August, a National Conference politician Yusuf Dalwai and on 14th September, Mr. Taploo of the Bhartiya Janata Party were killed. JKLF admitted the responsibility for these killings and proclaimed that these acts would continue until India left Kashmir.

In another reversal of fortune, Sheikh Abdulla's birth anniversary on 5th September was greeted with black flags and burning of his effigy. It was indeed a remarkable turnaround in the fortunes of man almost deified by Kashmiris till as recently as 1982! Farooq Abdullah's response to these events was a study in appeasement. Between July and December 1989, as many as 70 militants charged with various crimes were released on bail. Once out of jail they promptly went underground. On 28th September 1989, Mr. Shabir Shah of the Peoples League, a party that advocated merger with Pakistan, was ordered to be arrested. The civil servants responsible refused to sign the warrant and Government lawyers boycotted the courts. On 4th November, Mr. Ganju, the judge who had tried Maqbool Butt of JKLF for murdering an intelligence officer, was gunned down in Srinagar in broad daylight. The Farooq administration had ceased to exist and pro-Pakistani elements had taken over the rule. Most Kashmiris believed that a merger with Pakistan was around the corner and decided that they need not pay their electricity or telephone bills to the existing government. The worst was however yet to come.

The happenings in Kashmir were not an isolated instance of abdication of governance. The rest of India was also in the throes of a crisis since 1987 when Prime Minister Rajiv Gandhi's authority was seriously undermined by charges of bribe taking, in a defence deal with Sweden for purchase of 155 mm guns.

In this situation of drift, in 1989 the general elections held resulted in Rajiv Gandhi losing power and his erstwhile colleague Mr. V. P. Singh becoming the Prime Minister. V. P. appointed a Kashmiri politician Mufti Mohammed Syed as the new Home Minister. Kashmir and the violent uprising there became his responsibility. V. P. had promised during his election campaign that he would give priority to finding a solution to the Kashmir and Punjab problems. Mufti Mohhamed's appointment was thought to be a step in that direction. But within days of V. P. taking over the central government, the JKLF militants abducted the daughter of Mufti Mohammed on 10th December 1989. In return for the girl, the terrorists demanded release of five militants, then in prison. It is believed that Chief Minister Farooq Abdullah advised against the release of the terrorists. In spite of overruling objections, a deal was struck with the kidnappers. The release of jailed terrorists was rightly claimed as victory by the militants and Srinagar witnessed scenes of jubilation. Governmental authority ceased to exist and most Kashmiris felt that within a month Kashmir would either become independent or a part of Pakistan. Many fence-sitters jumped onto the bandwagon and Kashmir, remaining part of India, was thought to be a lost cause. The abject surrender by the Government to the kidnappers sent a signal to Pakistan that India lacked the will to hold on to Kashmir. This incident marks the beginning of the proxy war and insurgency.

It is believed that the Government knew about the location of the kidnapped daughter of the Home Minister all along. Even her daily meals were being sent by relations. It is very unlikely that in a closed society like the one existing in the Kashmir valley, the abductors would have caused any harm to the kidnapped girl. The motives and timings of the whole episode are shrouded in mystery. It can be however safely assumed that the armed forces were neither consulted nor kept informed about the happenings. The decision that plunged Kashmir into a full blown insurgency was that of Prime Minister V. P. Singh.

In the peculiar defence set-up prevailing in India, professionals have no place. As a telling example, Mr. T. A. Sheshan had just moved into the Ministry of Defence from the Ministry of Environment. Overnight he became the arbiter of India's destiny. All this while, the army continued to deal with the events in Kashmir as a simple 'law and order' problem. This author's request to visit Kashmir to study the budding insurgency, made in 1988, was dismissed by a bureaucrat with a cryptic note- "But there is no insurgency in Kashmir"

Earlier in the 1980s when the author was in the Eastern Army headquarters in Calcutta and dealing with the problems of internal unrest, similar resistance to recognition of reality, was encountered. At that time a violent movement by students in Manipur had all the makings of turning into a full-fledged insurgency. Yet in the Indian scheme of things, the armed forces had to wait till the problem turned really serious. Exactly the same experience was repeated in Kashmir. It seemed as if the local civil authority was actually hoping for the situation to deteriorate so that it could be then handed over to the army. India has no apex agency or institution to monitor and co-ordinate the various departments and fashion a response to crisis. Ad-hoc ism rules the roost. In a complicated matter like the Kashmir trouble, the policy finally adopted does not depend on any objective criterion but is dictated by the strongest personality on the scene and the views of the organisation s/he represents, prevail.

As expected, the release of terrorists was greeted with dismay by the rightist Bhartiya Janata Party (BJP), on whose support the minority V. P.

Singh administration was dependent. In another of those typical wild swings in policy, Mr. Jagmohan, a tough no-nonsense bureaucrat was appointed the new Governor of state at the behest of BJP and against the wishes of the Chief Minister. As a reaction, Farooq Abdullah resigned on 19th January 1990 and the state came under the direct rule of the Central Government, a rule that continued for six years.

In addition to the administrative changes, nearly two divisions of army, earlier located in the North East and specialising in counter-insurgency operations were inducted into the Valley. Over one hundred battalions of Para-military forces, the Border Security Force (BSF) and Central Reserve Police (CRPF) were inducted in the state. The Para-military forces were deployed mainly in urban areas and on static duties while the army stayed in its barracks and was given an offensive role. The Para-military forces in India do not have the training or discipline of the army to withstand the rigours of counter-insurgency. They also have no well-thought out rotation plan and the force is generally poorly officered. Living in the midst of a hostile population day and night and all the time fearful of a sniper's bullet or a grenade attack, these small pockets of isolated detachments were extremely vulnerable to over-reaction to provocation. The situation was tailor-made for causing civilian casualties in case the soldiers ran amok.

When the army began its operations in Kashmir in 1990, it suffered from various handicaps. The state of anarchy that had lasted from 1987 onwards had resulted in the total elimination of the police intelligence network. No information about the identity or plans of insurgents reached the troops. It was like a blind man trying to fight an unseen enemy at night. The armed forces went about their task in whatever way they could think right. Many people were picked up on suspicion and beaten up in custody. A large number of custodial deaths occurred during this period. While many of those who died belonged to the militant group JKLF, innocents also suffered. This ham-handed approach alienated the population even further from the government.

In tandem with the operations of the security forces, Mr. Jagmohan the newly appointed Governor also took tough measures to control vital resources like food and oil supply to bring the people to their knees. The security forces were helped in their task by the fact that since 1988, many of the JKLF activists were functioning openly. The JKLF was therefore the organisation that suffered the most during this period.

To counter the pressure of the security forces, the JKLF turned their ire against the 200,000 strong Hindu community. Living in isolated pockets and forming less than 3% of the population, the Kashmiri Pandits were vulnerable to terrorists. The ethnic cleansing of Kashmir valley by the JKLF began by selective murders of prominent people. On 27th December 1989, a social worker of Anantnag, Premnath Bhat was short dead in broad daylight. The victim lay bleeding on the road and no one dared to come to his rescue. Journalists, teachers and political workers were targets of this violence. Newspapers carried messages from terrorist outfits publishing lists and addresses of Hindus to be targeted the next day. The commonly heard cry in valley was, 'Leave your women and property and get out'. A massive exodus of the Hindus began on 21 January 1990. Many went to Delhi and stayed with their kith and kin. The poorer Hindus who had nowhere else to go came to Jammu and began life as refugees in their own country.

This massive tragedy, comparable with human rights violations in former Yugoslavia and ethnic cleansing in Bosnia, was largely ignored by the Indian media possibly under pressure of the Government. The government's logic being that news of exodus of Hindus may provoke reaction against Muslims in other parts of India. Indian media, though largely independent, has a tradition of co-operating with the government on sensitive security issues. Even in 1971, the best- kept Indian secret was the identity of majority of the nearly 9 million refugees driven away from the erstwhile East Pakistan (later the independent country of Bangladesh). Since these were Hindus, this fact was kept carefully hidden from the Indian masses to prevent communal rioting on religious lines. The same feat was repeated in the case of the plight of the Kashmiri refugees. While that rationale was laudable and even logical, its effect at regional and global levels, has been that terrorists who perpetrated one of the biggest post-Cold War ethnic cleansing operations and their supporter, Pakistan, were left free instead to blame India for violation of human rights. The West cynically exploited this faux pas on India's part to corner her inept and naive diplomats on various world forums. It is only in 1995 that the Indian government woke up to the mistake of this approach and began highlighting the plight of Hindu refugees from Kashmir. It is noteworthy that despite all the propaganda against the Indian security forces and their alleged atrocities, there has been no influx of refugees into Pakistan from Kashmir.

Most analysts agree that the 'insurgency' in Kashmir began in 1988/89. But such is the close nexus between the proxy war by Pakistan and domestic unrest in Kashmir, that the two are virtually inseparable. The initial impetus was definitely provided by the happenings in Europe, but a long-term reason was the long cultivated myth of the 'unique' Kashmiri identity. This was due to the defensive reaction of the secular Indian State and the cynical exploitation by the West and Pakistan. During the Cold War period, Kashmir could be used as a pressure point against the pro-Soviet Union India. The Afghan war against the Soviet occupation began winding down in the late 1980s. This was perceived as a victory for Islamists forces and the fighters that were freed from this war were directed towards Kashmir. As to the material support to the Kashmiri insurgents, this was the period when the US backed Pakistan to the hilt and made sure that the insurgents in Kashmir had the very latest weapons and equipment. Towards the early 1990s, Pakistan sought and got American support for its Kashmir venture as a sort of reward for its role in ousting the Soviet Union from Afghanistan. Seldom does one come across a case of insurgency where so many factors came together in time and space. Insurgency in Kashmir was a virtual certainty in 1988/89.

South Africa

No contemporary conflict has attracted so much world support and sympathy as the struggle of the black population of South Africa to overthrow the minority rule. The end of the 'Apartheid' regime in South Africa is regarded as the last of the struggles against European imperialism and is regarded as the end of an era of European domination. Ex post facto, the outcome is regarded as a virtual certainty and therefore not too much of outside research effort has been devoted to the 'armed struggle' and 'counter-insurgency' operations by the racist regime. As opposed to this, a large body of literature exists on the peace process that took place in South Africa post 1989. It is undoubtedly true that the peaceful transition from white minority rule in South Africa to the formation of a multi-party inclusive democracy is a fascinating subject. Yet it should not be forgotten that the seeds of this very welcome outcome were sown during the struggle itself.

The first watershed in the history of the struggle, was the famous 'Rivonia Trials' in the year 1963-64. These trials were the outcome of a raid by the South African Police on the farm Lilliesleaf at Rivonia, near Johannesburg, on 11th July 1963. The trial was the most famous in the history of South African political resistance. Nelson Mandela, Walter Sisulu, Govan Mbeki and others were sentenced to life imprisonment on 12th June 1964. This marks the virtual end of the peaceful struggle waged by the majority Black Africans and can be said to be the beginning of the armed struggle, not out of choice, but out of compulsion.

But the arrival of that spark for armed resistance took 12 long years! The South African regime with its repressive measures had successfully marginalised the ANC (African National Congress). With its leadership decimated and no direct access to South Africa proper, the ANC had become an 'expatriate' resistance movement. The revolt in the Johannesburg suburb of Soweto changed all that.

On 16th June 1976, some 20,000 Soweto school children marched in protest against the 'language rule'. The trigger was the government diktat that the Afrikaans language was to be the medium of instruction in all black schools. The credit for the new found confidence amongst the blacks to oppose the unfair conditions goes to the Black Consciousness (BC) movement that had started a few years earlier. The key founders of BC were Steven Bantu Biko and Barney Pityana, both of whom were heavily influenced by the 'Liberation Theology' that entered South Africa through the University Christian Movement and South African Council of Churches. Rev D. Allan Boesak was particularly influential in its spread.

Though the membership of the BC movement was small, there was great power in its message and it raised a deep emotional response. BC philosophy was readily spread to the masses with compelling slogans such as 'Black is beautiful'. This movement helped black youth overcome years of conditioned subservience to white domination. The result of all this was the revolt in Soweto.

Returning to the events of that fateful 16th June 1976- It was a sedate march to begin with, with a lot of slogan-shouting and placard-waving. The police rushed to the scene and ordered the marchers to disperse. But in the noise and din no one heard the order and demonstrations continued. Then suddenly a 13-year old schoolboy Hector Petersen was shot in the head from behind. There were no warning shots or tear gas. Several more youngsters were shot dead by the police. All hell broke loose. Police vehicles were set on fire; isolated policemen were dragged from their vehicles and burnt alive. The news of the riot spread fast and the entire township of Soweto erupted in a revolt. White business establishments were burnt, banks, post offices, shops were looted and then set on fire. Soweto began to resemble a war zone.

The revolt did not remain confined to Soweto but spread far and wide. In Cape Town, Kimberly and elsewhere, blacks went on the rampage, burning and looting. The youth were at the forefront of much of the violence. The black community organised an economic boycott of white businesses. Close to 550 people died in police action and thousands were detained in harsh repressive measures by the Government. The most notable leader to die in detention was Steve Biko. On 11th September 1977, a sick Biko, handcuffed and lying naked, was driven 1200 km in the back of a truck, ostensibly for medical treatment, from Port Elizabeth to Pretoria. On 12th September he died in prison in Pretoria. Students organised a school boycott and close to 10,000 young people escaped the country to join the liberation movement. The world was outraged and the UN in Nov 1977 imposed a mandatory arms embargo on South Africa and called for an end to Apartheid. The then US President Jimmy Carter came out openly in support of the Soweto students. South Africa was never to be the same again. The Soweto revolt can well be called the beginning of the armed struggle.

It is necessary to have a brief look at South African history to understand the events of the dying decades of the 20th century. The Republic of South

Africa is a country located at the southern tip of Africa, with a 2,798 kilometres coastline on the Atlantic and Indian Oceans. To the north lie Namibia, Botswana and Zimbabwe; to the east are Mozambique and Swaziland; while Lesotho is an independent country wholly surrounded by South African territory.

Modern humans have inhabited Southern Africa for more than 100,000 years. At the time of European contact, the dominant indigenous people were tribes who had migrated from other parts of Africa about one thousand years before. From the 4th-5th century CE, Bantu-speaking tribes had steadily moved south, where they displaced, conquered and assimilated the original people of southern Africa. At the time of European contact, the two major groups were the Xhosa and Zulu people.

In 1652, a century and a half after the discovery of the Cape Sea Route, the Dutch East India Company found a refreshment station at what would become Cape Town. Cape Town became a British colony in 1806. European settlement expanded during the 1820s as the Boers (original Dutch, Flemish, German and French settlers) and the British (1820 Settlers) claimed land in the north and east of the country. Conflicts arose among the Xhosa, Zulu and Afrikaner groups who competed for territory.

The discovery of diamonds and later gold, triggered the 19th-century conflict known as the Anglo-Boer War, as the Boers and the British fought for the control of the South African mineral wealth. Although the British defeated the Boers, they gave limited independence to South Africa in 1910 as a British dominion. Within the country, anti-British politics among white South Africans focussed on independence. During the Dutch and British colonial years, racial segregation was mostly informal, though some legislations were enacted to control the settlement and movement of native people, including the *Native Location Act of 1879* and the system of *pass laws*. Power was held by the European colonists.

In the Boer republics, from as early as the Pretoria Convention in the 19th century and subsequent South African governments, the system became legally institutionalised segregation, later known as *apartheid*. The government established three classes of racial stratification: white, coloured and black, with rights and restrictions for each. South Africa achieved the status of a republic in 1961. Despite opposition both in and outside the country, the government legislated for a continuation of apartheid.

The 1960s were a period when the various colonies of European powers in Asia and Africa were gaining independence. South Africa, or more precisely, the minority whites in that country, chose to go in the opposite direction. Racial superiority of the whites and segregation and discrimination based on 'race' was the foundation of the 'new' republic. For close to thirty years after this event, the South African state was an anachronism. The story of the downfall of this ideology is one of the fascinating stories of the 20th century liberation movements.[4]

But returning to the Soweto riots of 1976, serious as these disturbances were, they could not have had long-lasting effect but for the ready infrastructure of the ANC that was already in existence. Almost thirteen years before the Soweto revolt, in 1953, the ANC in its annual conference chalked out a plan to carryout underground violent struggle in case it was banned. Known as the M Plan (Mandela Plan), ground work was laid to carry out underground struggle on the lines of Communist revolts in other parts of the world. Going back even further in time, Ray Alexander Simons, a member of South African Communist Party (SACP) was trained in Latvia in former Soviet Union in 1929. The first plans for underground and violent struggle meant a change in the attitude of the ordinary workers of ANC.

The formation of volunteer corps wearing uniforms and swearing an oath during the Defiance Campaign of the 1960s, were the first tentative steps towards formation of the uMkhonto weSizwe (MK for short) that

---

[4] Communist Party of South African (CSA), 'The Path to Power', Johannesburg, Sep 1990.P. 48. In 1961 ANC plus CSA created MK the armed wing and national sabotage campaign was launched on 16 Dec 1961. The document lays bare the reasons/conditions that prevented a guerrilla war in South Africa,a) All military knowledge and weapons were withheld from blacks for centuries.

(b) 80% land was held by the whites and there was hardly any black peasantry.

(c) No rear bases available outside South Africa.

(d) Terrain was in favour of security forces.

(e) The Apartheid regime had efficient and mobile SADF (South African Defence Forces).

meant 'The Spear of the Nation'. There is an interesting parallel to the Indian experience. Subhas Chandra Bose as Congress President introduced uniform and military drills for the corps of volunteers when the Indian National Congress was committed to peaceful over ground struggle. It is no surprise that at a later date Bose went on to create the Indian National Army to fight the British.

The MK was envisaged as a hierarchical organisation with a clear 'top-down' character. In Nelson Mandela's words, 'The idea was to set up an organisational machinery that would allow the ANC to take decisions at the highest level which could then be swiftly transmitted to the organisation as a whole without calling a meeting.' At the same time the plan had important features promoting local initiative and participation.

The smallest unit was a cell, which in urban townships consisted of ten houses on a street. A steward was in charge of the cell. If the street had more than ten houses then there would be a cell steward and street steward. A group of streets formed a zone directed by a chief steward who was in turn responsible to the local branch of the ANC secretariat. Thus an elaborate and structured organisation came into being much before the ban on the ANC or the eventual armed struggle of 1976. One of the ironies of the M Plan was that it was actually the racist regime and its plans for segregated townships that helped it form secure bases for the underground work.

There was very little underground or armed activity following the formation of MK as the local conditions meant that the force had to be trained outside the country. But what M Plan did was to create the 'sea' in which the guerrillas could operate, once they managed to enter. While the ANC was banned and most leaders in exile, Radio Freedom, a clandestine radio station, was the main instrument to keep up morale and maintain presence. For example just before his arrest Walter Sisulu made a broadcast on the 26 June 1963,

'Sons and daughters of Africa, I speak to you from somewhere in South Africa. I have not left the country and do not plan to leave it.'

This had an electrifying effect on the people at large and raised their morale despite the repression unleashed.

Concerned at the lack of ability to infiltrate inside South Africa from its bases out side the country and the loss of momentum of revolution, the ANC sent a high-level delegation to Vietnam in 1978-79. The Vietnamese were flushed with their victory over the mighty US and gave valuable strategy tips to the ANC. Accordingly the initial emphasis of armed action was more on sabotage rather than taking on the state. On 1st June 1980, the MK attacked oil from coal facility in Sasol located in Orange Free State and East Transvaal using limpet mines. The total damage was worth Rand 58 million. It was an important target as South Africa was suffering from the oil embargo and this was a reminder of its vulnerability. Thus began the bombing and sabotage campaign as first part of the armed struggle.

Naxalism in Chhattisgarh

The 'Naxal' movement began in 1967 when long-suffering peasants killed a landlord, Naganrai Choudhuri, living close to Naxalbari village, in Darjeeling district of West Bengal. Years of oppression and injustice exploded into a violent reaction. This was the beginning of a movement of violent response to exploitation. The term 'Naxalism' is now synonymous with violent protests by tribals and landless workers all over the country. Throughout this book the term Naxals has been used in a generic sense and describes Communist insurgents of various hues who have many *avatars* as Maoists, People's War Group, and Socialist Unity Centre et al.

The state of Chhattisgarh came into being in the year 2000. The area comprising the state was earlier part of a larger Madhya Pradesh state. The problem of Naxalism in Chhattisgarh is not uniform. While the southern districts of Bastar have been affected for 25-30 years, northern districts like Sarguja and Jashpur have seen unrest in the last five to seven years. In the South, it is the spill-over of the agitation of the PWG (People's War Group) while in the North it is linked to the caste conflict in Bihar and more recently the anti-monarchy campaign of the maoists of Nepal.

Chhattisgarh, the 26th State of India was carved out of Madhya Pradesh on November 1st 2000. It is situated between 17 to 23.7 degrees N and 8.40 to 83.38 degrees E. It abounds in hilly-forested regions and plains and is surrounded by six Indian states: Madhya Pradesh, Andhra Pradesh, Uttar

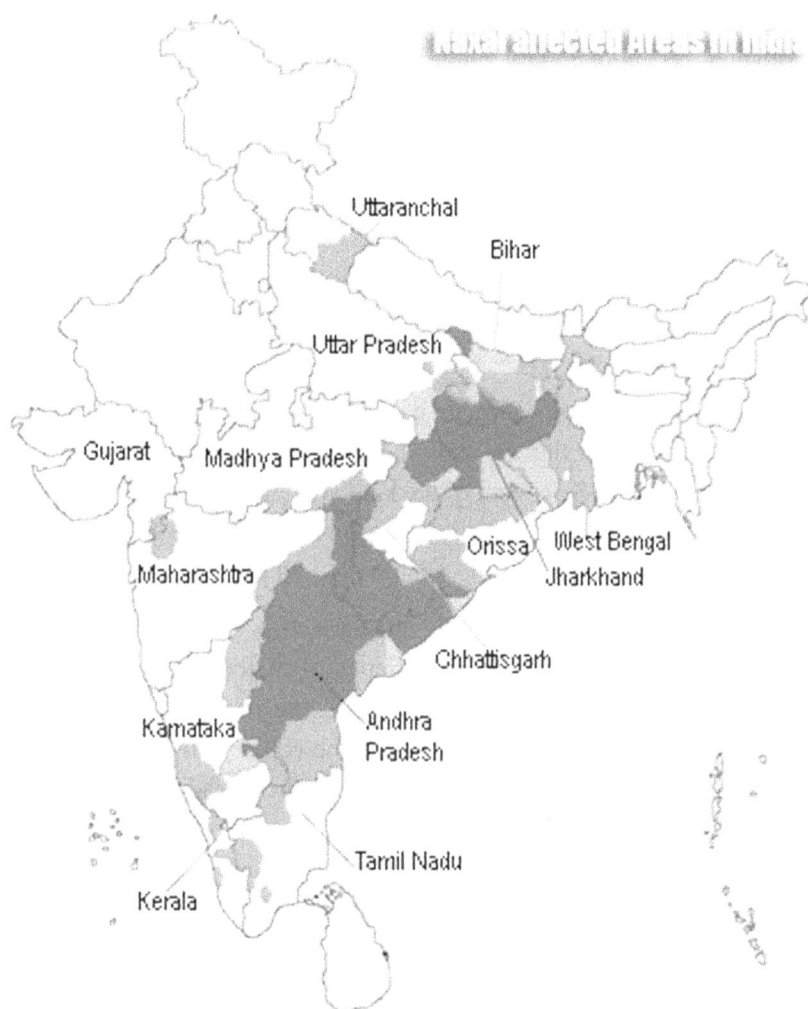

Naxal affected Areas in India

Uttaranchal

Bihar

Uttar Pradesh

Gujarat

Madhya Pradesh

Orissa   West Bengal

Maharashtra   Jharkhand

Chhattisgarh

Karnataka   Andhra
Pradesh

Tamil Nadu

Kerala

Highly affected (51)   Marginally affected (62)

Moderately affected (18)   Targeted (34)

Total affected districts - 170   States - 15

Pradesh, Maharashtra, Jharkhand and Orissa. It receives an annual average rainfall of 1500mm.

It is a predominantly tribal state endowed with rich mineral and forest wealth and has about 35 large and small tribes inhabiting the state. Of the total population, 37.1 per cent belong to the Scheduled Tribes and 22.3 per cent to the Scheduled Castes. According to the 2001 Census, 82 per cent of the total population of 20.8 million live in rural areas.

Forests account for 46 per cent of the total land area of Chhattisgarh region. Of the forests, Sal trees cover 46 per cent, followed by teak. Most of the timber is used for construction and accounts for 40 per cent of the total revenue, from the forest sector.

The rivers of Chhattisgarh are its lifeline and most cities and villages are situated on or near these rivers. The river Mahanadi and its tributaries provide water to 58.48 per cent of the land area of Chhattisgarh. Godavari and its tributaries provide 28.02 per cent, Ganga's tributary Sone, provides 13.24 per cent and Narmada, the remaining 0.90 per cent.

All of India's tin ore is in Chhattisgarh. It is very well-endowed in terms of mineral wealth, with 28 varieties of major minerals, including diamonds. It has almost the largest of all the coal deposits in India. Chhattisgarh has a fifth of the iron ore in the country and one of the best quality iron ore deposits in the world is found in the Bailadila mines in South Chhattisgarh. Rich deposits of Bauxite, Limestone, Dolomite and Corundum are found in the state. Major crops are Rice, Wheat, Maize, and Barley. Major forest products are timber, tendu leaves, mahua, medicinal plants etc. Chhattisgarh is popularly referred to as a "Rice Bowl". 85 per cent of the population is dependent on agriculture and 43.37 per cent of the total land area is cultivated.

Before division, Chhattisgarh was at one end of the state of Madhya Pradesh. Politically it was unimportant and the story of its neglect goes back 45 years. In addition the Government of the day, under the influence of Mr. B. D. Sharma, the district collector of Bastar, followed the policy of keeping the Tribals isolated so as to protect them from exploitation by plainsmen, with the result that no attempt was made to extend administration to the forest areas. The areas of Telangana in Andhra state had a flourishing Communist movement since 1947. The Peoples War Group (PWG), its latest incarnation, believes in violent revolution and consists of followers of Che Guevara. In the 1980s they carried out several attacks on trains and buses, forcing the Andhra government to crack down on them. Whenever under pressure in Andhra, the PWG moved into the forests of Bastar. The administration vacuum was filled by the Naxalites who established a virtual government in Bastar areas.

The situation in Bastar was tailor-made for the Naxals. The people-government interface at village level is based on Gramsevaks, teachers, talathi, and forest guards. These were mostly non-Tribal and exploited the illiterate Tribals. It was not unusual to find that money meant to build schools was used to build private houses. The Naxalites put an end to this and became popular among the Tribals. The Tribals had their own culture and tradition going back ages. They had their own trade and exchange methods and their own legal system. The administrative intrusion including the Panchayat Raj ordinance (village self government) actually reduced their participation and the Tribals felt a loss of power over their own destiny. This was projected as the government oppression by the Naxalites to turn the Tribals against the state.

The biggest cause of Tribal unrest in India is the Forest Act 1927 and its successor legislations. Jungles were divided into two groups by the Indian Forest Act 1927- Reserved Forests and Protected Forests. Every activity is prohibited in the reserved forest. Some rights were offered to the Tribal's in protected forests. Wood from the forest could be used for the purpose of house building. Use of small jungle products for self-use was permitted, but commercial sale was restricted. In short, the habitat of the Tribals was nationalised by the government without paying any compensation to the original owners, the Tribals.

Post independence, the injustice continued and the Forest Policy of 1988 was a re-hash of the original British design. People were forced to live as strangers in their own land. The Tribals were deprived of their living. The Indian Forest Act- 1927, Wildlife Protection Act- 1972, and Forest

Conservation Act - 1980, criminalised the Tribals' way of life. This Forest Conservation Act – 1980 denied all the basic rights of the Tribals. It treated the Tribals like criminals by conducting an inquiry under the Unlawful Activities (Prevention) Act 1967. This gave unparalleled power to the Forest guards, who ruthlessly exploited and oppressed the Tribals. The support for Naxals in forests originates in this basic injustice.

But the Naxals have a national level aim: to overthrow the existing government and bring in a 'People's Republic' with single party rule. The administrative vacuum and Tribal grievances were a means to enter the forests and convert them into sanctuaries for the armed struggle against the Indian state. Thus began the saga of Tribal predicament of being caught between the Naxals and the State.

Review and Reflections

Few insurgencies have had a dramatic start like the one in Mizoram. Typically, insurgencies begin as low-key agitations against the Government that escalate to armed struggle. But why bother about the 'origin' is a right and logical question. A wise old Indian saying advises, *One should not attempt to trace the source of a river or the ancestry of a Sage (Rishi)!*

There is indeed a lot of wisdom in the above saying. Any person who has trekked in the mountains and tried to trace the source of great rivers will testify to the fact that the discovery of some small stream and the fact that it has merely a trickle of water is a disappointment. The river only attains its size when many other streams join it. The source is both obscure and irrelevant. The same logic applies to tracing the background of a Sage! It is often very ordinary and undistinguished. The greatness of the Sage is in what he has made of his humble background and not the background itself. This logic applies equally forcefully to the origins of an insurgency. It is often obscure and irrelevant to the present.

Yet it is worthwhile to trace the origins and beginnings as in virtually all insurgencies and revolts, there is a constant chorus to 'deal with the root causes'. As we proceed further in our enquiry we can either support or falsify the theory of 'Root Cause' that is so popular amongst some peace advocates. Equally important is the question, Could it have been avoided? Could some measure by the Government have forestalled the revolt? This is not a mere academic question but has policy implications in terms of who should have taken what action.

It is quite apparent that the Mizo revolt was an exception in terms of a dramatic beginning. It was not anticipated. It points to a clear failure of the Government apparatus to fathom and warn about the impending storm. But if we look at the insurgency in neighbouring Nagaland, we can come to a conclusion that the Nagas gave enough warnings as well as opportunities to the Government, that they were restive and there was a sense of alienation. But with the diametrically opposing goals- the Government of India wanting to integrate Nagaland with the rest of the country while Nagas insisted that they were not Indians, there was very little middle ground without either party giving up its basic premise. Superficially this appears to be true and like a Greek tragedy, Nagaland seemed destined to go through a violent phase in its history. But a nagging question remains-what if the President of India had been more forthcoming in meeting the Naga delegation? What if, instead of unilaterally deciding that Nagaland would be part of India, a liberal Nehru, the first Prime Minister of independent India, had invited the Nagas to join the great Indian family? Reading the accounts about the start of Naga revolt by various administrators one is struck by the sheer insensitivity of the Indians towards Naga pride.

Once the armed struggle begins, with its inevitable loss of lives, atrocities and destruction of property, in place of the original cause, revenge occupies centre stage. Armed conflicts of this nature then acquire a dynamic and momentum of their own. But does the perception of 'separateness' alone start an insurgency? The answer is a resounding no! In the North East itself, areas of Manipur or the tribal population of Khasi and Jaintia hills (now forming a part of the state of Meghalaya) did nothing of that sort, though admittedly civil disturbances are endemic in those areas. Here one realises that the experience of Second World War, during which Nagaland and Mizoram saw live action, had a lasting impact in terms of perception of ability to fight for independence. In addition, the vast arsenals left in the jungles by the retreating Japanese and later the Allied forces (British and

Americans) provided the ready 'means' to launch an armed struggle. Thus mere perception of separate identity is not a sufficient reason for an insurgency to begin in a given area- other contextual factors like availability of means and recent memories of armed conflict are equally important.

Insurgency in Kashmir valley on the other hand had a strong link to external stimuli that helped it 'evolve' a sense of grievance and begin an armed struggle in 1980s. This is independent of the Pakistani claim on Kashmir that has been a dispute between India and Pakistan since 1947. The rise of 'Islamism' during the Afghan war of 1980s influenced the opinion in Kashmir valley. The planned withdrawal of the Soviet forces from Afghanistan was seen as victory of Islam. The proliferation of *Madrassas* (Islamic schools) funded by the Waahabi sect of Saudi Arabia played a role in it as did the fall of Berlin wall. The interesting point is that there was no major change either in political/economic or social status of Kashmir within the Indian union in 1980s. The insurgency in Kashmir began purely and wholly in response to the changed international context- rise of Islamism and in later periods, the clash of civilisation post the '9/11' terror attacks on the US in 2001. The inept local administration and tepid response from the Indian government were merely added factors, by themselves insignificant and either way could not have forestalled the insurgency.

But it is important to realise that the roots of insurgency in Kashmir go back to the ever -present feeling of 'uniqueness' of Kashmiri identity. This myth has never been seriously challenged. Other than religion, how was Kashmir different or unique from the remaining states of the Indian Union? Each of these states, has its own language, culture and history but yet does not have the urge to secession! In a sense, Kashmiri separatism is a self-fulfilling prophecy that India itself encouraged. Seen in this light there is inevitability to the happenings in Kashmir, with the international context or Pakistani support, merely an adjunct reason. The original sin was Indian acceptance of secession based on religion that saw birth of Pakistan. Having once conceded the creation of separate state on the basis of religion, how can India oppose a similar demand by the Kashmiris?

The Sri Lankan insurgency by the Tamil minority was not inevitable despite the thousands of years of rivalry. This became inevitable after the Sri Lankan government changed the basic parameters of its nationhood from territorial/historical to religious. Ironically, it was the democratic structure and competition for political power that was responsible for the unleashing of the primordial emotions of the Sinhalas. The person most responsible for it, late SWRD Bandarnaike, himself had Tamil ancestry and was British-educated and thoroughly westernised. Not unlike another person in the subcontinent- MA Jinnah who created Pakistan, SWRD Bandarnaike was personally secular. But once he decided to ride the tiger of religious passion, getting down was impossible and he paid the ultimate price with his own life when he was assassinated by a Buddhist monk. Jinnah would have possibly met the same fate but died early due to disease.

But Bandarnaike's divisive politics succeeded because of another factor, the sense of economic deprivation amongst the Sinhala people despite being a majority. The relative prosperity and advanced educational achievements of the Tamil was a red rag to Sinhala chauvinism.

Due to the historical memories of invasions from South India, the Sinhalas had a lingering suspicion of the threat from India. The close family links between the Lankan Tamils and Indian Tamils were an added factor. The rise of Tamil parties in the Indian state of Tamil Nadu and their encouragement of Tamil separatism in Sri Lanka fuelled Sinhala suspicions about the dual loyalties of the Tamil people. It is difficult to determine which came first- Sri Lankan 'exclusive' nationalism or the Tamils looking towards India as a saviour! Suffice to say that the two factors operated simultaneously and fed on each other. The dogmatic Sri Lankan obsession with a unitary state and a refusal to look at a federal solution was also a major factor in generating violent response. In May 2009, the Sri Lankans had won a military victory over the Tamil Tigers. But it was still going to be a hasty conclusion to assert that the insurgency in Jaffna was over.

The South African insurgency is different from the other examples. Here was an oppressed majority that was being ruled by a minority on the dubious and archaic principle of racial superiority based on the colour of one's skin. The Afrikaners who seized power in the aftermath of the decline of the British, were themselves oppressed by the English, since the days of the Boer wars. But instead of following the trend of democratisation, the white minority regime went back in time and thought it could resurrect the country into an 18th century model. The fact that this absurdity lasted well into the 20th century, owes much to covert Western support. The fight of the Africans for a majority rule soon got entangled in the politics of the Cold War and the white regime exploited the American fear of Communist influence. But once the ANC declared its intention to have a multi-racial and just society, and not just a black-dominated one, the ideological ground slipped from under the white regime. Interestingly, while the white regime remained militarily strong right to the end, it lost all international credibility. Here was a case where international pressure sustained the fight against all odds.

The Naxal revolt in Chhattisgarh state of India is a classic case of 'creeping revolution'. The rebels entered an un-administered area and made it their own. Neglect and political irrelevance even in a democratic state were the main causes. The most unfortunate consequence of this was that tribals- simple forest dwellers were caught between two opposing and irresistible forces. But the original sin was committed when the forests were nationalised and the Tribals became refugees in their own habitat. For the Tribals, this a fight for existence. Naxals stepped in to exploit the situation but did not create it.

The one common factor in all these events is the various divides within a state. The existence of racial, linguistic, economic, religious and societal differences is a factor common to all insurgencies. These divides provided the driving force for the violence. Boundaries played a major role in all these conflicts. The effect of these divides or boundaries on the internal cohesion and peace within a state is the issue that we will tackle in the next section.

Note:

EN Rammohan , a police officer of Assam cadre has a different take on the history of Assam.

"The Mongolian peoples of the Northeast, Bhutan, Sikkim, Nepal and Tibet and also of Burma and the other Southeast Asian countries were presumed to have migrated from North West China thousands of years ago. Those who settled in Assam were the Boro Cacharis, Sonowal Cacharis, Dimasa Cacharis, Thengal Cacharis, Rabhas, Rajbongshis, Borahis, Mech, Chutiyas and Morans. Later the caste Hindus from the Gangetic valley migrated and settled in the Brahmaputra valley. The caste Hindus intermarried with the Mongolian tribals and these are the Assamese caste Hindus of today. In the 12th century, an army of the Slave kings entered Assam and clashed with a Hindu Kingdom in Kamarupa. They were defeated by one Prithu, a Raja of the Hindu kingdom. Thw army of the Slave kings retreated from Assam. Some of the castes Hindus were converted to Islam during their sojourn. They are the Assamese Muslims of today. In the 12th century, a Shan prince from Burma, had differences with his brother, the King of the Shan kingdom, took about a hundred odd elephants and along with his followers came west crossing the Pataki hills and entered the Brahmaputra valley. They fought with the Shuteye and Moran rulers of upper Assam and established their kingdom in Sibs agar district. Since they did not bring any Shan woman from Burma, they intermarried with the local Moran, Borsht and Chutiya women and this new community came to be called the Ahoms. Incidentally the Ahoms never subdued the Naga villages of the Naga Hills south of Ahom country, but had continual fights over control of the salt licks which were only in the hills."

Section 3 - The Divide: Existing, Created & Exploited

Boundaries: Natural and Manmade!

Differences between and within species is a law of nature. It is impossible to find the 'exact' replica of a tree, a flower, a dog or a human. There are varieties of the same species and yet there are individual differences. Man has added to this natural diversity by creating further divisions based on religion, politics, perceived ethnicity and economics. Thus there are two types of boundaries or fundamental divides - natural and manmade.

The first amongst the boundaries is the natural or geographic one. Geography is the single most important determinant for group formation and a sense of alienation. In the case of secessionist insurgencies in the Indian North East or Kashmir, geography plays a very vital role. Mountain ranges and forests of the North East make movement of people difficult and result in both a real physical isolation from others in the larger expanse of the state and its consequent perception of separateness. As movement of people and goods is confined to the small area, it creates restricted economic linkages as well. Thus what was essentially only the problem of people also merges into an economic boundary! When this has persisted over a long period of time, a distinct isolated racial group arises.

Kashmir, or more accurately the state of Jammu and Kashmir (J&K in short) offers an even clearer example of the influence of geography on perceptions. Jammu and Kashmir is a divided entity that got formed into one political unit by an accident of history. As one travels north from the plains of Punjab, the area up to the 4000 metres high Pir Panjal ranges, is the Jammu division. Linguistically, ethnically and from a historical point of view, the fate of this area was closely linked to that of Punjab and the hill areas to the East. The Kashmir valley at the height of over 5000 feet that lies beyond Pir Panjal range is to the North bound by the Great Himalayan range and to the east and south by Ladakh and Zanskar range. Both these ranges rise above 18000 feet and are formidable barriers to normal movement. The natural route to the Kashmir valley is through the Jhelum gorge that opens up towards the west.

To the east of the valley of Kashmir is the Kargil and Ladakh region. Ladakh is mainly Buddhist, has historical links with Tibet and remains cut off for over six months from the rest of the state. To the north of the valley are the areas of Gilgit and Baltistan with affinity to the Central Asian region. West of Kashmir is the district of Mirpur that is Punjabi-speaking and more akin to Jammu division than Kashmir. The epicentre of insurgency is in the Kashmir valley.

The Kashmir valley is thus surrounded by areas that are ethnically and linguistically different. The mountain barriers ensured that the Kashmir valley developed in isolation from the rest of the area. Easy defendability and fertile land gave rise to a rich culture that produced some of the best literature in Indian history. Isolation and lack of external threat also made internecine quarrels frequent and the greatest threat to political stability came from within.

This brings home the fact that within a geographically isolated region itself, there is further diversity and division. Nagaland or the Nagas are similarly divided into tribes that inhabit distinct areas within Nagaland. Like J&K, communication between these tribes was minimal and dictated by geography; the tribes had their own distinct language and culture. The composite Naga identity is a modern political creation. In this creation of identity, both in case of J&K and Nagaland, religion that was common to the areas and different from the rest of the country played a role, Islam in the case of J&K and Christianity in case of Nagaland.

Mizoram on the other hand is unique in having a single dominant tribe, the Lushai, which, despite geography, is similar to that of Nagaland. In its heyday, this weighed heavily on the minds of Indian policymakers facing secession and the Mizo insurgency was regarded with greater alarm than the Naga one.

But here, in case of both the North Eastern India and J&K, one must hasten to add that neither of these areas were a 'Shangri-La', and though limited, contact with the surrounding areas was the norm even before the modern communication revolution. The history of Kashmir was linked to that of the rest of the country and there were numerous kingdoms that included this area. Even in the North East, the isolation due to geography was nowhere near the total.

In the centre of India, straddling across the boundaries of Chhattisgarh, Orissa, Andhra and Maharashtra states, is a forested area that is home to a population of forest dwellers, variously called Tribals or Adivasis (original inhabitants). The forests in these areas are certainly dense but not very difficult so as to not permit penetration of the state administration. But here, an interesting fact of political geography comes into play. These areas lie on the fringes of very large states (provinces) and were neglected. Here politics intervened to create isolation when no such thing should have occured. It is true that racially the people of this area are distinct, but they had enough interaction with others so as to not be an isolated community.

The isolation of the tribal areas was also a result of deliberate administrative action, such as the permit system to enter these areas. In North Eastern India as well, the 'Inner line Permit System' that prevents citizens from other parts of the country to travel or settle there, is in existence. This measure was taken by the administration to 'protect' the tribals from depredations of the rapacious plainsmen. The benefits these measures achieved was doubtful but one thing they surely did achieve and that is they froze the existence of the forest dwellers to the earlier centuries. The natural process of integration and change in lifestyle was interrupted, somewhat on the lines of the 'Indian Reserves' in the US. This policy of enforced isolation of communities created divides along economic and ethnic lines. As the communities so isolated remained backward, they were easy prey for Leftist and Communist ideologues who wished to use them to foment rebellion in the country.

It is indeed amazing how an administration in its misguided and romantic zeal to 'safeguard' culture ends up creating a divide that coincides with ethnic, economic and geographic boundaries thus making an area ripe for violent secessionism.

In the case of Sri Lanka, though the Tamils were indeed concentrated in the North and East, in the modern era there were no geographical barriers that stopped interaction. Here the boundaries were more political and linguistic. But the fact that in spite of lack of physical barriers, separatism developed in Tamil-dominated Jaffna shows that geographical isolation is not necessarily the precondition for secessionist movements. Here again, the religious divide between the Hindu Tamils and Buddhist Sinhalas, played its role. But the factor of religion cannot be overstated in this case, since on the one hand the Tamil rebels were not only Hindus but also Christian and Sinhalas had also in their ranks, followers of Christianity. The admixture of religions on both sides, makes it difficult to assign primacy to the factor of religion, though it certainly played a role.

South Africa, on the other hand, presents a totally different picture. Here the African tribes did have their dominant area-the Zulus, the Xhosas and Bantus, yet there was no great geographical barrier to stop the intermingling. The white and black Africans, in any case, shared the entire landmass. In the 1950s and 60s, it was the white regime that attempted to create a racially divided country by the policy of so-called 'Reservations' and 'Bantustans' by shifting population of Black Africans to these areas and creating exclusively White areas.

Economic necessity and the need for African labour however torpedoed this move and the total isolation of Black Africans could never be achieved. Instead the white regime ended up by creating safe havens for the insurgents. Another interesting facet of the South African situation is the commonality of religion. Since the arrival of missionaries in the 17th century, most of the Africans had been converted to Christianity. Thus religion as a dividing factor was absent in this situation. The divisions in South Africa were based predominantly on race and culture. Language was the divisive factor between the Blacks and the Whites. But on the other hand, the Black Africans themselves were also divided on this score. On the other hand the compulsion of Afrikaans language, as medium of education, was resisted by the Blacks and added to their grievances against the White minority government.

The South African regime did create an economic division by depriving the Blacks of fertile land and education, thus keeping 75% of the population economically deprived and poor while the Whites controlled the economy. Only poorly paid menial jobs were available for the black Africans. More than anything else it was this economic deprivation and the vast economic gulf between the whites and blacks that led to the revolt.

But none of these offer any conclusive evidence about the causal link between boundaries and revolt. For instance, in case of India, the trans-Himalayan areas of the state of Uttar Pradesh, i.e. the Garhwal and Kumaon hills as well as the region around Shimla that is now the state of Himachal Pradesh, have geography similar to J&K. In fact the geographical layout of these areas is even more daunting and there was less communication with the plains. Yet there is no separatist movement in these areas.

Similarly, like the North East, areas in Central India are forested and inhabited by Tribes, the Gonds or the Santhals. There is indeed unrest in these parts, but that has its basis in economic stagnation and resistance against economic exploitation. There is no secessionist movement.

This brings in an interesting hypothesis that, to engender secessionism and related violent movement, more than one boundary has to coincide. In case of both Nagaland and Mizoram, the geographic boundary also roughly corresponds to the racial and religious divide. Thus three divides coincide. In case of J&K, the geographical divide is reinforced by religious divide. Thus we can safely reason out that when more than one boundary coincides, there is a possibility of secessionist movements.

In the pre-industrialisation era, communication was difficult and hills posed a formidable obstacle to movement of goods, people as well as armies. Thus geography created political units that could and did exist for a long period in history. This in turn, produced a distinct culture and language. But as mentioned earlier, common religion played an integrating role by linking the difficult areas with the rest of the country, as in the case of the Garhwal and Kumaon hills. While in case of Kashmir valley that is mainly Muslim or the North East that is predominantly Christian, religion played a divisive role.

In the case of Sri Lanka and the Tamil separatist movement, the geographic divide between the Sinhala and Tamil populations was a result of history, in fact ancient history. A turning point in the history of Sri Lanka was in the 13ᵗʰ Century, when fed up with the constant threats of invasion from South India, the Sinhalese abandoned their capital at Anuradhpura and moved further south into the central mountain highlands as that area offered better protection. The collapse of the irrigation-based Sinhala kingdoms marks the political separation of the North and East of the island. As the Sinhalese retreated into the mountains, a large number of Tamils came over from South India and settled in the northern areas of Jaffna. The Tamils occupied areas right up to Anuradhpura.

According to the British historian Toynbee, the constant invasions from South India and incessant strife sapped the will of the Sinhalese to go on repairing the irrigation works and these fell into disuse. Ultimately overcome by the tropical jungles, today they are areas infested with malaria and unfit for human habitation. The invaders from South India deliberately cut the embankments and bunds as shortcuts to military victory. Even the original names of these tanks are lost; one tank bears a name that in Tamil means the tank of great breach.

Later on in 1411 A.D., Parakrambahu VI brought the whole island under his rule. Yet the respite was too brief to reclaim the lost irrigation works and the fertile plains. The shift of the capital into mountainous areas to the south, weakened central control, so essential to running an intricate irrigation system. Even in modern times it has been the experience that a highly organised civilisation that is dependent on effective government is vulnerable to civil strife. The decline of Sinhalese irrigation-based civilisation was thus a direct result of the invasions from South India.

The small Tamil kingdom of Jaffna became a virtual province and a satellite of the Chola and the Pandya kingdoms. It could only survive by aligning itself with the Indian kings. As the Sinhalese power retreated south, the tropical jungle invaded the once prosperous irrigated zone that was the centre of the Lankan civilisation. These jungles then formed a natural barrier to movement and helped further consolidate a distinct Tamil identity in the North and East of the island. Thus history created geography.

The Jaffna peninsula and South India are separated by the narrow and easily navigable Palk Straits. Thus the interaction between peoples of the northern Sri Lanka and the Tamils of mainland India was intense and extensive including marital relations, trade and commerce and culture. For all intents and purposes, northern Sri Lanka remained an extension of South India.

The predominant Tamil population of Jaffna is Hindu. Lanka finds mention in the Indian epic of Ramayan, estimated by most scholars as dealing with the events of 1500 BC, if not earlier. There is enough tell-tale evidence to support the view that the Lanka of King Ravana of Ramayan is the same as the present day Sri Lanka. Aside from the name, there are many sites associated with Ramayan to be found in Sri Lanka. The rocky outcrop connecting the tip of India with Sri Lanka closely resembles the description of the bridge built by Ram to carry his army into Sri Lanka. There are also sites that correspond to the Ashok van, a garden where Ravana had imprisoned Sita. The story of Ravana, King of Sri Lanka finds mention in Mahayana Buddhist texts. Medical texts written by ancient King Ravana, such as "Ark Prakasika" and "Kumara Tantram" have survived in Sri Lanka's rich Ayurvedic tradition. Archaeological evidence dating back to 500 BC based on the iron implements and burial practices shows unmistakable connection with the Tamil country in India. Another Buddhist text, Rajavaliya says that the Ramayana war took place exactly 1884 years before the birth of Buddha. Tamils are acutely aware of their ancient inheritance and to the existing geographic, economic, linguistic and political divide, religion was added.

In all insurgency movements, religion has played a very major role, both for and against. While the causes of revolts in North Eastern India, Northern Sri Lanka and Kashmir are many, one issue stands out and that is religious difference between the rebel provinces and 'heart land'. The author was told time and again that in South Africa, Christianity played a major moderating role in the conflict and its ultimate peaceful resolution.

Even in the Indian North East, after initially sympathising with the rebel cause, towards the late 1960s, the Christian church increasingly distanced itself from the rebels. The main reason for this shift was that the rebels had begun to seek support from Communist China, and the church saw this as a threat to Christianity. Many peace initiatives were blessed by the church and a fair amount of credit for the eventual peace can be given to the efforts of the church.

The Tamil revolt in Sri Lanka was not a religion-based conflict, yet it is worth speculating whether the vehemence or violence that engulfed Sri Lanka all these years would have been this intense had the two sides shared a common religion! In Kashmir on the other hand, the support by the Muslim clergy for secession has made any peaceful resolution difficult.

Of all the world's ideologies, religion is possibly the oldest. It is also a universal phenomenon, in that there is virtually no human being without it. In this calculation, the negation of religion, Agnosticism and Atheism, by themselves could be classed as religions. Thus the main reason for the importance of religion as a factor is due to its universality. One acquires religion at birth and is brought up in its tradition. While it is true that in day-to-day life, religion as factor plays a very minor role, yet its influence in forming attitudes, mindsets and behaviour is crucial. Since behavioural and attitudinal change is the aim of counterinsurgency, one cannot ignore the factor of religion.

Politics and Leadership as Catalysts

Various boundaries and divides are necessary but NOT a sufficient precondition to generate an insurgency. Geography and its consequences create conditions of separate identity but it is the leadership and political organisations that catalyse it into a movement. Politics and the desire for power on the part of an individual and/or a group, play the role of a catalyst.

In case of Nagaland, it was the untiring efforts of the late Mr Z A Phizo that united the diverse Naga tribes for the demand for independence. Dormant organisations like the Naga Club played some role. The tribal traditional organisations like the *Ho Ho* or meetings of tribal elders and village headmen provided the basis for the subsequent formation of Naga Federal Government. In addition, at least in the early period of the Naga revolt, the Church played a role from behind the scenes, encouraging separatism, if not actually endorsing violence.

But it would be unwise to attribute the Naga troubles to the leadership of Phizo alone. Phizo had been in exile for a prolonged period and yet the Naga struggle continued without him. Over time he became a mere symbol and hardly had any control over or communication with the Naga insurgents. This indicates two things- the strength of the organisation i.e. the Naga Federal Government and the popularity of the cause that had widespread support. As we look at other cases these three elements are in different balance. The correct identification of the balance between these factors is a necessary precondition for successful counterinsurgency.

Likewise in the case of the Mizo revolt, late Mr Lal Denga's thwarted political ambition to come to power was a major motivation. The *Mautam* or the flowering of bamboo and subsequent rat invasion provided an ideal opportunity. The Mizo Famine Relief Front that was created to organise relief became the perfect vehicle for Lal Denga to organise an underground organisation. Large number of de-mobilised veterans from World War II filled its ranks. Lal Denga himself was an ex-soldier and found it easy to capture the leadership of this organisation. Lal Denga virtually personified the MNF (Mizo National Front) and was its unchallenged leader. Unlike Nagaland, Mizos had no internal divisions and there was no serious rival to the MNF. It is no wonder therefore that while it lasted, the Mizo insurgency was regarded as a far greater threat than Nagaland, which was bedevilled by tribal divisions, leadership contests and multiple organisations (NFG, Socialist Council and Khaplang group et al).

In the case of Kashmir it was the leadership of Sheikh Abdullah that undoubtedly sowed the seeds of separatism. For nearly half a century Sheikh Abdullah strode as a giant on the political scene in Kashmir. It will not be an exaggeration to say that the whole politics of the Kashmir issue resolved around him. A clearer understanding of the ideological preferences of the Sheikh is necessary to understand the political ferment in Kashmir.

Sheikh Abdullah was a charismatic personality with of the image of a father figure. Standing 6 feet 1 inch tall, he carried a halo of martyrdom acquired by undergoing long periods of incarceration, with charm and ease. His oratorial skills and personal courage led to him being known as the 'Lion of Kashmir' (Sher E Kashmir). But his leadership was in the form of two-way-traffic. As much as he moulded the Kashmiris, their aspirations, urges and sentiments affected his politics. In 1965, when he went on a 'Haj' pilgrimage, in his application for an Indian passport he refused to describe himself as an Indian. 'Kashmiri Muslim', is the term he used for himself. That about sums up his politics and also the Kashmir dilemma. As a hero of Kashmiri nationalism he refused to subsume his identity in Islamic Pakistan. Yet as a Muslim he was a Pan-Islamist, in the same mould as another illustrious son of Kashmir, poet Allama Iqbal.

Sheikh Abdullah was born at Soura, near Srinagar on 5th December 1905. His father Sheikh Mohammed Ibrahim died a fortnight before Abdulla's birth. Sheikh Abdullah was the youngest of five brothers and two sisters. His father was a small-time businessman dealing in wool. In these difficult circumstances, Abdullah, a bright student, completed his education in science. He did his schooling at Government High School Srinagar, graduation from Jammu and Islamia College in Lahore. He completed his masters in Physics from Aligarh in 1930. Given the low level of education prevailing at that time amongst Kashmiri Muslims, this was a singular achievement.

Almost immediately after his post graduation he plunged into active politics. He worked as a school teacher for a brief period but was soon dismissed for agitating to get a better representation for the majority Kashmiri Muslims in Government jobs. Most of the jobs went to the Kashmiri Pandits or the Dogras of Jammu. Large tracts of land were similarly owned by non-Muslims. Sheikh Abdullah soon joined the Muslim Conference, a political party of Kashmiri Muslims that fought the Dogra rulers for Muslim rights.

Sheikh Abdullah was a devout Muslim and was influenced by his deeply religious mother. According to his autobiography, he was also influenced by the writings of Allama Iqbal, Nehru, Gandhi and Kemal Attaturk, the Turkish revolutionary. With his radical ideas, he found little that was common between him and the conservative and aristocratic leadership of the Muslim League. He began drifting towards Indian National Congress and particularly its young leader, Jawaharlal Nehru. To get national-level support for his fight against the Dogra rulers, he modified the constitution of his party, the Muslim Conference and converted it into a secular organisation called National Conference in 1939. In his fight against Dogra rule, Sheikh often used highly communal language and spewed venom against Hindus. After 1939, this tendency was modified by him but would come up time and again, when he was out of power. Sheikh Abdullah made no secret that his goal was an independent Kashmir. Secularism and alliance with Indian National Congress were tactical ploys to achieve that aim.

In 1947 as Independence drew near, there was hectic manoeuvring in the state. Sheikh was in jail at the time, but his emissaries, Bakshi Ghulam Mohammed and G. M. Sadiq tried to secure the agreement of Indian and Pakistani leaders for an independent Kashmir. The response of both the sides was negative. Pakistan was however not prepared to wait and launched a thinly disguised attempt to annex Kashmir by force. Sheikh was in a dilemma, a dilemma that continues to plague Kashmir to date. While he did not want to join India, neither was he in favour of joining Pakistan. He wriggled his way out of this by accepting a 'temporary' and limited accession with India and sought Indian help to protect the valley from the depredations of unruly tribals.

Once the danger of Pakistani annexation passed, he began plotting independence for Kashmir, this time with the sympathetic Americans. This led to his landing in prison once again in 1953. After eleven long years, he was again released in 1964. Nehru was ailing and already had suffered a stroke. At this time Sheikh was entrusted, by Nehru, with a delicate mission to broach the idea of an Indo-Pakistani confederation as a lasting solution to the Kashmir problem. But before this could take any practical shape, on 27th May 1964, Nehru died and the promising effort was put in cold storage.

The 1971 Indo-Pak war that led to separation of East Pakistan and formation of the independent country of Bangladesh finally made Sheikh Abdullah give up his dream of an independent Kashmir. This was a clear recognition of the Indian predominance and Sheikh realised that the time had come for giving up the old game of playing India against Pakistan to secure Kashmiri interests. The result was the 'Delhi agreement' of 1975. Sheikh Abdullah became the Chief Minister of Jammu and Kashmir province and remained in that position till his death in 1982. While Sheikh gave up his dream of independence, others took over the leadership of the separatist cause.

In Sri Lanka, the Tamils had organised a strong political party, the Federal Party to protect their interests. This met with a Sinhala backlash. Brushing aside Tamil objections, based on the support of her Parliamentary majority, Mrs. Sirimavo Bandarnaike ushered in the new Republican Constitution on 22nd May 1972. Ceylon now became the Democratic Socialist Republic of Sri Lanka. To oppose the move to make Tamils second class citizens, all the Tamil parties came together to form the Tamil United Front. This party had representatives of both the Jaffna Tamils as well as the plantation workers. The Tamils of Lanka organised strikes and began preparations for 'direct action'. The situation was again reminiscent of the happenings of 1958. It was the start of a violent Tamil revolt led by young Prabahakaran, who went on to form the LTTE.

Out of all the cases of insurgency/counter insurgency being studied here, South Africa is the only case where the insurgents succeeded. With the hype surrounding Mr Nelson Mandela's imprisonment, an impression has gained ground that his leadership was instrumental in getting rid of apartheid in South Africa. Nelson Mandela was more a symbol of South African resistance rather than the cause. In ANC, the South African black majority had a very powerful organisation to pursue their cause. Over time an impression has been created that the ANC was always the all powerful and sole voice of the African resistance. This is far from true as we shall see presently.

The African National Congress was initially less of a political party and more a freedom movement. But the peculiar condition of repression within the country, an official ban and a virtual *cordon sanitaire* around South Africa made sure that it had only a marginal presence within the

106

country. The struggle against apartheid received a shot in the arm on 20th August 1983 when the UDF (United Democratic Front) came into existence. A thousand delegates, representing close to 500 organisations, attended the meet at a community centre in a coloured area at Mitchell's Plain. The prominent organisations that came together were the SACP (South African Communist Party), Trade Unions, Black Consciousness Movement activists, Church organisations supporting liberation theology, student activists and white activists opposed to Apartheid. The notable exception was the Inkatha Freedom Party led by Chief Buthelezi that claimed to be the sole representative of the Zulus.

The ANC was also not a one person organisation and a galaxy of leaders like Oliver Tambo, Sisulu, Bishop Tutu and Maharaj. The South African struggle thus differed from the other models in that there was no personality cult or single leader unlike say Phizo for Naga's, Prabhakaran and LTTE for Lankan Tamils or Sheikh Abdullah in Kashmir.

Of all the insurgencies, the South African one had the greatest degree of legitimacy. Increasingly even the Afrikaners saw Apartheid as absurd. During the 1980s, the South African whites increasingly began to become international pariahs[1]. Almost a reverse Apartheid began to take shape. A South African academic Pierre du Toit wrote in his book *'South Africa's Brittle Peace'*

"The country was barred from Olympic Games, UN General Assembly and ousted from many other venues of international recognition and prestige. The psychological deprivation provided a powerful stimulus towards negotiating a new political order."

There is a myth that sports and culture are immune to politics and should be kept separate. In the early 1970s, spearheaded by the newly independent African nations, there was a worldwide sports boycott of South

---

[1] This author passing through Heathrow airport in 1991 July, encountered this. During a long layoff between flights, the author was sitting next to a white man and struck up a conversation. Right at the outset, the individual apologetically informed him that he was from South Africa with an unstated assumption that he would understand if after knowing his origins one would not wish to converse with him!

African whites. The International Olympic Committee (IOC) withdrew its invitation to South Africa, to the 1964 Summer Olympics when interior minister Jan de Klerk insisted the team would not be racially integrated. In 1968, the IOC was prepared to readmit South Africa after assurances that its team would be multi-racial; but a threatened boycott by African nations and others, forestalled this. The IOC adopted a declaration against "apartheid in sport" on June 21, 1988. South Africa was formally expelled from the IOC in 1970.[2] To a sports-loving nation, the sports boycott was particularly hurtful and many talented sportspersons emigrated to UK or Australia to escape this.[3] Wide-ranging discussions with countless South Africans, Afrikaners and English during the author's visit to that country in Sep 2009 and the many people that the author talked to, confirmed the perception that the isolation of South Africa in the sports field, hurt the racist regime badly.

Right until the end when the Apartheid regime gave in to the ANC and ushered in a multiracial nation concept, militarily the regime remained undefeated. In fact throughout most of the period of the struggle, the ANC was extremely weak, militarily. South Africa had a ring of buffer states around itself and insulated the mainland from any direct military threat. The inevitable conclusion is that international events and international pressures were decisive factors in the victory of the ANC-led struggle.

There is hardly any insurgency that has been even marginally successful that did not have some form of external linkage. The Kashmir revolt has been encouraged and supported by neighbouring Pakistan. The LTTE and the Tamil rebels in Sri Lanka enjoyed political and material support from the Indian state of Tamil Nadu most of the time and even from the Central Government for some time. The same is the case of the Naga or Mizo insurgency that was patronised by Pakistan (when East Pakistan existed before seceding and becoming Bangladesh) as well as China, to a limited

---

[2] Rogers, Thomas (April 15, 1988). "U.N. Reports Contacts with South Africa". New York Times. "International Convertion Against Apartheid in Sports". Office of the High Commissioner for Human Rights. 10 December 1985.

[3] A conversation with peace activist Ms Susan Collins Marks in American Centre, Mumbai (India) in the year 2000, confirmed this effect on the South African whites' psyches.

extent. As seen in case of South Africa, the external factor plays a very important role in success or failure of an insurgency.

The External Dimension

The rise of insurgency wars in the post-Second World War era was directly linked to the Cold War that followed it. The Cold War between the U.S. and erstwhile Soviet Union was a drive for power that had an ideological dimension of the fight between Socialism and Capitalism. It was a tool used by the 'weaker' Communist bloc to change the global power balance under the shadow of threat of nuclear destruction. Open confrontation carried the risk of escalation and the communist powers were at a disadvantage in the field of technologies of conventional weapons. At the other end, at the level of combat, the insurgents lacked heavy weapons and therefore made use of guerrilla tactics. Thus, the communists successfully managed to dictate the terms of engagement. Captain B. H. Liddell Hart, in his foreword to the book on Mao's thoughts on guerrilla war, says,

"Campaigns of this kind, (revolutionary wars) are more likely to continue because they fit the condition of modern age, while at the same time well suited to take advantage of social discontent, racial ferment and nationalistic fervour."

Insurgency warfare using the tactics of a guerrilla war, is thus a low cost, low risk option for a weaker power to change the territorial map despite an adverse power balance. These tactics and their adjunct terrorism, continue to be used as an instrument of state policy by nations that want to change the status quo. Pakistan's interference in Kashmir is a classic example. In addition, protection of human rights has emerged as an issue of global concern. Since the guerrillas operate with some support of the masses and within them, it is often impossible to distinguish between an innocent citizen and a guerrilla fighter. In the era of instant media coverage and omnipresent television, the counter insurgency forces are at a distinct disadvantage as they cannot clearly identify the guerrilla while the guerrilla can identify the soldiers easily. Often the guerrillas can provoke a fire fight in a crowded area and virtually paralyse the reaction capability of the security forces. This has added a new dimension to the potency of guerrilla warfare.

Ever since the dawn of the industrial era, a major change has occurred in the military balance. Unlike in the past, when barbarians regularly defeated the settled area, once fire arms and industrial power became the predominant force, the State, armed with modern conventional arms became all-powerful. Critics may point to the Vietnam and Afghanistan wars as examples where seemingly agricultural or pastoral powers defeated super powers like the US and Soviet Union. But this is a fallacy as the Vietnamese had the full might of the Soviet Union backing them, while the Afghan Mujahedeen had American technology and modern arms provided to them via Pakistan.

External help is crucial due to two other reasons. Insurgencies are invariably a long-drawn-out affair and fighters need sanctuaries and rest areas. In addition, the fact that an established state is in support, is a great morale booster for the insurgents. In conversation with late Mr. Lal Denga, the supreme leader of the Mizos, in 1988 this issue came up. Mr. Lal Denga mentioned that the MNF deliberately floated the rumour that they had the support of the US in their fight against India. While meeting Chou En Lai, the Chinese Premier, Mr. Lal Denga emphasised that the Mizos wanted 'open' as opposed to covert Chinese support. The effect of open external support on morale has been crucial in keeping the embers of violence burning in Kashmir. The lack of the same in case of the LTTE, led to its military defeat by the Sri Lankan army in 2009.

The South African case provides the clearest example of impact of external forces and events on the struggle. It is clearly established that the ANC enjoyed the support of the erstwhile Soviet Union right from the early 60s. The support included finance, arms and ammunition, training and advice.

A senior-level delegation of the ANC, SACP and the armed wing MK, visited Vietnam to learn from their experience. The delegation was led by the ANC President Oliver Tambo along with the armed wing commander Joe Modise, chief of staff Joe Slovo and SACP General Secretary Chris Hani. On 8 Jan 1984 Oliver Tambo outlined the ANC strategy of 'making South Africa ungovernable.' Alongside this the ANC also launched a campaign to work for economic isolation of South Africa. The ANC was careful that while it took the Soviet Union's help it also kept its links with the

Western liberals. In 1984, the Nobel Prize for peace was awarded to Bishop Desmond Tutu, a leader of the UDF. This marked a high point in the success of garnering international recognition and support for the anti-Apartheid struggle. The Free South Africa movement began daily demonstrations against the South African Embassy in Washington DC. The campaign soon spread all over the US and in January 1985, over 600 people including 15 Congressmen were arrested in the US. President Reagan came under increasing pressure to re-think his policy of 'constructive engagement' with South Africa.

The South African Government fully exploited the American paranoia about the spread of Communism, by pointing at the support of Soviet Union to ANC. But the ANC skillfully used the contacts of Bishop Tutu with Christian groups to convey that while the ANC were Socialists they were not Communists and believed in a multi-party democratic system. Such was the worldwide support to the ANC cause that 'Free Mandela' concerts and events became a global industry. Wearing Nelson Mandela T-shirts became a fashion statement. Artists and sportspersons were in the forefront of this campaign. In 1980, the United Nations began compiling a "Register of Sports Contacts with South Africa". This was a list of sports people and officials who had participated in events within South Africa. It was compiled mainly from reports in South African newspapers. Being listed did not itself result in any punishment, but was regarded as a moral pressure on athletes. Some sports bodies disciplined athletes, based on the register. Athletes could have their names deleted from the register by giving a written undertaking not to return to apartheid South Africa to compete. The register is regarded as having been an effective instrument to enforce a sports boycott of South Africa even amongst those who were closet supporters of racism, since it meant ruining one's international career.

1980s also saw a major proxy clash between the Soviet Union and US in Afghanistan. With paucity of resources, the Southern African operations were out-sourced to the Cubans by the Soviets. The US also became less concerned over the prospects of ANC-rule in South Africa, as the endgame of cold war began with the ascent of Gorbachev and his Perestroika and Glasnost polices. As a part of easing of tensions between the two super powers, the conflicts in Namibia and Angola were wound down. Both the countries having won their independence, the proxy wars were ended with victory of forces of liberation. This set a trend in Southern Africa with South African racist regime, the last *domino*.

The case of total military defeat of the LTTE in Sri Lanka in May 2009 shows how world events can impact insurgencies. While the ANC struggle was aligned with that of the Afghans where the insurgents triumphed, the LTTE got categorised as a terrorist organisation. In the post 9/11 world, LTTE found no sympathy or backers. The Kashmiri separatists are similarly caught in the time warp. The world is not prepared to accept another haven for radical Islam that Kashmir may well become. Fortunately for the Kashmiri separatists, the Indian government is also equally behind the times and has not been able to tap on the international insecurities against the surge of Islamist revolts. Skillful Pakistani diplomacy has linked the Kashmir issue with help to NATO forces in Afghanistan, but the greater blame lies on the Indian inability.

The effect on insurgencies in Northeastern India, Nagaland and Mizoram, of the changes in external environment is even starker. In December 1971, exploiting the discontent in the majority of population in erstwhile East Pakistan, India intervened militarily and created a new state of Bangladesh. With the end of East Pakistan, the source of external support and arms supply to Mizo and Naga insurgents dried up. The Indian army destroyed the insurgent camps and the bulk of the leaders had to escape hastily to inaccessible areas of Chittagong hill tracts in neighbouring Myanmar. The Nagas and Mizos never recovered from this mortal blow and the Naga insurgency more or less ended in 1975-76 after the Shillong Accord was signed by Mr. Zoheto. The Mizos entered into serious peace negotiations and ended their struggle in 1988.

Review and Reflections

This was an exercise in trying to find out the why and how of insurgencies. Boundaries or divides, when more than one, are a logical cause for alienation and secessionism. The geography of an area cannot be altered, but isolation can be ended with the development of communications. Similarly, economic linkages can dilute isolation and promote emigration and immigration, leading to integration. A careful study of the boundaries and efforts to mitigate their effects would be an effective measure for counterinsurgency and can promote peace and conflict resolution. In short, rather than solving the conflict, this can undercut the very basis of conflicts thus removing the root cause.

Our extensive discussion on role of leadership and organisation is meant to clearly identify dominant element in any insurgency. At the risk of oversimplification, one can classify insurgencies as leader dominant, organisation dominant or cause dominant. It could be represented by a triangle.

Cause & Ideology

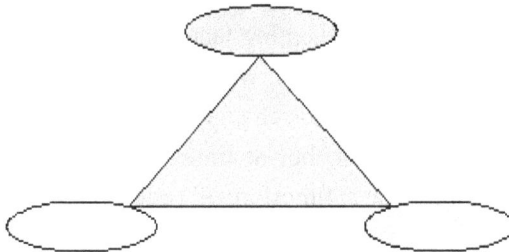

Leadership   Organisation/Structure

This is not a static relationship but is ever-changing. To counter the insurgency, one has to have a keen eye to spot the changes in the relationship. For instance, in case of Nagaland, it was the untiring leadership of Z. A. Phizo that was instrumental in starting the revolt in Nagaland. Equally, Lal Denga, galvanised the Mizos. But over time, at least in the case of Nagaland, the organisation (Naga Federal Government) became the dominant factor in the insurgency. Despite Phizo's long absence from Nagaland and later his demise, the Naga movement continued. This also shows the difficulty in negotiations with multiple actors. Today it will not be an exaggeration to say that it is the vested interest of the insurgent organisations that has kept the struggle going in Nagaland, despite the lack of a charismatic leader and weakening of the cause. In the case of Kashmir, after Sheikh Abdulla, the prime movers of the insurgency have been the various organisations and sustained support to the cause from Pakistan, which keeps the fires of unrest burning. If we look at the South African example, it becomes clear that the *cause* was uppermost and primary all through the anti Apartheid struggle. It is indeed true that Nelson Mandela and his continued imprisonment on Robben Island fired the world's imagination and his release became the *cause celebre,* but this was incidental to the larger picture.

The problem this poses to counter insurgents is that if the relative importance of the three facets is not correctly assessed, then one ends up on the losing side, by living in the past. Far too many negotiations have foundered on this rock of uncertainty of the exact status of the inter-relationship between these three fundamental factors.

There is yet another complicating factor; the three facets themselves also undergo changes. For instance, while a revolt may have begun as a quest for independence, it may soon change its goal to autonomy. This is not merely *shifting of goal posts,* but at times a total game changer. The changes in leadership are a function of time and changes within an organisation, as there is often a power struggle based on personalities or approach or ideology. Thus there are hardliners and moderates or pro peace or pro violence leaders in virtually every organisation. The organisations or structures of insurgents may similarly change with the political wing dominating over the armed wing or vice versa.

All this explains how an insurgency is different from a military problem that deals with certainties. Failure of a purely military technique is thus inherent in the nature of this type of conflict.

Understanding of environment and understanding the role of each of the motivational forces, is essential for a successful conflict management. Strategic control over the environment in which the conflict is taking place is possible in case the country has the ability or the power to do so. Else, aligning one self with the trends is essential. Otherwise one would end up a victim like the LTTE, Apartheid regimes or North Eastern insurgents.

Our study of insurgency has also shown that in about two decades the revolt begins to fade. This is directly related to the insurgencies in which *Leadership* is a dominating factor. It seems that as the leaders begin to age, there is an urge to see a conclusion within one's lifetime. An aged insurgent leadership is then ready for compromise. However this theory of *shelf life of insurgency being two decades* does not work when the revolt is sustained by the strength of the cause or organisation/external support.

It is common wisdom that the counter insurgency must adopt a multi-pronged approach. This is true at the policy level in the sense that the war has to be fought on five fronts, namely economic, social, political, psychological and military. But at the strategy level as well, the approach has to be three-pronged, to aim at the cause, leadership and organisation. Weakening of only one or even two facets of the insurgency does not result in peace. In Nagaland, for instance, after Z. A. Phizo, there has not been a leader who commanded the loyalties of Nagas, of all tribes. Yet such has been the strength of the *structures and institutions (*the Naga Federal Government) that despite the absence of a charismatic leader and weakening of the cause, the insurgency (although at a low level) continues unabated. What has happened is that the armed wing has developed its own vested interest and strength that is independent of the leadership. Insurgency is now a means of livelihood through extortion and crime. Not unlike Nagaland, in Kashmir as well there has been multiplicity of bickering leaders, each with limited influence. The Army's operations, over the years, have disrupted the organisations of the insurgents, yet the insurgency is far from over because the cause, basically secession, based on religion, is alive and kicking. The very existence of Pakistan nearby, as an *Islamic State* is sufficient to keep the separatist cause alive. The fact that Pakistan continues to provide help, support and sanctuaries is an added reason, but even without that the cause would survive. This author was told an interesting incident of 1980s when a Kashmiri told an Indian Army officer that while everything else in Kashmir or India was fine, he preferred Pakistani *salt.* In the Indian subcontinent, salt is equated with loyalty. What the Kashmiri meant was that irrespective of the economic and other goodies that India may provide to Kashmir, his loyalty would be to Pakistan, that he sees as a *homeland for Indian*

Muslims. A well known Indian Muslim reformer, late Hamid Dalwai had a similar tale to narrate when he mentioned that a simple *Shikara (a small boat) man* told him that while he had everything else in India, he also had to care for the *flag of Islam.* The point that ought to be understood is that mere disruption of organisation or elimination or buying of leaders may not lead to success in counterinsurgency as long as the cause and ideology is not countered or neutralised. This brings home that neutralising rebel leadership and/or organisation with the military is not sufficient to win peace.

But what happens in the course of long-drawn-out conflict is a fascinating subject of study. Why do some insurgencies end in successful negotiations and peace while some like the Kashmir go on and on? We will examine the conditions that lead to negotiations and peace in the next chapter. The duel between insurgency and counterinsurgency in all its aspects, peace process as well as use of force, is what will be tackled next.

Section 4 - Quest For Peace: An Integrated View

Counter insurgency is a much-misunderstood concept. It is seen primarily as a military operation and has often been confused with wars of colonial domination. Colonial powers freely used the term insurgency to describe freedom struggles. Purists of the conflict resolution school and members of peace organisations look at it with suspicion. The author was a victim of this when in 1998 a Pakistani peace activist opposed the author's participation in the XIII World Peace Congress in Melbourne in December 1998. His objection was that as a specialist in counter-insurgency in Kashmir, the author was unfit to attend the Peace Congress (Fortunately, the organisers did not accept this). Not only peace activists but some of the militaries world over, engaged in these operations, also see it in purely military terms.

Counter insurgency is holistically defined as a quest for peace or for enforcing peace. War, on the other hand, is essentially a tool of politics that aims at acquisition, of territory, influence or economic resources. Peace, in that case, is a consequence of victory and not an aim of war. Warfare also follows the methods of maximising the efficiency of use of force through principles of concentration, flexibility and offensive action. Since the basic aim of the two differs, so does the methodology, as we shall see presently.

If insurgency is 'armed politics' or an armed challenge to an established state, then the component of the use of force is an integral part of dealing with it. But counter insurgency is a much wider term and is inclusive of the peace process or vice a versa. The peace process in this case could consist of socio-economic measures, negotiations, ceasefires, political concessions, propaganda and other measures to foster integration and absorption.

As seen earlier, violence faced by the state and the challenges to it, can have their roots in social conditions, economic issues, internal politics, external interference or psychological factors like alienation. Violence is a symptom while the cause of the disease lies elsewhere. Use of force or counter violence is thus merely one of the instruments to bring about the desired results. According to late Lieutenant General Eric Vas, an authority on insurgency, the battle has to be fought on five fronts simultaneously, namely economic, political, psychological, social and military. Use of force is thus only one of the fronts and to be successful it has to be in consonance with the other four. This has to be clear right at the outset.

That does not mean that force is unimportant. In fact, in order to get the other measures and strategies in place, control over violence is a pre-requisite. The relationship between the factors that generate violence is neither precise nor static. This brings us to the conclusion mentioned in the introductory chapter, that there is no one uniform formula for success or a universal strategy applicable at all times and at all places, even in the same country. One can however, have enduring principles that would be applicable in most situations.

There is however a fundamental difference between the use of force in counterinsurgency and in regular warfare. Defeat of the 'enemy' is the ultimate goal of war while in case of counter insurgency; there is no enemy, only a section of population that is alienated. Thus phrases like 'search and destroy missions' are out of place in counter insurgency. That these tactics were regularly used in the context of Vietnam operations was both the cause and consequence of the illegitimacy of American operations in Vietnam.

As mentioned earlier, in a situation of internal violence when a group is using violence against the state it is, ipso facto, also challenging the monopoly of the state to use force. In this scenario both the parties to the conflict are using force and in this case the issue of legitimacy is not simply a moral or an ideological factor but has direct effect on the effectiveness of the force, so used.

Two of the most significant conflicts of the last century were undoubtedly the Vietnam War that lasted from 1960-1976 and the one in Afghanistan that lasted from 1979 to 1987-88. Both of these were termed as 'Insurgencies' or 'Freedom Struggles' depending on which side of the

Cold War divide one was on. But it is crystal clear now that the American involvement in Vietnam was essentially an outcome of the so called 'Domino' theory. This theory postulated that if the Communists were to win in Vietnam, the whole of South East Asia would turn Communist. This was an outcome that was not acceptable to the US, as it saw in this, a threat to its domination of the Pacific Ocean area. The war had nothing to do with the aspirations of freedom of the Vietnamese or the defence of freedom. So the Americans invented leaders, actually their puppets, like Diem, Thieu or Nguyen Cao Ky, installed them in Saigon and pretended that they were actually defending the South Vietnamese against the 'aggression' of North Vietnam.

The other super power, the erstwhile Soviet Union repeated the folly of the Americans, this time in Afghanistan. In 1979, the Soviet Union entered Afghanistan in order to take advantage of the turmoil in Iran and likely American intervention there. It was a defensive measure to protect their soft underbelly. The local Afghans saw this as foreign invasion and fought the Russians. In 1988, the Soviets had to beat a retreat from Afghanistan much like the Americans had to leave Vietnam.

In both the cases, external aid played a major role in the ultimate outcome. Both the conflicts became a part of the then-ongoing Cold War. Yet the results showed that lack of legitimacy and its by-product, public support or lack of it, played a crucial part. It also showed the efficacy of the guerrilla tactics in an asymmetrical conflict, in terms of coercive power. Today the Taliban faction of the Afghans is using similar tactics to checkmate the Americans. Again, the conflict in Afghanistan is being termed as insurgency. The reason Americans entered the country and virtually occupied it, was to hunt for Al Qaeda. The illegitimacy of American actions may well come to haunt them in the coming years.

The moral dimension of 'legitimacy' is important in conflicts of this nature since these tend to be long drawn out. Over a long period, in the absence of legitimacy, the conflict becomes unpopular (as the Vietnam War was) and saps out, the will of the country engaging in it.

The Indian counterinsurgency operations in the North Eastern tribal regions offer a glaring contrast to these purely externally controlled operations. The North Eastern revolts by the Naga and Mizo tribes had an element typical to primitive tribes living in a harsh, mountainous terrain. Throughout the nearly two-decade-old violent conflict, the tribals maintained a steady code of honour in the selection of their targets. At times, the conflict almost came to resemble a competitive sports event! Many parts of the world, particularly Afghanistan, resemble the conditions of North East. In the Kashmir conflict, on the other hand, there have been no 'rules of the game' and violence is ruthless, even women and children are not spared. The religious idiom is used both as justification of violence and as a motivating force. Establishment of the rule of *Sharia* (the Islamic Law) has often been invoked as the goal of the insurgents. In Sri Lanka, the issue of identity as Tamils, essentially a linguistic/cultural/racial/historical concept, has predominated and religion has taken a backseat. The Tamil rebels are also the virtual pioneers of suicide attacks in the modern era. One President, two defence ministers and one ex-Prime Minister have fallen victims. In one particularly effective attack the entire Defence Ministry building in Colombo, Sri Lanka, was destroyed by Tamil suicide bombers.

In classical Clauswitzian[1] formulation, insurgency technique relies on 'resistance' over long periods and wide spaces, to ultimately cumulatively overcome the adversary. Counter to this is the limiting of the space and the attempt to lower the intensity of 'friction' and also reduce the timeframe. There appears to be some evidence, from the preliminary studies, that insurgencies do have a 'shelf life'. In this sense it is also a contest in stamina.

Mizo Rebellion 1966-1686

Out of all the violent movements, the insurgency in Mizoram that lasted from 1966 to 1986 is a classic open-and-shut case. The supreme leader of the Mizo National Front (MNF), the late Mr. Lal Denga, himself became the first elected chief of the State of Mizoram in 1987. A case study of Mizoram yields interesting insights into Indian methods in the use of force. In the 20-year struggle, Mizoram went through virtually all the stages of

---

[1] Clausewitz talks of strategy of decisive blow or large numbers of small battles, fought over a longer period of time, leading to the same result. The insurgencies belong to the second category in terms of strategy.

classical insurgency, from open warfare to low intensity war to terrorism directed at non-Mizo individuals. At the height of insurgency, as in Kashmir, MNF flags used to fly from every house on India's Independence and Republic days. From this extreme to Mr. Lal Denga swearing allegiance to the Indian Union was indeed a long journey. How it all began has already been elaborated in the second chapter. Suffice it to say that when it all began it caused a great shock to the nation.

In 1844, the British had penetrated the plains to the north of Mizoram. Their interest was confined to tea plantations in the plains. The war-like Mizos launched frequent raids against the plains' settlements. The British colonial policy was not to get involved in administering the difficult mountain areas of very little economic significance. After each raid by the tribals, an Expeditionary Force would be sent to punish the tribals. It would advance to the offending village and burn it. These punitive expeditions took place at regular intervals of ten years from 1849 till 1888. In order to find a solution to the recurring problem, the British established a fort at Lunglei in 1888. In 1891 the village chiefs were co-opted into the local administration.

Every time a punitive expedition would go into the interior, it would be accompanied by Christian missionaries. Promising peace, security and salvation, by 1891, the population of the entire area was converted to Christianity by the missionaries. The British colonial policy actively discouraged missionary activities in the plains but was supportive of conversion in the tribal areas. According to a long term plan, the tribals were sought to be used against the politically active plainsmen. Under a plan named after a civil servant Coupland, the British toyed with the idea of an independent tribal state in the North East. Since 1873, the British administration enforced a system of an 'Inner line' in the tribal areas. Under these regulations, citizens from other parts of the country needed a permit to enter the tribal areas and could not buy property there. With minor modifications, this restrictive system is still in force.

The Christian missionaries helped convert the Mizo dialect into a written language using the Roman script. They also established hospitals and schools. Education was however, confined to reading religious hymns and secular subjects like science and technology were neglected. At the time of Indian independence, Mizoram had a high literacy rate of 80 %. The Mizos took to Christianity with gusto and harmonised their tribal religion with the new faith. The village priest along with the Chief became an influential power centre.

In 1914 at the time of the First World War, the British recruited around 3000 Mizos to form a labour brigade. This brigade served in France. This was their first ever large-scale contact with the outside world. The retired labourers formed the first nucleus of a political party in Mizoram, the Mizo Union. Since 1891, the British also followed a policy of strengthening administration and district headquarters were set up at Aizwal.

In 1942, as the Japanese advanced into Burma, Mizoram was thrust onto the front line of fighting. The British recruited Mizos on a large scale, to fight the Japanese. Owing to the difficult terrain, the Japanese did not attack Mizoram. The area was however used as a jump-off point by the British for their offensive in the Arakan province of Burma. The Second World War led to the building of a rail line to Silchar and also the development of an airfield. At the end of the Second World War, 3000 trained Mizos were de-mobilised. They found little chance of employment in their areas, in the absence of any industrial development.

In 1947, after India attained independence, all the tribal areas in the North East, including Mizoram, became part of the newly created province of Assam. The capital Shillong, was located 500 kms away and by virtue of their numbers, the administration was dominated by the plains' Assamese. The hill people's, including the Mizos', demand for a separate province was turned down. The tribal areas were given a District Council setup with limited administrative powers. The forest lands, in effect, most of the areas, were kept out of the jurisdiction of the District Councils, thus making them an ineffective body. No sooner was the province of Assam formed, than the provincial Government imposed Assamese language on the unwilling tribals. The tribal aspiration for self-rule remained unfulfilled.

The Indian Army had undertaken contingency planning since 1963 and had earmarked brigade strength if it needed to quell a rebellion. The troops were located outside Mizoram, at Agartala. As the news of the Mizo revolt reached Delhi, the army was ordered to 'take back' Mizoram. A force of eight battalion strength began advancing into Mizoram on 4th March 1966. The preponderance of ex-soldiers among the Mizo rebels led them to adopt classic positional defence at various points. The veteran Indian army units who had successfully fought the Japanese in the Burma theatre, faced little difficulty in overcoming the resistance and within 8 days, all the posts were relieved and towns retaken. In the operations, the army suffered 110 casualties while the rebels lost an estimated 500. Over two hundred rebels surrendered. The losses suffered by the rebels led to a change of tactics from open confrontation to hit-and-run raids conducted by small bands. The main tactic was ambush along the vulnerable and sole road that linked Aizwal with Silchar in the plains.

To secure communication, an operation was launched, to control the population that lived along the road. The Mizo pattern of living in small villages was changed and 50,000 people from 32 villages were shifted to ten re-grouped villages. Each centre had a security post, dominating the population. Identity cards were issued to all villagers and all food grain stocks outside the centres, were destroyed. In the re-grouped villages, people were given free food for six months. The new centres also gave access to medical facilities, postal services, electricity, etc. Small-scale industries and services to give improved seeds as well as livestock, were established. This task was completed by the end of 1967. The people were initially reluctant to move to the new centres. But they soon came to realise the advantages of effective administration and by next year 10,000 people living in 21 villages, volunteered to be re-grouped.

As the grip of the administration tightened over the population, the rebels established bases in the neighbouring East Pakistan that had a Government, sympathetic to the Mizo cause, as part of its zero sum politics vis a vis India since 1947. The main operation was confined to trans-border raids and ambushes. Rebels would infiltrate into Mizoram, carry out the task and ex-filtrate. Despite the re-grouping of the population, rebels easily slipped in and out of the villages due to the support and sympathies of the populace.

In August 1968, an amnesty was declared that lasted until November. Nearly 2000 cadres took advantage of the offer. It was noticed that those who surrendered were mainly old people and were being 'pensioned off' by the MNF. No major leader surrendered.

In 1971, tensions between India and Pakistan reached a breaking point and an internal revolt took place in East Pakistan. Most of the troops were withdrawn from Mizoram to fight in this campaign. In August 1971, another amnesty was declared in Mizoram, but very few took advantage of it, as the MNF appeared to be awaiting the outcome of the impending Indo-Pak war. In December 1971 in a two-week campaign, East Pakistan was defeated and a new nation, Bangladesh, friendly to India, emerged on the western border of Mizoram. The rebels now, not only lost their sanctuary, but also support. The first visible effect of this was seen on 25th December when a group of 350 rebels led by the Number Two man in the MNF hierarchy, Lalnunmavia, surrendered. It was however noticeable that the surrendered weapons were mostly old ones of World War II vintage. The second amnesty lasted till 30 September 1972.

Along with the amnesty, the Mizo district was granted the status of a Union Territory, a halfway position between a district and a full-fledged state. Elections were held in April 1972 and the old guard of village elders represented in the Mizo Union party, came to power. The MNF boycotted the elections. In the early months of 1972, flushing operations were launched in the newly independent Bangladesh. Most rebels managed to escape to Burma.

Since 1970, the MNF and Lal Denga were in touch with the Chinese through the latter's embassy in Dacca. After the demise of East Pakistan, the rebels sought Chinese help. Mr. Lal Denga himself had been to China earlier and met Chou en Lai, who assured him of all material support. China, however, refused 'open' political endorsement of the Mizo cause in a world forum, like the UN. The arms aid by the Chinese was however forthcoming. Two groups of strength of over one hundred, went to the Yunan province of China, traversing through the difficult terrain of North Burma.

The rebels were in total disarray due to the shock of loss of their bases in East Pakistan (now Bangladesh) and were lying low. Encounters with the army were avoided and the principal emphasis was on infiltrating Government and police forces and a drive to collect taxes. As law and order was under the popularly elected local Government, curfew and night movement restrictions were relaxed. Secret contacts were made with the rebels by the local Government as well as intelligence agencies and talks began.

In June 1974, a retired brigadier of the Indian army, T. Sailo, himself a Mizo, launched a human rights movement in Mizoram. Every time security forces launched operations, the movement collected details about atrocities committed and launched prosecution in Indian courts. Army operations and the use of cordon and search methods were greatly hampered by judicial intervention. Many of the captured rebels were set free for lack of evidence, by the courts. In February 1976, direct talks with the MNF began in Delhi. Lal Denga himself led the Mizo delegation and was given guarantees of safe conduct. Just as the talks were on, a group of rebels returned from China. In view of the ongoing peace process, the group was persuaded to remain inactive at a place named Balakote and await the outcome of the talks while the army surrounded it. In October 1976, the peace talks broke down. The China returned rebels were tipped off on the impending breakdown by the Indian Government and they escaped into jungles. After the breakdown and escape of the Chinese-trained rebels, intensive operations were resumed by the army. The escape of the rebels caused a major controversy but the then Army Chief General T. N. Raina maintained that the word of honour given to the rebels was more important than any tactical setback.

The peace talks in Delhi were bogged down by the rebel leaders' insistence on treating MNF as the sole organisation representing the Mizo people and their demand, to be given power without elections. In May 1978, in the elections held for the local assembly, the trenchant critic of the Government's human rights record, Sailo and his Peoples Conference party, won an absolute majority.

In order to keep up the support and keep the movement alive, MNF turned to xenophobic actions against non- Mizos. In June 1979, the MNF issued a notice for all non-Mizos to quit Mizoram. Many school teachers and Government servants were killed in cold blood. Security forces, now supported by Sailo and his popularly elected Government, again launched intensive operations. Cordons and searches were resumed, putting people through a great deal of hardship.

The ding-dong battle between terror tactics and peace talks continued through 1982. In April 1982, Lal Denga left India and went back to the UK. The MNF issued the third Quit Mizoram notice in June 1982, leading to a large scale exodus of non-Mizos from the state. The elections in April 1984 brought the Congress party to power, on the platform of resuming peace talks. It promised to make Mr. Lal Denga the Chief Executive of the state. Peace talks resumed and the Mizo Accord was signed on 25th June 1986. After nearly a quarter century, several elections and many changes in the Government, it can be safely said that peace in Mizoram has held out.

Kashmir

The Kashmir insurgency cannot be understood without the dimension of inter-state conflict between India and Pakistan.

The 1947 partition of India into two states and after 1971 into three states has not solved the problem of historical animosities. Pakistan claims that India has never accepted the Two Nation theory that propounds that Muslims of the Indian subcontinent are a separate 'nation' and that Pakistan is their 'homeland'. It feels that India has been doing everything possible to undo Pakistan. It blames India for the separation of Bangladesh. Not accepting the merger of Jammu & Kashmir with Pakistan is another proof of Indian ill-intentions.

India argues that the conflict is not communal; it is a mini cold war being fought between a secular, democratic and pluralistic society and a barely disguised theocratic autocracy.[2] Though India has accepted Partition as a fact, it cannot accept the Two Nation theory as that would impact the minorities in India. In view of the country's vast diversities, it can only survive as one entity on the basis of secularism.

This background of ever-increasing spiral of mistrust between the two countries, makes the problem of Jammu & Kashmir intractable.

The events in Kashmir in 1947 were also propelled by historical forces. The main force was the unique character of Kashmiri Islam. Kashmiris are the most 'recent' mass converts to Islam in the Indian subcontinent. The largest majority were forced to give up the religion of their forefathers in the 17th and 18th centuries under the rule of Mughal Emperor Aurangzeb. Even to date, the most common family name in Kashmir is Butt, a distortion of Bhatt, a Hindu surname, most common amongst the Brahmins in India.

Kashmir has the largest number of Dargahs or graves of holy men, in total violation of the strict Islamic code that prohibits such practices. Many of the saints are worshipped by both the communities. The patron saint of Kashmir- Nurrudin is known as Nand Rishi to Hindus. Sufi saints of Kashmir continued the tradition of learning and tolerance. Kashmiri Islam is closer, emotionally and culturally, to secular India rather than a strict Wahaabi Islam that has come to dominate the Indian subcontinent. On the basis of its Muslim-majority and geographic contiguity with Pakistan, Jinnah and the people of Pakistan felt that Kashmir rightly belonged to them. Even the tribal invasion of Kashmir in 1947, must be seen in the light of what India was doing in Hyderabad and Junagarh. In these cases, Muslim rulers of predominantly Hindu population were coerced to accede to the Indian union through the use of overt and covert force. Pakistan lost Kashmir when the tribals advancing towards Srinagar forgot their military objective and instead spent time in loot and rape. In less than two months time, the raiders were driven out of the Kashmir valley. In 1948, Pakistan dropped all pretences and its soldiers openly fought the Indian army. Poonch and Kargil were recaptured by India in 1948 and the fighting ended on 31st December 1948, when India proposed a cease fire. Nearly one third of Jammu and Kashmir remained under Pakistani control.

India took the Kashmir issue to the UN on 15th January 1948. It was the Indian complaint of Pakistani invasion of Kashmir that was the original

---

[2] Toynbee, Arnold J & Ikeda, Daisalea, 'Choose Life: A dialogue', Michigan University Press, 1976, p.125.(Has to go as foot note of next page.)

issue. But the blasts of the Cold War and the Indian decision to stay away from alliances, infuriated the west. The original issue of Pakistani aggression and Indian complaint got converted into a dispute over the state of Jammu and Kashmir, as a territorial dispute between India and Pakistan. In 1947 Pakistan was militarily weak. It could not afford to risk its existence for the sake of Kashmir and it did not escalate the conflict. Once it became a Western ally, the inflow of modern arms began in 1956. India continued to neglect its defence. In 1962 when a border dispute with China erupted in an armed conflict, India suffered a major debacle. Pakistan, fearful of the subsequent Indian military build-up, launched a second attempt to annex Kashmir in August 1965. The operation code named 'Gibraltar', envisaged sending in armed infiltrators to the Valley and Rajouri - Poonch areas. There, in co-operation with locals, the infiltrators were to carry out sabotage, cut off lines of communications and take over the Government. The Pakistani army was to then march in to support the 'liberated' Kashmir. Pakistan was encouraged to carry out this adventure by the chaos that had engulfed the Valley in December 1964 when the holy relic of the Prophet Mohammed went missing. The resultant civil strife convinced Pakistani leaders that Kashmir was ripe for a revolt. The Indian Army's dismal showing against China also gave encouragement to Pakistan. In the Valley, infiltration began in the first week of August along the Pir Panjal route as well as northern gullies, with the objective of reaching the Valley. A smaller force also infiltrated in the areas of Rajouri- Poonch and occupied some hill features on the cease fire line as well areas in depth. The infiltrators received some support in Rajouri- Poonch sectors but did not receive much co-operation in the Valley. Pakistani Brigadier Gul Hasan (later Lt. General and Commander in Chief) admits as much in his memoirs. Another Pakistani miscalculation came to the fore when the Indian defences on the ceasefire line held firm. On 28th August 1965, Indians captured the strategic Haji Pir pass on the main route of infiltration. Along with the capture of the Raja post, north of Poonch, the Indian army eliminated the Haji Pir bulge and opened an alternate all-weather route to the Kashmir Valley.

Indians inducted additional forces in the depth areas to deal with the infiltrators. The incessant operations launched from August onwards saw the infiltrators on the run. Out of the total force of 8000, nearly 1/4th was eliminated. Many captured men were publicly paraded in front of the media. On 1st September 1965, Pakistan attacked with regular troops supported by tanks in the plains, west of Jammu.

In April 1965, Indian Prime Minister Mr. Lal Bahadur Shastri, issued a warning to Pakistan that any attack on Kashmir will be considered as attack on India. On 6th September 1965, India launched an all-out attack against Lahore, the second largest city in Pakistan. India thus, widened the scope of the conflict and fighting in Kashmir assumed secondary importance, thereafter.

After 22 days of fighting, a UN-sponsored cease-fire came into effect on 23rd September. The cease-fire was observed only partially. The fighting stopped only after 10th January 1966 when an agreement was signed in Tashkent under the auspices of the Soviet Union. In Tashkent, both sides agreed to give up their respective territorial gains and promised to resolve the dispute, peacefully. The next day, Mr. Shastri died of a heart attack and within two years, General Ayub Khan lost power. The Tashkent agreement remained a dead letter and Indo-Pak hostility continued unabated.

The last fifty years have seen many violent shifts in public opinion in Kashmir. Immediately in the aftermath of the tribal invasion of 1947, anti-Pakistani feelings ran very high. Soon the pull of Islam and constant Pakistani propaganda made for a sea- change and by 1953, Nehru realised that the results of a referendum may well favour Pakistan.[3] For close to two decades, due to his oratory and anti-India rhetoric Z. A. Bhutto was a popular figure in Kashmir. On 4th April 1979, when he was hanged on the orders of late General Zia of Pakistan, there were anti-Pakistan riots in Srinagar. A congregation in the Hazaratbal mosque held on 6th April, thanked the Allah that Kashmiris had made the choice of joining India and not Pakistan in 1947. The cadres of JI and their leader, who was vehemently anti-India, sought shelter with the Indian Army! In 1987-88 the clock had turned full

---

[3] Prime Minister Nehru sent one of his close confidants, Mr. Haribhau Pataskar on a secret visit to Kashmir to gauge public opinion. Pataskar reported that the pull of Islam was strong and majority of Kashmiri Muslims would vote to join Pakistan. This came as a jolt to Mr. Nehru.

circle and General Zia and Pakistan were seen as saviours to bring 'Azadi' (Freedom) to long-suffering Kashmir. Zia's be-medalled photographs began to adorn many public places in Kashmir. In contrast, rioting took place in Srinagar over the installation of a statue of Mahatma Gandhi.

Sheikh Abdullah and later his son Dr. Farooq, remained undisputed leaders in Kashmir right till the 1980s. But as the Sheikh's party, the National Conference tasted power and their rule saw widespread corruption and inefficiency, support began to evaporate. In 1989, Shiekh Abdullah's birth anniversary was observed as a black day and his grave in Srinagar had to be put under massive security to save it from the wrath of people who intended to vandalise it.

The year 1987 marks the beginnings of the present cycle of violence in Kashmir. Essentially the revolt that began in that year, spearheaded by Jammu Kashmir Liberation Front (JKLF) was a home-grown phenomenon. Kashmiris were tired of the mis-governance of Dr. Farooq's administration. But even more fundamentally, the new generations of Kashmiris grew impatient with their lot. Kashmir has one of the highest rates of population growth of around 6 percent. The Constitutional restrictions on investment under Article 370 of the Indian Constitution had the effect of stalling any industrialisation in the state. The literacy rate in Kashmir was a dismal 18 percent (as compared to the national average of 63%). The combination of these factors, along with massive corruption in public administration ensured that nearly 20 billion Rupees worth of developmental aid went into the pockets of a few. Successive generations have seen their standard of living fall. In this situation, some politicians sold the dream of independence or a merger with Pakistan as the panacea and a revolt began.

Pakistan claimed that the uprising in Jammu & Kashmir was a people's revolt and the Indians had suppressed it with brutal force. The cause of a merger with Pakistan was championed by the Muslim Conference. This had its popular base in the Muzzafarbad/Mirpur areas that are presently under Pakistani control.

The changes in Eastern Europe had their own effect in raising expectations of 'freedom' from Indian rule. At that time, the violent campaign for an independent Sikh state in Punjab was also at its height. In an election held in 1989, a coalition Government took over in Delhi and within a week, Kashmiri separatists scored a major victory when they kidnapped the daughter of the Union Home Minister (himself a Kashmiri Muslim). In a weak-kneed move, the new Government released several violent separatists. The expectations in the Valley were that it was only a matter of time before Kashmir merged with Pakistan.

Pakistan decided to take full advantage of the situation and launched a major operation to help Kashmiri separatists. Pakistan was euphoric over its success in helping Afghans successfully fight the Soviet forces and was also confident of being able to take on ten-times-larger India in a military confrontation, thanks to the massive American military aid that had flowed in. In terms of deployable force and sophistication, by 1989, Pakistan had achieved near parity with India. The Indian Army's performance in Sri Lanka (1987-89), wherein it fought Tamil guerrillas of the LTTE and suffered 1,100 casualties, had also not gone unnoticed in Pakistan.

In 1987 when Pakistan got actively involved in Kashmir, the late General Zia Ul Haq was very clear that this could only succeed if the Kashmiris played the major role. This was indeed the case till 1992-93. Over a period of time though, the Kashmiris have taken a backseat, with Afghans and Pakistanis fighting the Indian Army in Kashmir. These foreign mercenaries have often carried out atrocities on Kashmiris and rapes by militants are not an uncommon occurrence. The Indian security forces on internal security duty also sometimes went beyond the bounds of necessity. Nearly two hundred soldiers and other ranks have been punished for their crimes. The reason for the quick change in public mood was that the firm handling of the situation in 1990 and 1991, led to evaporation of the euphoria of 1989 when most Kashmiris expected a merger with Pakistan. The presence of the Army in the Valley was also a new factor. Ever since 1947, the Army's presence was confined to the border areas and the Valley was left alone. But after 1990 when the Army's presence became a reality, many a shrewd Kashmiri revised his opinion about the efficacy of revolt.

In October 1993, in a major confrontation with the Indian security forces, over 20 militants holed up inside the Hazaratbal shrine in Srinagar tamely surrendered. Just at the time when the attention of world was focussed on the happenings at Hazaratbal, Sopore town, the headquarters of the pro-Pakistani Jamaat E Islami, was cleared of all militants.

1993 also saw the emergence of Hizbul Mujahideen as the most dominant group in Kashmir. The JKLF was the largest and the most active militant group till then, but relentless pressure by the army had depleted its strength. JKLF stood for 'independence' of Kashmir, while the Hizbul was in favour of a merger with Pakistan. 1993 marks a watershed year in the insurgency and the beginning of a decline in violence. The surrenders were yet to start, but it would be safe to say that the seeds of loss of morale were sown in the successful clearance of Sopore and Hazaratbal.

After 1994, Harkat Ul Ansar emerged as the strongest militant group in Kashmir. The strength of this outfit was estimated to be around 1500 to 4000. Majority of the members of this group are non-Kashmiris- Afghans, Pakistanis, Sudanese, Algerians and Egyptians. They have no local political affiliations and instead are linked to pan- Islamist organisations, Harkat ul Mujahideen and Harkat e Jihad e Islami. Both of these claim to be international organisations, with branches and fighters in Chechnya, Bosnia and even Philippines. With this group becoming prominent, the ISI (Inter Services Intelligence wing of Pakistani army) had taken a direct control of the fighting in Kashmir. Their areas of influence were the Doda, Anantnag and Batamaloo localities of Srinagar. Destruction of educational institutions and opposing all measures of normalcy, irrespective of the cost incurred by the people has been their attitude and there have been frequent clashes with Kashmiri militants. This group is lavishly armed with rockets, machine-guns and efficient communications.

In the beginning of 1995, militants led by Mast Gul, Jamaat E Islami followers from Pakistani occupied Kashmir, entered Charar E Sharif, a shrine dedicated to the patron Saint of Kashmir, Sheikh Nuruddin to Muslims and Nand Rishi to Hindus. Most of the militants holed up inside the Charar E Sharif were supporters of Jamaat E Islami. On 11th May 1995, the militants set fire to the shrine and in the ensuing melee, many, including Mast Gul managed to escape to Pakistan. This incident helped the average Kashmiri turn against the militants.

On 4th and 8th July 1995, militants of Al Faran, a front for the Pakistani controlled Harkat Ul Ansar, took six Western tourists, hostages in the upper reaches of Pahalgam in South Kashmir. On 13th August, a Norwegian, Hans Christian Ostro, was beheaded and his headless body thrown out by the captors. His Jewish origin and also the fact that Norway is a small country, apparently went against him. One American hostage managed to escape. Four more westerners, a German, a British and two Americans have never been traced.

On 26th August 1995, encouraged by the response to its overtures, the Government announced a generous surrender package. Cash rewards ranging from Rs.8000 for a machine gun to Re. 1 per round of ammunition surrendered, were announced. In addition, militants were promised vocational training for rehabilitation and a stipend of Rs. 1500 per month. During the next four years, over 1100 armed militants surrendered. The Indian army was also able to capture over 9000 AK-47 rifles, 900 machine guns and several rocket launchers from the militants.

Since 1997-98, the militants shifted their attention to the areas of Doda and Rajouri/Poonch. They also began killing at random. In early 1998, marriage parties of Hindus were attacked and so were the road construction workers. The tensions within the State and cross border movements of terrorists often led to clashes between the two armies, deployed on the line of actual control. In the first week of August 1998, the two armies exchanged artillery fire across the entire stretch of the line of control. In this round of firing, over 100 people died on the Indian side and an equal or greater number on the Pakistani side.

The decade of the Nineties saw several events that radically altered the world and regional situation. The three most significant events were: overt demonstration of nuclear weapons by India and Pakistan through tests carried out in May 1998, withdrawal of Soviet forces from Afghanistan and the collapse of Soviet Union leading to the end of the Cold War.

In these altered circumstances, Pakistan was no longer a key partner in US global strategic plans. US financial and military aid to Afghan guerrillas dried up. Pakistani army units already deployed in Afghanistan continued to provide military support to the Taliban. However many of the Pakistani-sponsored militia forces which could no longer be financed, were forced to leave Afghanistan. Pakistan was engulfed by hundreds of seasoned mercenaries, who had been operating under their control. Among these were gangs which were being funded by the proclaimed terrorist leader Osama Bin Laden. All were well armed and religiously motivated. Their morale was high as they had fought and defeated the powerful Soviet forces. Pakistan decided to clandestinely use the Afghanistan-returned militia to infiltrate into J&K, using them as reinforcements for their proxy war against India.

By the 90s, Indian security forces had redeployed and evolved new tactics to deal with infiltrators who found shelter in inhabited towns and villages. Also by then some of the locals were with brutal Afghan, Pathan and Arab mercenaries who demanded free shelter, food and women. The army began receiving accurate information about the movements of intruders from some local sources. This enhanced their success rate against infiltrators. About 20 mercenaries were being killed or captured every week. By 1995, it was evident that mercenaries who infiltrated into Kashmir, were having a difficult time.

Nawaz Sharif had been elected Prime Minister of Pakistan by a two-thirds majority on a "friendship with India" election manifesto. His political opponents disapproved of his moderate policies. They believed that India was not serious about finding a just solution to the problem. They welcomed the influx of militants from Afghanistan and sought their support for a more fundamentalist approach to social problems. In order to offset domestic pressures, the Prime Minister announced that he was introducing the Sharia Law. His critics were not satisfied with this. They were unhappy that friendly overtures were developing between India and Pakistan. They knew that a direct military confrontation with India was impractical. They demanded that Sharif at least display a more aggressive approach towards India. They wanted Pakistan to continue the policy of infiltrating mercenaries and whipping up insurgencies in the state or to create a military incident, which would impel international intervention in J&K.

In order to keep restless unemployed militia groups' busy and political opponents quiet, Pakistani strategists suggested a scheme wherein the army supported by militia groups, would establish a small enclave across the LOC at a place which would be tactically strong and hurt India. They believed that India's conventional military superiority had been neutralised by Pakistan's nuclear weapons. There was therefore little risk of a modest incursion escalating into a full-fledged war. They were sure that this would result in the intervention of the US and UN and a reopening of the J&K issue to Pakistan's advantage. Nawaz Sharif accepted the concept in outline

The border skirmish between India and Pakistan at Kargil from 25th May to 26 July 1999 was one of the most serious post-Second World War conflicts. Since the nuclear tests of 1998, both countries were 'declared' nuclear weapon powers. This was the first ever 'battle' between the soldiers of two nuclear weapon armed states. During the entire Cold War era, the Soviets and the Americans were careful to avoid direct confrontation, with the exception of the 1962 Cuban Missile Crisis. Pakistan broke the unwritten first commandment of the nuclear game, "Thou shall not directly confront another nuclear power!"

Kargil was not just an attempt to gain a tactical advantage. The idea was to seize Kargil town and isolate Ladakh in the East. Through terror tactics and ethnic cleansing in Doda area and Poonch district, in combination with the Kargil thrust, Pakistan hoped to obtain the Valley. Though it continues to lay claims to the whole of Kashmir for public consumption, it appears that it has settled for control of the Kashmir Valley as the minimum strategic prize. Sympathy for Pakistan's claims on Kashmir was virtually wiped out by international perception that its leaders flirted with nuclear disaster in Kargil. Pakistan was not able to win Western or Chinese support, nor get the US or UN to intervene directly in J&K.

History has been repeating itself in Kashmir. In 1947 and 1965, Pakistan tried to seize Kashmir by sending irregular forces led by its soldiers and tried to pass them off as 'Kashmiri Freedom fighters'. In the Kargil skirmish as well, it tried the old trick. But decisive change was to come over in Kashmir in 2001. The attack by Al Qaeda on the US, changed the West's attitude to the Islamic insurgency in Kashmir, for the first time.

Meanwhile, the newly-formed Rashtriya Rifles effectively garrisoned the Kashmir Valley. The Indian Army also completed the fencing of the border. Along with the induction of effective night-vision equipment and better surveillance devices, the external influences on the situation within the Valley, began to wane.

The Government also undertook many economic initiatives to better the lot of the average Kashmiris. The result of all this is that in the year 2010, Kashmir had the lowest number of people below poverty line (at just 3% of population) in the entire South Asian region. In the early 90s, rural poverty was a major issue in J&K. At a village in Uri (Kamalkot), the author remembers an Indian soldier pointing out at the new slippers a woman was wearing …a sign that she was getting money from her husband, who she claimed was missing. The army believed that her husband was acting as an ammunition carrier for the insurgents! Such was the desperate state of people that they risked their lives in cross-border trips for merely Rs. 200. At the root of much of the unrest in Kashmir (the term is used in a generic sense and it includes Jammu, Kashmir and Ladakh) were socio economic problems- a combination of high population growth, no industry and no employment.

The improvement in the situation in Kashmir has to be credited to improved governance and the restoration of democracy. The last decade has seen peaceful elections conducted in Kashmir and genuine representatives of people coming to power. The voting percentage, especially in local elections, has been impressive and even the most rabid separatists have not questioned its impartiality.

All this led to desperation in Pakistan and among the terrorist organisations based there. Whatever the world may think, for the Jihadi organisations like LeT (Lashkar E Toiba) or Jaish E Mohammed based in Pakistan, 9/11 was a great success. In order to keep the fires of unrest burning in Kashmir, the Pakistan-based organisations increasingly took to terror attacks inside Kashmir and elsewhere in India. The attack on the Indian Parliament in December 2001 nearly led to a war between India and Pakistan. As an aftermath of this crisis, in February 2002 the Pakistani government gave an assurance, backed by the US that its territory would not be permitted to be used by terrorist groups, to attack India.

This led to a composite dialogue and peace process between India and Pakistan, in which Kashmir was one of the issues discussed. This was in view of the reality that the Kashmir insurgency was essentially a Pakistan-sponsored activity with some local support. But this was merely a change of tactics and no real change of heart. As the American difficulties in Afghanistan began to spin out of control and the US began to rely more on Pakistan to pull its chestnuts out of the fire, Pakistan demanded its pound of flesh in terms of concessions by India on Kashmir. At this point in time, in 2011, it seems difficult to predict what shape this would take. One thing is however certain, India is in a far stronger position now as compared to 1963, which was the last time the US attempted to pressure India on Kashmir, in the wake of the Chinese threat to India and the Indian need for US aid and support. India is now unlikely to yield to American pressure. For the foreseeable future, the terrorist campaign is likely to continue with some success.

The peace process in Kashmir has been a multi-pronged effort and has been following several tracks. Right from the days of Nehru, the first Prime Minister, Kashmir has enjoyed a 'Special Status' in the Indian Constitutional scheme. The local legislature has a virtual veto in applying Parliamentary Acts to the state. Though the earlier nomenclature, where the state Chief Minister was designated Premier has been done away with, the substance of autonomy remains. Kashmiris enjoy a virtual separate citizenship and no Indian is permitted to settle there or acquire the privileges of 'Kashmiri Citizenship'. This measure of isolation was meant to assure Kashmiris of their so called 'unique' identity and assuage fears of being swamped by the majority. The second track of this approach was the extremely generous federal aid and funding that the state received. Year after year, close to 70% of the state's expenditure was borne by federal grants. These grants were for developmental efforts as well as current consumption. Thus, articles of daily consumption have been heavily subsidised by the Indian government grants. The policy of economic isolation had long term consequences that came to surface only much later, i.e. in 1980s.

The problem of civic unrest in Kashmir was basically rooted in the lack of economic development. It is true that one does not come across the kind of grinding poverty that one sees in other Indian states, yet the fact was that despite natural resources, a vast numbers of Kashmiris were poor.

Unchecked population growth, running at 5% per annum with declining death rate has tremendously increased the population pressure on land. Article 370 and the internal isolationist policy that it engenders, xenophobia instigated by petty leaders and ineffective administration have resulted in a situation wherein there is a total lack of industrial development. The combined result of these two factors has been that an average kashmiri has seen his standard of living declining over the last two generations. It is not poverty or social disadvantage that triggers a revolt, but loss of hope. The Kashmiris felt trapped in their circumstances, between the threats and forces by militancy and its counter, the security forces.

To address the socio-economic roots of the Kashmir problem, INPAD[4] launched 'Project Hope' in 1996-97. This author as the co-ordinator was fully involved in this effort. The idea was to introduce modern methods of agriculture, horticulture and animal husbandry in selected pockets of Kashmir. During one's army career as an infantryman and staff officer, the author spent close to a decade serving in Kashmir, mostly in mountainous areas. It was difficult not to like the average folk, simple, God-fearing and hardworking. A soldier's contacts were mainly with the hill folk and NOT the valley Kashmiris-ask any Gujjar or Bakarwal or Jammu people about them and you will get a volley of unprintable invectives.

A common Soldier's relationship with the civilians was always cordial and friendly. All this was of course before the poison of religious fanaticism got injected in the body politic of Kashmir in the 1980s. One vividly remembers the years from 1975-76 when the Sher-E-Kashmir, late Sheikh

---

[4] INPAD or Initiative for Peace And Disarmament is an independent think tank affiliated with Bharatiya Vidya Bhavan Pune Kendra. This was established on 2 October 1995.

Abdullah was Chief Minister and there was a mass movement in Pakistan occupied Kashmir to march in to join India. The Sheikh's call for 'return' had such an effect that the Pakistan Army used bullets to stop the pro-India march. It was amusing to see that in 2009 some Kashmiri 'Leaders' organised a march to Muzzafarabad to go and join the failing state of Pakistan, to face American drones, suicide bombers and the Taliban! As an aside, when asked the question as to when Pakistanis are preparing to jump off the sinking ship of that state (many influential Pakistanis have moved their assets abroad)[5], why do Kashmiris want to go on board, one is met with an embarrassed silence.

In October 1991, the author had started his second career as researcher and teacher at a University. At that point the author was approached by the Indian army headquarters to counter the adverse media propaganda. The author went to Kashmir and visited villages and remote areas (not merely Srinagar) and wrote about it all. As an add-on, an independent assessment was sent to the Army Chief. Thus began a journey that lasted nearly 8 years, till 1999.

There was acute poverty at the village level in Kashmir. These observations were shared with a Pune industrialist and a Gandhian, the late Navalmal Firodiya (of Bajaj Tempo, now Force motors). He suggested that something should be done about it and offered generous financial help. Thus was born Project Hope under which INPAD inducted computers in Kupwara area (used 286s given by Cummins company) and arranged the visit of a team of scientists to Rajouri-Poonch area to explore horticulture and biotechnology that could be inducted to improve the lot of people. Success was limited and the impact not very visible, but the seed was sown. After about ten years, the army launched a full-scale Operation Sadbhavana along similar lines.

---

[5] 'The Dawn' Karachi, 25 June 2011 'Escape route',by Themrise Khan. 'But since early this year, following the backlash against support to repealing the blasphemy law and more recently, the OBL takedown, the rush towards immigration to countries like Canada and Australia, has seen a massive surge among Pakistanis of various economic backgrounds. This includes those from within Pakistan's minority Hindu, Christian and Ahmadi communities who are desperately (now more than ever) trying to seek asylum in countries like India and Thailand.'

At that time, the proliferation of *madrassas* (religious schools) was a major worry. INPAD's view was that it was pointless to ban them-that would only force them underground. Instead it was suggested that the army (that has a presence in every nook and corner of Kashmir) establish 'English-medium' schools as a counter magnet. The idea was accepted by the then Chief and the first of these was opened in the village of Trehgam in North Kashmir. Trehgam, the birth place of Maqbul Butt, (founder of JKLF who was hanged) was a hotbed of militancy and anti-Indian sentiment. The Brigadier was doubtful whether any student would come! This was in 1993. The following year on a visit, one was told that the school was a grand success and even known militants had sent their children to the army run school…In 2011 one does not even hear of the *Madrassa* problem in J&K .

The army went about establishing schools in big way and by 2010 *Army Goodwill Schools* dotted the state and were long-term solutions to the Kashmir issue. As a symbol of hope and change, in the 1990s INPAD had also campaigned for the Valley railway to be constructed at the earliest. The argument was that a link to the national network would take time, but an isolated Valley rail line was easy and doable. That is now a reality. Another of the suggestion was to effectively 'garrison' the valley by creating a force like the Assam Rifles, permanently stationed in population centres. The idea was also to induct the local youth in this force, thus solving the unemployment problem to some extent and also bridging the gap between the army and the people.

There was global apprehension about Kashmir becoming a nuclear flash point in 1998 after both countries went overtly nuclear. At a World Peace Congress organised by Physicians Against Nuclear Weapons (IIPNW) in Melbourne from 4th to 8th Dec 1998, a roadmap was proposed by INPAD to address the issue. The gist of the proposals made is given below,

- Both sides accept that they have a case and are in a no-win situation. Any measures that are taken in the interim do not detract from this basic stand i.e, the claims of both sides remain intact.

- Without prejudice to their enduring positions regarding the Jammu and Kashmir state, both sides agree to promote peace in Kashmir. The two countries could form a joint team with equal representatives of each country and one each from the SAARC countries to monitor the human rights situation and cross border terrorism in the entire state of J&K (on both sides of the LOC). This team should be given unfettered access to all areas and could make its finding public and also present them to both the governments.

- Having thus taken care of the issue of human rights violations and cross-border terrorism, both countries could open the borders to Kashmiris to visit either side.

- Once this is put into practice for a period of six months or so, as a next step, the border should be opened for limited trade in local produce. This should hopefully prompt the direct trade between the two countries. The reality is that today billions of dollars of trade is carried out between the two countries via Gulf countries. Direct trade will benefit all.

- Once contact at the people to people level is established in Kashmir, as well as elsewhere, after five years time, the issue of what should be the status of Kashmir, should be examined. As a teaser, one can propose a 'de-militarised' Kashmir as an interim goal.

- Simultaneously, with the establishment of a joint commission and parliamentary committees, both India and Pakistan should cease interference in each other's country. Service personnel of other SAARC countries could head the observer groups as well.

After many rounds of Track II diplomacy and negotiations, this is the 'solution' that seems to have a chance of being accepted by all the parties.

While the end of the Cold War saw its ramifications in Kashmir, it also had one beneficial effect. All these years, with firm Western support to the Kashmiri separatists, the Indian Government had ensured that dissidents were kept out of the electoral process. There were some instances of outright electoral rigging. However, especially post the Kargil clash in 1999, the US changed its stand on Kashmir and the rest of the Western world followed suit. This permitted a free play to democratic forces and the last few elections in Kashmir have been accepted as free and fair. What this did to the political aspect was akin to what happened in Mizoram in 1975-76. There, Brigadier Sailo's People's Party, that made human rights a major issue came to power and restored the faith of the Mizos in Indian democracy. Something similar happened in Kashmir with the People's Democratic Party that championed the human rights issue, sharing power in Kashmir. This essentially marginalised the separatists and also established the democratic credentials of the Indian state. Improved governance saw economic development at a faster pace and a reduction in corruption. At the same time, the instability and anarchy in Pakistan made the merger with Pakistan, a very unattractive proposition. It was due to a combination of these factors that by the end of first decade of the 21st century, the insurgency in Kashmir seems to be on its last legs.

But there is an important caveat. While the insurgency is on its last legs in Kashmir, peace will continue to be illusive since the ideology of separatism is not being challenged by politicians, both the ruling party and opposition. The present Chief Minister of the state, Mr. Omar Abdullah, in a memorable speech in the Parliament some years ago, had spoken of his identity as a Kashmiri, a Muslim and an Indian. It is politicians in a democracy who have to take the lead and take on the separatists' ideologies. The armed forces can reduce violence, even help in development, but the political battle has to be fought by nationalist Kashmiris. The window of opportunity may not last too long before an insecure Pak muddies the waters with another terror strike and Kashmir goes back to square one.

Sri Lanka

The incessant fighting in the Northern Sri Lanka for nearly 30 long years came to an end at around 3.30 pm on Sunday, May 17, 2009 with the announcement by the LTTE's Head of International Relations, Selvarasa Pathmanathan, that the Tigers had finally decided to silence their guns. Sri Lanka's war against Tamil extremism in all its forms, had been going on for the last three decades. Out of the 38 insurgent groups that came into being in this period, barring the Janatha Vimukthi Peramuna (JVP), the predominantly Sinhala group that attempted a Marxist insurgency, all others were of Tamil origin. They were fighting against what they perceived as the Sinhala oppression. Almost all Tamil groups considered the carving out of an independent Tamil nation – the Tamil Eelam – out of Sri Lanka's traditional Tamil inhabited areas, as the only path of redemption for Tamils to preserve their language, culture and identity.

Only the LTTE had managed to survive the military onslaught of the Sri Lankan state against Tamil insurgent groups from 1983 till 2009. It had also weathered active Indian political and military intervention in Sri Lanka between 1983 and 1990. In its bid to emerge as the sole standard-bearer of the cause of Tamil Eelam, the LTTE did not hesitate to eliminate thousands of militants and leaders of rival Tamil groups. In his bid to emerge as the unchallenged leader of the Tamils, Prabhakaran eliminated important Tamil political leaders including Appapillai Amirthalingam and Dr Nilan Thiruchelvam of the Tamil United Liberation to emerge as the only viable Tamil organisation, with political and military clout.

The Indian Peace keeping force (IPKF) interlude in this long saga of conflict is significant in many ways. It was the first Indian attempt to intervene militarily outside its borders, and ended in failure. This is not the last time that such interventions have been attempted. A close look at the IPKF operations is thus of relevance, beyond the Sri Lankan experience.

The Indian Peace Keeping Interlude

Indian intervention in the affairs of Sri Lanka dates back to ancient times. The Sinhalese, in such situation, have generally played one side against the other and survived. With modern India, a united entity, the scope for such a response is limited. Even so, during India's intervention in 1987, Sri Lanka successfully pitted the Tamil Nadu Government against the Centre and the DMK, an ally of the National Front against the Congress Party. However, the final outcome of the intervention was largely determined by India's below-par leadership and institutional weaknesses.

Indian military intervention in the Sri Lankan conflict was a spur-of-the-moment decision by an inexperienced Prime Minister, who also had the biggest Parliamentary majority in Indian history. It was to prove a lethal combination. The Indian system has consistently resisted the formation of an institution to deal with national security and the entire politico-diplomatic approach was based on assessments by India's non-specialist bureaucracy at the Defence and External Affairs ministries. For instance, the Indian Consul General at New York was overnight pitch-forked into the role of chief negotiator with the Tamil Tigers. Even when the crucial briefing was going on for the top military commanders for an impending operation in Sri Lanka, the single map used was of 1937 vintage. The first maps obtained for planning were tourist maps, purchased in a Delhi market by a three-star General's aide. In order to keep secrecy, the General told the aide to pick these up from different shops so as to not raise suspicions. It is to the credit of Indian army's professionalism that in spite of the handicap of short notice and lack of higher direction of war, it performed as it did.

The IPKF operations can be divided into three phases. The first phase lasted from 30 July 1987 to 8 October 1987. The second phase lasted till Dec 1988 and the final phase before the withdrawal in 1990.

Phase I: 30 July -8 Oct 1987. The Peace Keepers.

In May 1987, the Sri Lankan army had launched a major offensive against the LTTE and Jaffna town. The tactics of the Lankan army were to make the civilians pay if any guerrilla activity took place. The killing of civilians in Jaffna produced a flood of refugees and an outcry in Tamil Nadu. An impending provincial election in Tamil Nadu made it a sensitive issue for the Congress party, anxious to retain its support in the state. The Lankan Government also imposed an economic embargo on the Jaffna peninsula, leading to great hardship for the people of the area. On 3rd June 1987, a small flotilla of ships carrying relief materials to Jaffna was stopped by the Lankan Navy. The Indian Government decided to intervene at this stage and five AN-32 transport planes of the Indian Air Force escorted by two Mirage 2000 fighters dropped 25 tonnes of relief supplies in the Jaffna peninsula. The Indian action was a clear violation of Lankan sovereignty. But this action sent a message that India would not remain a bystander while the Sri Lankan Army carried out its campaign to crush the Tamils. Simultaneously, contact was established with the Lankan Government to end the conflict in Lanka on terms that would guarantee Sri Lanka's integrity and a position of honour for the Tamils. Prabhakaran was flown to Delhi on an Indian aircraft and met the P.M. Rajiv Gandhi on 28th July. Meanwhile anti-Indian riots broke out in Colombo.

On 29th July 1987, the Indian P.M. arrived in Colombo and an accord was signed that tried to end the conflict. India agreed to keep peace in the Northern and Eastern province. The Lankan army was to remain confined to camps. Sri Lanka agreed to create a Tamil majority province in the North and the East. On getting regional autonomy, the Tamil rebels were to lay down arms. India also extracted a promise from Lanka that the port of Trincomalee would not be leased to external powers.

Divisional strength forces began landing in Kankesanturai port in the expectation of a peace keeping role that the Indian army had performed so admirably in Congo, Gaza and other places under the UN. Though the troops did not sport blue berets of the UN, the troops of the IPKF landed as a consequence of signing the Indo Sri Lankan Peace Accord on 29th July 87 by Lankan President Jayawardhane and Indian PM Rajiv Gandhi. The initial approach of the Indian troops as well as military leaders was to treat it like a UN peace keeping operation.

It was an accord forced on the Sinhalese by the Indian might. During the initial stages, there was an apprehension that the Sri Lankan Army would oppose the move. To safeguard the Lankan President against a military coup, a battalion of Indian commandos was stationed in Colombo harbour on-board an Indian Naval ship. Contingency plans were made to fight the Lankan army, should it oppose the landings. LTTE was to fully co-operate with the Indian army.

On 30th July 1987, the Indian army began taking over areas from the Lankan army. There was no resistance. The force was built up to division strength. Indians were welcomed in Jaffna as saviours and given all help by the Tamil Tigers. The top Tiger leaders even stayed in the Indian Army messes. Pallali Airbase near Jaffna became the hub of Indian Air Force operations.

The path to peace was not easy. Anti-Tamil riots had broken out in various parts of the island and the Tamil tigers carried out reprisal killings. There was reluctance on the part of the Lankan Government to release political prisoners and pressure was brought on the LTTE to lay down arms before the peace process could progress further. Amidst this tension, Prabhakaran, the LTTE supreme repudiated the July 29 accord. He however agreed to go along as long as the Lankan Government kept its side of bargain. On 5th August, the lay down of arms by LTTE began with Yogi, Prabhakaran's aide symbolically giving up his pistol. The tension was palpable as he neither shook hands with anyone nor was there any spirit of letting bygones be bygones. It soon became clear that the LTTE was only handing over old and useless arms, keeping heavy weaponry in hiding.

In order to speed up the surrender of weapons, the Indian High Commissioner in Colombo began building pressure on the LTTE through the Indian Army. To counter this and also to test the Lankan Government's intent, LTTE demanded release of its cadres, languishing in Lankan jails. Mr. Thileepan, the Tiger's propaganda chief began an indefinite fast on this issue on 15th September. He died on 25th September. His death was blamed on the Indian Government and its policy of appeasement of Sri Lanka and bringing pressure only on the Tamil Tigers, while leaving Sri Lanka free to pursue its military option. The local Indian army commander in Jaffna was close to the LTTE and appreciated their anxieties over the peace process. But diplomats in Colombo, used bluff and bluster to force the army to act against Tamil interests. In the absence of direct communications between the local army commander in Jaffna and Delhi, a local diplomat assumed command of operations in field. The Indian Foreign Ministry continued to pressure the Indian Army to expedite the laying down of arms by the LTTE. A breach with the LTTE was now imminent. The last straw in this sordid drama was the suicide of 12 LTTE cadres on 3rd October. These LTTE men were captured earlier and were in the custody of the Indians. On orders from the Indian High Commissioner they were to be handed to the Lankan authorities, where they would almost certainly face torture and brutal treatment. Despite the pleadings of the local military commander, this

146

was done and resulted in their deaths. Earlier the Indian diplomat in Colombo had a stormy meeting with Prabhakaran. The egotist diplomat did his worst to antagonise the LTTE leader. The last-minute efforts of the Indian General in charge of operations, well- aware of ground realities, were to no avail in the face of the ignorant obduracy of the Colombo-based Indian diplomat. The LTTE now began reprisal killing of the hostages held by them. To assess the situation, the Indian army chief General K Sundarji arrived in Sri Lanka. It was decided to bring the LTTE around to negotiations and support the Accord by use of force. The IPKF was given orders to shoot at sight. A massive airlift to induct two more divisions in Lanka began. General Sundarji made an astonishing statement that the Indian Army would finish the LTTE in a week. Indian troops were rushed on civil airlines from peace time cantonments. Many of the soldiers had barely been in their peace time locations for a few months, after a hard tour of duty on the border. They were now to spend their time in fighting in Lanka. The faulty assessment by the Army Chief about the nature of the operation- a short and swift one- ensured that the units and formations arrived with minimum logistic support and were ill-prepared for a long stay. Soon the situation came to such a pass that Indian troops who had come with limited clothing were fighting battles in their underclothes. A flash demand was passed on for 10,000 pairs of trousers!

Second Phase: Oct 1987 to Dec 1987. Cutting LTTE down to size

The Indian army was virtually a friendless force in its operations against the LTTE. Few Tamils supported this action. It also meant total lack of intelligence, so vital to fight the insurgency. The Indian Army followed a tactic of virtually saturating the area with troops and hoping that with this overwhelming presence, encounters would necessarily take place. In these encounters the Indian Army was expected to come out triumphant due to its superior training and fire power.

The first assumption proved right. Numerous encounters took place between the two sides. Without exception, in all the encounters, the Indian Army suffered more than the LTTE. The Tigers proved themselves to be a first-rate fighting force at the tactical level. In addition, the Indian Army found that its infantry was armed with inferior weapons compared with the

AK-56 of the LTTE. Lack of intelligence meant also that the Tigers had the initiative to choose the time and place of the encounters while the army mainly reacted to situations.

On 25th October 1987, after a week of hard fighting the Indian Army captured Jaffna town, but India paid a heavy price for this success. While fighting in a built-up area, the Indian Infantry showed exemplary courage and professionalism. The loss of Jaffna was a big blow to the LTTE. The Indian Army, because of its numbers, had a greater capacity to take casualties. The combined effect of these two factors was that despite tactical-level success towards the end of 1988, the LTTE was in a much weakened position.

On 19th December 1988 Presidential elections were held in Sri Lanka and a known opponent of the Indo - Lanka accord, Mr. Premadasa became President. The peaceful holding of elections was a major triumph for the Indian Peace Keeping Force.

Phase III: Waiting to go home

No sooner had Mr. Premdasa come to power, than he demanded the withdrawal of the IPKF. Meanwhile in India too, the DMK Government in Tamil Nadu, known to be sympathisers of the LTTE, voiced similar sentiments. Mr. V.P. Singh, a former Defence Minister of Rajiv Gandhi had broken with him and had mounted a political challenge to the Congress party. In the run up to the 1989 general elections in India, V.P. Singh made the withdrawal of IPKF, an election issue.

As the inevitability of withdrawal dawned on to the Indian Government apparatus, a last-minute bid was made to retain a meaningful influence in Lanka after the withdrawal. In order to do this, the army was used to build a political party that was pro- India and a force that could counter the LTTE. Both the tasks were clearly out of the reach of the army. As soon as the Indian Army left Sri Lanka in 1990, the 'Tamil Army' raised by it, melted away and the political party functionaries fled to India to be hunted down by the LTTE.

In the second phase as the army was clear that it was pursuing a lost cause, morale suffered. Most operations were conducted only on paper to keep up appearances. The LTTE was sure of itself and refused to compromise. The year 1989 saw the reputation of the Indian Army plummet. Pakistan, watching the goings-on from the sidelines, drew hasty conclusions and embarked on Operation Topac in Kashmir to do an 'LTTE" on India in Kashmir.

The Indian intervention in Sri Lanka was inevitable and in its enlightened national interest. Unfortunately the conduct of politico-diplomatic operations was faulty. The break with LTTE was unnecessary. The attempt to do the job of ending insurgency was in any case out of reach of India, as the Lankan Government never kept its side of the bargain. India lost Tamil support without gaining gratitude of the Sinhalas. The Indian intervention had all the hallmarks of an attempt to try out a military solution to a political problem. While India had the LTTE under control militarily, it had no influence on the other three fronts, namely political, economic and social. On the psychological front it failed due to the obdurate bureaucracy that did not give the freedom to local commanders to interact with the media. Thus India also lost the propaganda war. The late pathetic attempts to raise a rival force or create divisions within Tamils were a result of a typical 'escalation of expectations' from the armed forces that invariably happens when success on the military front engenders intervention in other unfamiliar areas. This is not peculiar to India and many foreign armies have found themselves involved in tasks as diverse as education and nation-building.

With the offensive against the LTTE, India threw away the only card it held to pressure the Lankans to give concessions to the Tamils. The Sri Lankan Government was the biggest gainer. While the Indian army battled the LTTE, there was very little progress on the political front. But for the naïveté in Delhi and mishandling at Colombo by the diplomat, the break with the LTTE was entirely avoidable. India did then and continues to pay a heavy price for that folly. The P.M., Rajiv Gandhi paid with his life. At the end of two years campaign, the Indian Army had 600 dead and nearly 2500 wounded. The egotist diplomat, mainly responsible for this blunder, continued to prosper and retired as a foreign secretary.

The Final Push by the Sri Lankan Army

Sri Lanka Security Forces (SLSF) could not achieve decisive results against the LTTE in the three rounds of war from 1983 to 2002. However, in their victorious Eelam War IV in 2009, the SLSF killed as many as 15,000 LTTE cadres and destroyed or captured millions of rupees worth military and civil assets of the insurgent group. In addition to this, the SLSF captured over 9000 LTTE cadre.

The military defeat of LTTE is indeed a significant event. It was made possible by the defection of Colonel Aman Karuna, the number two man in the LTTE, in 2004, due to popular disenchantment with constant fighting amongst the Tamils and changed international circumstances. Sri Lanka was helped with weapons and equipment by Pakistan and China. Indian help to Lankans was indirect in the sense that India did not intervene on the side of the LTTE, despite growing clamour to do so in the Indian state of Tamil Nadu.

Since Karuna's area of influence was in the jungle clad east, his defection bottled up the LTTE in Jaffna peninsula. As a consequence the LTTE was denied the sanctuary of jungles to retreat to. Earlier in 1986-87 when it successfully faced the onslaught of the Indian Army, it had made full use of the Eastern sanctuary. Prabahkaran and LTTE paid the price of obduracy and lack of political flexibility when they failed to read the writing on the wall in the wake of lack of international support and sympathy in an environment of the 'War on Terror' that began in 2001. LTTE became a designated terrorist organisation and its finances were choked, supplies dwindled and support from the international Tamil Diaspora dried up.

With the death of Prabhakaran and decimation of most of the leadership of LTTE, Sri Lanka has declared victory in Jaffna. The existence of LTTE as an organised body that was a 'virtual' government in Northern Sri Lanka seems to have come to an end. But it would be hasty to come to a conclusion that it also means an end to the Tamil insurgency and return of peace to Sri Lanka.

The LTTE made several cardinal mistakes. The assassination of Rajiv Gandhi turned Indian public opinion against it, so much so that even when the Congress was not in power, the NDA government itself did not dare deal with it. It needs to be noted that in 1987 when the Indian Peace Keeping Force (IPKF) went to Sri Lanka, it went there to save the Tamils from the genocide by the Lankan army. On a visit to Jaffna in 1989, the author was told that till the time the break did not take place, the LTTE top brass used to dine in the Indian Army mess! LTTE misread the Indian intention, which was to save Tamils but NOT help create a separate Tamil Elam. India has been steadfast on its support to Sri Lankan unity.

LTTE forgot that Eelam was a means to an end, which was a place of honour to Tamils and a preservation of their identity and culture. By obdurately focussing on an 'all or nothing' strategy, the LTTE lost everything and brought untold misery upon the Tamil people of Jaffna.

The LTTE also failed to see the altered world situation after the 9/11 attack. In the aftermath of that attack, a world consensus has been built around zero tolerance for terrorism and secessionism. Sri Lankan diplomacy was skilful and successful in hiding its own obduracy and painted the LTTE in the darkest possible colours. It must be noted that in the last several years the LTTE had more or less stopped its terror attacks.

Finally, Prabahkaran paid the price of forgetting cardinal rules of insurgency. It is true that LTTE had reached the last stage of its guerrilla struggle and was capable of open confrontation with the regular Sri Lankan army. But as Sri Lanka built its military muscle with Chinese and Pakistani help, LTTE ought to have ceded territory and gone underground to survive to fight another day. Instead it chose open defiance and annihilation. In the closing stages of the last Sri Lankan offensive, the LTTE found that it was friendless. The Sri Lankan Army also cleverly timed their offensive to coincide with Indian elections when Indian decision-making went into limbo, giving the Lankans ample time to finish off the LTTE, militarily. The defection by Karuna, with his base in the East, was possibly the last nail in the LTTE coffin. It will be interesting to see if Karuna also meets the fate of other Tamil leaders, who attempted to reach a compromise with the Sinhalese.

If reports in Western media are to be believed, close to 20,000 Tamils have been killed in the last offensive. The whole of Jaffna was turned into a concentration camp. While the LTTE may have been neutralised, an organisation like the Palestinian 'Black September' may well have taken birth. It was Black September, born in the aftermath of the Jordanian offensive against the Palestinians that pioneered aircraft hijacking and started a cult of terrorism in the Middle East. There is real fear that the brutal tactics of the Sri Lankan Army may produce a similar result. In its six-decade-long experience of dealing with insurgencies, India has NEVER used heavy weapons like artillery or air power against insurgents. In this the Lankans seem to be following the Pakistani example of using fighter jets and artillery in Swat and other tribal areas.

A few years ago, during a discussion with a European diplomat involved in the peace process in Sri Lanka, the diplomat mentioned that both sides were obdurate. While the LTTE has been rightly criticised for its demand of Eelam, the Sri Lankans have escaped censure. Sri Lanka has steadfastly refused to give the federal structure a chance. While talking to the late Foreign Minister Karmadigar (later assassinated by LTTE) in 1996, the author mentioned that a status like that of Kashmir in the Indian union would certainly satisfy most Tamils. Unfortunately the mass of Sinhala opinion in Sri Lanka equates national unity with a *unitary form of government.* Such is the vehemence of Sinhala opinion on this issue that all talk of federal solution is denounced as treachery.

If the Sri Lankans do not show pragmatism and accommodate Tamil aspirations, the island nation is in for a long winter of violence.

The Indian approach to Lanka has been timid and indecisive, partly out of the memory of Rajiv Gandhi's assassination but more due to the shrewdness with which the Lankans have used the bogey of China and Pakistan against India. While in the short run the Lankans may have succeeded, they could suffer in the long run if they got involved in the potential big power rivalry in the Indian Ocean area. They may yet discover that a giant India is far more benign than the Chinese dragon. The Chinese are building a deep sea port at Hambantota, in the deep South of the island. The port has hardly any hinterland and there is no economic rationale for it. It is obviously part of the Chinese 'String of Pearls' strategy of having naval bases in the Indian Ocean area. The westernmost end of it is the port of

Gwadar in Pakistan. How the US and India react to this 'venture' by Sri Lanka would impact on Sri Lanka, whose economy is in tatters- with its attendant fears of popular unrest. If the Sri Lankans are not careful, their involvement in big power rivalry may well give an incentive to major powers to prop up a resurgent LTTE.

South Africa

Of all the insurgencies being studied in this work, the South African example is unique since it is the only instance where the insurgents won. Right at the outset it must be conceded that for sheer 'illegitimacy' of the regime, South African Apartheid has no parallel. It is somewhat ironic that the very Afrikaaners, who in the post World War II era, wrested control of their country from the domination by the minority English-speaking population, should turn into the oppressors of the majority of blacks. Like the LTTE or Kashmiri separatists, the South African regime was out of sync with world events and trends. When the process of de-colonisation was in full swing in the rest of Asia and Africa, the Apartheid regime was busy passing elaborate race laws and segregating people on the basis of race. A Professor at University of Johannesburg put it,

"South Africa had an ideology based on pigmentation of skin."[6]

The strict race laws and a need to interact with the rest of the world that had moved on, presented some interesting dilemma to the regime. For instance in dealing with the Japanese- what was to be their classification? The South Africans found an interesting way out by creating a category of 'honorary Whites'.

But despite all this, the task before the ANC and insurgents was not an easy one as the South Africans had built one of the world's most formidable military machines. Much intellectual enquiry and rigour has gone into studying the difficult transition of South Africa from a racist regime to a democratic one. Our aim here is however, to study the process only up to the dismantling of Apartheid.

---

[6] World Congress of IPPNW in Melbourne in 1998 December.

Logically, the day President Botha and later President FW De Clerk decided to free Nelson Mandela, they knew that this marked the end of the Apartheid regime. What were the forces, circumstances, strategies and tactics that brought about this outcome is not merely a subject of intellectual curiosity but of immense practical use. For this can show us the broad contours of how a similar illogical ideology could be defeated. The lessons are of particular relevance when the world faces the threat of Islamist ideology- based violence. South Africa teaches us what should not be done.

The beginning of the South African 'People's War' can be traced to the events of March 1960. On 7th March, sixty nine blacks protesting against the notorious Pass Laws of the country were shot dead by the police at Sharpeville, south of Johannesburg. This led to riots all over the country and the South African government led by Prime Minister Dr. Hendrik Vervoerd passed a law banning the ANC (established in 1912) as well as its rival Pan-Africanist Congress (PAC). On 31st May 1961, South Africa became a Republic and broke its relationship with the British Empire. All restraint on racial discrimination was now removed. Dr. Vervoerd, the architect of Apartheid declared that he was a man of granite and that the Apartheid system brooked no changes. The Cold War then raging between the West led by the US and Soviet Union- led Communist block, saw South Africa take a firm pro-US stance. The US needed the South African base at Cape of Good Hope as well as its mineral wealth. Curiously, many strategic minerals that are needed in nuclear and space programmes are shared equally by Russia and South Africa. For strategic as well as ideological reasons, the Soviet Union had been taking a keen interest in the politics of South Africa and was a staunch supporter of the ANC since 1956. Ironically, just when South Africa was tightening the Race Laws in 1960, over 17 countries of the African continent gained independence from colonial rule. South Africa was out of sync with the rest of the continent. The armed wing of ANC *Umkhonto we Sizwe or* the Spear of the Nation (MK for short) was established in 1961 in collaboration with the SACP. The initial targets of the MK were *Bantustans* or the so called African homelands established by the Apartheid regime as a part of its policy of racial segregation.

But the initial resistance was short-lived and in a raid in July 1963, the South African police arrested several SACP leaders and Nelson Mandela. They were charged with high treason and sentenced to life in what has come to be known as the Rivonia trial. Due to internal repression and effective police action, most of the ANC and MK cadres fled South Africa and established camps in friendly neighbouring countries like Tanzania.

The period of the 1960s and 70s was a difficult one for the ANC. It had at its disposal, 500 trained guerrilla fighters based in Tanzania but it was very difficult to enter South Africa proper since it was surrounded by British and Portuguese colonies. In August 1965, at the promptings of the Soviet Union, the ANC took a crucial decision that MK would fight for the liberation of Angola, Mozambique and Southern Rhodesia (later to become independent Zimbabwe). This was to be the long-term strategy of 'hacking their way home'. It was hoped that this way the ANC could create the African version of the 'Ho Chi Minh trail' (a legendary line of supply built by the Vietnamese through Laos-Cambodia to supply Vietcong guerrillas fighting inside Southern Vietnam.) The first such venture was in collaboration with the ZAPU (Zimbabwe African Peoples Union) of Joshua Nkomo. The campaign had a limited success since the MK relied on conventional tactics.

The South African struggle entered a new phase in April 1969 at a conference held at Morogoro in Zambia. Here it formed a larger body, the Revolutionary Council to co-ordinate the underground and over-ground activities, thus broad basing the ANC. In addition the ANC took a momentous decision to admit whites, coloureds and Indians to its general membership and all its decision-making bodies. This was a major departure from its practice since its inception in 1912, as till then the membership was confined to black Africans.

But while the ANC remained ineffective inside the country, support for it at the international level grew. Since the 1960s a large number of newly independent countries had become members of the UN. These countries along with the Communist bloc pressed for anti-Apartheid resolution. Apartheid was equated with Nazism and the objections of Western countries that it was the 'internal' problem of South Africa, were rejected.

155

In 1974, the General Assembly barred South Africa from taking part in its proceedings and accorded observer status to the ANC and PAC. The ANC also began receiving humanitarian aid from the world over. Funds began to flow from Western countries as well after 1969 when the World Council of Churches established a programme against racism.

In April 1974, a military coup took place in Portugal and the Salazarist Prime Minister was overthrown. The Socialists who came to power in Portugal promised early independence to their colonies of Angola and Mozambique. The independence of Mozambique proceeded rapidly, as there was only one organisation and President Samora Machel of FRELIMO established a one party State on 25th June 1975. The independence of Mozambique opened yet another avenue for ANC to infiltrate into South Africa.

The Angolan situation was complicated by the presence of three contenders for power, MPLA of Agostinho Neto, FNLA of Holden Roberto and UNITA led by pro South African Jonas Savimbi. As the scheduled elections in mid-1975 approached, fighting broke out between the three. MPLA, the largest and most popular faction appealed to the Soviet Union and Cuba for help. Soon a force of division strength of Cubans landed in Angola and the Soviet Union helped the MPLA government with arms and supplies. Taking this as an attempt by the Soviet Union to establish its foothold in Southern Africa, the US weighed in on the side of UNITA and FNLA. The American intervention was through South Africa. It is not the author's intention to go into the course of the Angolan Civil War, but suffice it to say that it drew the South African Armed Forces into combat away from their homeland. The meagre manpower resources of the Afrikaner community proved to be inadequate to fight on more than one front.

The South African Defence Forces (SADF for short) had developed an interesting strategy to deal with the threat posed by the ANC and MK. Primacy was given to maintaining a *cordon sanitaire* around South Africa by intervention in Angola, Namibia (then South West Africa) and Mozambique. Conscious of its lack of manpower, the SADF decided to fight the war on its own terms. It never sought to dominate the area of operations or establish any kind of permanent presence in the area of conflict. Instead it organised company level hard-hitting teams using helicopters, tracking vehicles or airborne mobile columns. The basic tactic was to launch raids on ANC bases in neutral countries. These raids forced the ANC to locate itself further and further away from South Africa. The SADF also decided that it was not going to get involved in infantry fighting and instead relied on mechanised forces in which it had an edge. The South Africans keenly watched the American war in Vietnam and wished to avoid fighting battles on terms, dictated by the enemy. But the basic assumption behind the military strategy of the SADF came unstuck in 1987. The theatre of war was Angola.

In August 1987, the MPLA regime in Angola launched a major offensive to capture a strategic town Mavinga that would cut off direct access for UNITA to South Africa. The offensive was launched with nearly a division strength supported by tanks, MIGs and Sukhoi fighter aircrafts gifted by the Soviet Union. In the wake of spirited resistance by UNITA, backed by over 3000 South African soldiers, the offensive failed to achieve its objective and the MPLA forces were forced to retreat to Cuito Cunavale.

The SADF and UNITA advanced towards the town of Cuito Cunavale and engaged the MPLA forces there. In the battle that took place in October 1987, the MPLA combined forces successfully held on to their defences and thwarted all attempts made to take it. This was regarded as a great defensive victory. It was for the first time that the SADF had been check-mated militarily.

There are two views on the impact of battle Cuito Cunavle on the course of the conflict in Southern Africa. South African defence sources tend to downplay the importance of this battle and point to the comparatively low absolute casualties suffered by the SADF. But as the SADF operated with a small population base, these losses were indeed telling. Even more importantly, the blacks, for the first time, felt that they could hold their own on the field of battle, against the South African whites.

Hidden behind the happenings at Cuito Cunavale, another major change took place. For the first time the South African Air force met its match. An informal arms embargo against South Africa was in place since 1963. The situation took a turn for the worse and on November 4, 1977 the Security Council adopted a mandatory arms embargo. The Carter administration, under pressure domestically and internationally, cast the U.S. vote in favour of the embargo. The South African aging fleet of Mirages was no match for the advanced MIG 23 and Sukhoi 22 supplied by the Soviet Union. It is true that the embargo was seldom seriously implemented by the US, and Israel had a clandestine relationship with South Africa. But once in place as a Security Council measure, it became increasingly difficult for the SADF to maintain its dominance in the air. With air dominance likely to be lost, the retaliatory strategy of SADF was in serious jeopardy. One is reminded of the *Tet offensive* carried out by the Viet Cong in 1968 during the Vietnam War. The Americans weathered the attack itself quite well, but the political repercussions of that attack were long lasting and the US public, long lulled by the American rhetoric of *light at the end of the tunnel*, was disillusioned. A similar sense of doom spread in South Africa once the news of the battlefield reverse, reached home.

South Africa operated a conscript army and also maintained a strict censorship internally, about its involvement in Angola. But returning soldiers told horrid tales of fighting in Angola and the difficulties they faced and soon it was common knowledge. The Afrikaner supporters of the Apartheid began to have serious doubts about the conflict's continuation.

While the regional military situation worsened for South Africa, internally the ANC's campaigns, such as the strikes by miners and the consumer boycott of white businesses had great impact on blue-collar workers and small traders. This was the very constituency from which the white supremacist National Party drew its strength.

The cumulative result of all these happenings was that Nelson Mandela, who had by then, become the symbol of anti Apartheid struggle, was moved from the Robben Island prison to Paarl where he was given his own cottage and allowed to meet visitors. This was a prelude to his release. The rapprochement was facilitated by Mandela's assurance to the interlocutors of South African intelligence (Dr. Neil Barnard) that majority rule would be balanced by guarantees to protect minority groups and prevent black domination. Mandela's visitors were impressed by his lack of bitterness and statesman-like approach. Nelson Mandela was set free on 11th February 1990 and, the rest, as they say, is history.

Naxalism in Chhattisgarh

Since the beginning of the 21st century it has been widely accepted that India is on a growth curve of over 8% annual economic growth. Many analysts and particularly the economist Prime Minister, Dr. Manmohan Singh are of the view that many of the major problems faced by the country such as poverty and related law and order issues would get solved automatically once equity and growth are ensured. Naxalism, an euphemism for Left Extremism perhaps poses the greatest challenge to this dream of a prosperous India. Naxalism, which has spread to five states, may well spoil this dream. Here the focus is on Chhattisgarh state.

The Naxalites for years have attacked and looted armouries in the Bastar division. Kidnapping of tribals has been a common tactic to intimidate people. Chhattisgarh, located at the geographical heart of the country and containing unknown and vast mineral wealth, presents both a challenge and an opportunity. With its geographical location at the centre, unrest here can jeopardise East-West and North-South communications that could have grave repercussions on the national economy. Also, the use of the mineral wealth of Chhattisgarh is essential for the industrial growth of the whole country.

The Naxalite movement is possibly the weakest in Chhattisgarh, providing a great opportunity to end this menace in the state. Being located in the geographic centre of the areas affected by Naxalism, success by counter insurgents in Chhattisgarh would break the contact between the extremists in the North and South, making any coordinated action difficult. The basic weakness of the Naxalites is the fact that while they aim at 'Revolution', the Tribals are looking to end exploitation by Forest Guards and economic development. The fact is that the top leadership of the Naxalites is dominated by 'outsiders'. This can be of great help in dealing with Naxalism. This provides the state with an opportunity to wean away the Tribals from extremists and isolate the Naxalites.

In any counterinsurgency study, there is no shortcut to field work. The author led a team of 15 persons to Chhattisgarh for a fortnight in 2006. The Naxal threat was seen in terms of the author's studies for over two decades and experiences in North East India, Sri Lanka, Kashmir and Northern Ireland. But Chhattisgarh was a reminder that comparisons are of no avail. The Chhattisgarh experience made all the theories stand on their head! Chhattisgarh's Naxal problem confronts one with a sense of astonishment. For where else could one find imported leadership, revolutionary rhetoric and cynical exploitation of people as cannon fodder? That the city-based leftist intellectuals accept Naxal rhetoric about welfare of the poor while turning a blind eye to the reality on ground, where blowing up schools and hospitals by Naxals is common, adds to the sense of unreality.

The stark reality of the phony Naxal rhetoric for revolution, assaults one all along a drive from Dantewada to Bijapur, the heart of the Tribal area. On both sides of the road there are typical makeshift refugee shelters, similar to those seen in migrant colonies in Delhi during the height of the Punjab unrest (1980s) and seen even today in Jammu where the hapless Pandits eke out a living. By a conservative estimate, around ten thousand Gond tribals have fled their homes, due to the fear of Naxalites.

This possibly, is the first instance in Indian counterinsurgency experience where a people's movement against Guerrilla fighters is seen taking place. The author participated in one such rally on 25th September 2006. One was quite skeptical, as it could well be a Government-orchestrated move and the participants could have been forced to attend by the police! But the genuineness of people's anger against Naxals had to be seen to be believed. The author walked with the Gond tribals for nearly 15 kms through the forests, chatting and sharing a bidi smoke. There was no doubt about the genuineness of the marchers.

In a sense this breach between the Naxals and the Tribals was inevitable. While the Naxals aim at revolution and overthrow of the existing Government in the country, the Tribals had modest expectations and were attracted to the Naxals as the only way to end the oppression of Forest Guards and local officials. Once the state of Chhattisgarh came into existence, the Tribals and their area was no longer on the margins and became politically important. Electoral arithmetic dictated that political parties and the Government could not ignore the issues of development or the Tribals' grievances. As the State Government began to aggressively pursue the development agenda and also got the bureaucracy under control, the Tribals began to aspire for economic betterment. The Naxalites whose sole interest in the area was to get safe sanctuaries were alarmed and opposed roads, electricity and schools. The Naxals also began extorting money out of poor Tribals' earnings from activities such as Tendu leaf collection. This appears to be not so much for the sake of money but to impose their will and also ensure that the Tribals did not become 'rich' and happy. For that would spell the end to their dominance. Salwa Judum is the Tribals reaction to this Naxal dog in the manger attitude.

It is believed that the movement against the Naxals began on a quiet note nearly 15 years ago. A people's awareness movement was launched to organise village level groups to resist Naxalites. It was launched in areas of Gidam, Bhairamgad and the other worst-affected areas in the Dantewada district. The movement had a positive thrust for peace and was not merely negative in the sense of being anti-Naxal. On 5th June 2005, in a role reversal, during a Salwa Judum meeting in the villages of Ambeli, the assembled Tribals charged and punished 5 Sangham (over-ground sympathisers) members, much on the lines of the Naxal 'People's Court'. There were several such meetings in the villages of Talmendri, Kotarapal and Jungla. The Naxal reaction was violent and on 20th June 2005, they attacked a village and killed 8 Tribals and took away 45 others. But the momentum of the revolt against Naxals seemed unstoppable and each gathering became bigger than the earlier one. A meeting attended by approximately 5000 in an area that is sparsely populated is no mean achievement.

The Salwa Judum was truly a people's movement and no political party really initiated it. Mr Mahendra Karma from the Congress Party and leader of the opposition in the State Assembly began participating in it. He paid a heavy price for it, when the Naxals, in retaliation, killed his brother and burnt his village house.

To the credit of political parties, on this issue, the two main parties in the state, the Congress and BJP have come together in support of the people's movement. The Government and the police forces began to provide protection to the Salwa Judum rallies. This further raised their morale.

Mao had once famously said that the guerilla and popular support are like fish and water. Without the support of the masses, the guerilla cannot survive. Salwa Judum targeted the Sangham members, hitting at the weak point of the Naxals. Their armed strength is useless without Sangham members and passive masses. The fact that all the top leaders of Naxals are non-Tribal was a major factor in this breach between the two.

The truth is that the Naxal revolutionaries, either of the Peoples War Group variety of Andhra Pradesh in the South or the Maoists from Bihar in the North are not there to solve the problems of Tribals. They are there as the forests offer sanctuary for training and rest. The general neglect of the area, callous forest guards and police and a power vacuum made the task of the Naxals easy. Having once helped Adivasis through their 'Robin Hood' methods, they now intend to milk the Adivasi support for the 'higher purpose' of ushering in the Marxist Revolution through out India.

Do the Naxals seriously believe that 'revolutionary conditions' as described by their Guru, Guevara, really exist in India for their revolution to succeed? All this leads one to the conclusion that essentially the Naxals are a gang of thugs and robbers much on the lines of the Sandalwood smuggler Veerappan,[7] who also put up a charade of 'Tamil Pride' to hide his criminal activities.

It is in this context of Naxal cynicism about the interests of the Tribals that movements like 'Salwa Judum' can be understood as revolt against oppression of the Naxals and not counter revolution.

Alarmed at the erosion of popular support and fearful of being isolated, the over- ground wing of the Naxals in cities and the capital Delhi launched a fierce campaign against the Salwa Judum. The media with its inherent leftist bias went to town over alleged atrocities by Salwa Judum members. The courts, Human Rights Commission and civic activists were used to

---

[7] The Times of India, 19 October 2004.Veerappan, a brigand who operated in the jungles of Tamilnadu and Karnataka state and had committed nearly 120 murders was finally killed by the police after eluding the state for over ten years.

defame the resistance. It was dubbed as the State Government's attempt to get Tribals killed by Tribals. Everyone conveniently forgot that village defence forces being organised to fight rebels, has a long history in India and outside. The Central Government, with woolly-headed thinking and to get Naxal help in the national elections, ultimately succeeded in winding up the potent movement.

Emboldened by the 'victory' over Salwa Judum, the Naxals went about consolidating their hold over forest areas and four years later, ie by 2010, were bold enough to take on the Paramilitary forces in open confrontation.[8] At the time of writing, the Government is on the back foot and is re-re-learning the lessons learnt elsewhere. In India, the govt has reinvented the wheel several times over. It is difficult to predict the outcome of the present campaign against Naxalism. It is likely to soon get embroiled in the Indo-Nepal problem, since Maoists are likely to come to power there. The one dimension to Naxal issue, foreign support, that was lacking all these years may change in coming years. Through the conduit of Nepal, China may soon begin to fish in the troubled waters of Central India.

The problem of Naxal-induced violence lies in the richest mineral belt of India, which is also close to the very heartland of the country. This adds to seriousness with which the problem needs to be tackled. The roots of the problem lies in alienation of the Tribals on two counts-One, due to the unfair forest legislation with respect to forests- their natural habitat and second, due to the glaring gap between the lifestyles and living standards of the Tribals and plains-people. Extreme sensitivity is required to tackle the issues involved. Rough and ready methods of using force may prove counterproductive in the long run. Thus there is a dilemma of sorts, while urgency demands action whereas the sensitivity to Tribal identity merits caution and preparation. Standard administrative structures that can support the extension of Government rule have to be identified carefully. If needed, a completely new model of administration could be evolved, based on sensitivity, realism and continuity. A re-look at the erstwhile Indian Frontier

---

[8] The Times of India, 10 April 2010. In a major ambush of the CRPF policemen near Dantewada, over 80 personnel were killed in an ambush by the Naxalites.

Administrative Service may be worth while in the light of India's experience of repeated administrative failure in these areas. The rule of law must replace the rule by outlaws. The quality of the administrator and law enforcer would matter a great deal. Tribals are war- like people and proud of being so. The history of Gonds and Santhals in resisting all manner of invaders should never be forgotten, nor their stand in support of late Pravir Chandra Bhanjadeo.[9] In bringing the Tribals to modernity, care must be taken to be gradual and the transition should not be from no-clothes to a three-piece-suit.

Review and Reflections

The insurgencies and peace process in each of the cases that we have looked at so far have their own unique dynamics. The Naga issue was essentially a political one whereby the Nagas' demand for independence was based on the perceived past of never having been ruled by Indians. The Mizo revolt on the other hand was a reaction to socio- economic problems and the need for local autonomy, though the rhetoric was that of independence. When asked about this, Mr Lal Denga was categorical and mentioned that, to garner support he had no choice but to put forward the demand for independence.

In Kashmir, on the other hand, hidden behind the façade of the slogan of *Azadi* (independence) is the desire to create a mono-religious state. Often the propaganda and bleeding heart media have portrayed a picture of great deprivation, leading to revolt. In most cases that is far from reality. In the early 1990s, poverty was indeed *a* problem. But good governance and huge inflows from Central Govt has totally changed the picture today. INPAD played a small role in introducing modern education (computers) in villages in Kashmir. The impact of the Army's 'Goodwill Schools' has been such that the issue of proliferation of religious schools or *madrassas* is virtually

---

[9] Pravir Chandra Bhanj Deo 'Pravir, King of Bastar' ('Pravir Chandra Bhanj Deo' 25 June 1929 - 25 March 1966) was the last king of Bastar who was killed in 1966 by the then congress government of Madhya Pradesh, for championing the cause of his subjects. He fought for rights of the tribal people. He was killed along with 12 others of his family and associates. The exact cause of his killing remains a mystery to date. It is rumoured that the reason for his killing had to do with lease of immensely rich Bailadila iron ore mines.

non existent. The valley rail line, promoted by INPAD also, is a symbol of hope and change for the better in the valley.

While in the Indian context, socio-economic measures and political concession have been an integral part of the peace process; its absence in the Sri Lankan case is glaring. In the case of South Africa as well, the Apartheid regime tried the concept of *Bantustans* , but the whole idea of cramping 80% population in less than 13 % land (mostly barren) was so outrageous that it was seen to be a mere gimmick. At a later stage, the South African regime also tried the Tri-cameral Legislative structure, one each for whites, Indians and coloureds. But this was seen as an attempt to divide the opposition to Apartheid and not a genuine reform.

There is widely held view that economic development can serve as an antidote to insurgency. The late Field Marshal SHFJ Manekshaw had once remarked that the day Nagas begin to wear shoes, the insurgency will be over. The logic behind this was that it is poverty that is the *cause* of insurgency. It is true that poverty and unemployment indeed help the cause of insurgency by providing willing recruits and foot soldiers to the rebel organisations. But many recent studies have shown that insurgencies are not quelled even when economic development improves the standard of living of the people. Both Nagaland and Kashmir in India have the lowest poverty levels today… Approximately just 4% of the population is now below poverty lines in these states,[10] yet this has had no impact on the support for insurgency, which continues unabated, while in Mizoram, the insurgency is over and the state is one of the most peaceful in the Indian union. The mechanical linkage of poverty with insurgency needs a rethink.

Out of all the violent movements, the insurgency in Mizoram that lasted from 1966 to 1986 is a classic open-and-shut case. The supreme leader of the Mizo insurgents, Lal Denga himself became the first elected Chief of the Indian state of Mizoram in 1987. A case study of the Mizoram insurgency yields interesting insights into the Indian doctrine of the use of force. In the

---

[10] In 2011 the Indian Planning Commission and some other economists differed on the estimates of poverty. The figures were reviewed upwards on a shaky basis, since close to 51% of the consumption was left out. See 'The Business Standard', 23 June 2011.

20-year struggle, Mizoram went through virtually all the stages and phases of classical insurgency, from open warfare to low intensity war to terrorism directed at non-Mizo individuals. At the height of the insurgency, MNF flags used to fly from every house on India's Independence and Republic days. From this extreme to Mr. Lal Denga swearing allegiance to the Indian Union, was indeed a long journey.

Violence in Mizoram lasted 20 years and in this contest, the Indian state and its Army proved to the Mizos that independence through violent means was unattainable. Counter-violence by the state was highly discriminate. Weapons and tactics that could cause collateral damage were not used, except in the initial phase. Indian soldiers often termed this as a 'war fought with one hand tied'. Success was bought at high human cost, with the casualties' ratio between the Indian forces and rebels being fairly even throughout. The Indian superiority displayed was essentially a superiority of numbers and skills, and not much of technology. It was brought home to the insurgents that the Indian state had the will, the manpower and the resources to fight on endlessly. Once the cause was clearly seen as unattainable, it lost its support and popular appeal. In addition, the Indian Government gave continuing proof of its intentions of granting generous autonomy by holding free elections. This not only gave locals a say but also permitted a known rebel sympathiser to come to power. This reasonableness and wide acceptability of the option available, further eroded support from the extreme, though emotionally still attractive cause, of total independence. The autonomy granted to the Mizos, which included many restrictions and disabilities imposed on non-Mizo Indians, was in fact so generous that a section of Indian opinion considered it surrender and a sell-out. The Mizos, according to this view, got independence, in all but name.

The Indo-Pak war of December 1971 saw the destruction of East Pakistan and the emergence of an independent nation Bangladesh, friendly to India. This was a major blow as it cut off external aid and removed the sanctuary in the erstwhile East Pakistan. The refusal of the Chinese to give open political support meant that Mizos could not access international public sympathy and support. Lal Denga and the Mizos soon realised that the interest of external powers was to serve their own ends, and were unreliable.

While talking to this author Mr. Lal Denga mentioned that their insurgency was like a controlled flame for the Chinese, to be increased or decreased as per their interest. Once the Mizos realised this, disillusionment set in. At this stage, the second best option of preserving the Mizo identity and getting provincial status gained favour. Once these conditions were created, it was only a matter of time, before the violence ended.

The Indian Government never used sustained military pressure. Every major operation was followed by a prolonged period of cease fire and amnesty. While this was clearly against orthodox military wisdom, it proved fatal for the insurgents. Once people got used to the life in peaceful conditions, resumption of violence became increasingly difficult. Popular support to the rebel cause was, in the last stages, more an expression of clan loyalty than anything else. But clan loyalty or rosy dreams cannot withstand harsh realities for ever.

One of the reasons that in Mizoram the insurgency had *closure* was the fact that the insurgents made a clever use of the signing of the Mizo Accord as a symbolic victory. The absence of such a defining moment in neighbouring Nagaland has meant that a residual insurgency has remained. In South Africa as well, the regime change was complete and clear cut with Mr. Nelson Mandela becoming the President of the Republic. In Sri Lanka on the other hand, the State has gone in for a purely military solution with the death of LTTE leader Prabhakaran as the culminating point of the Tamil insurgency. The jury is still out on whether this would mean the end of the Tamil struggle. An outcome becomes stable when it is mutually acceptable. In the ongoing insurgency in Kashmir, while the yearning for peace and end to violence is a dominant public sentiment, peace will remain illusive till a mutually acceptable *solution* is found. In the case of Kashmir, it could well be autonomy. But since Kashmir insurgency is not merely a Kashmiri fight, it is also seen as a Pakistani war; therefore what may be acceptable to Kashmiris may still not usher in peace.

Why do some peace processes succeed, while others fail? Can there be some principles along the lines of the Principles of War that can guide counter insurgents? Essentially, for the insurgency to end, either or both the combatants have to be convinced that they are in a *no win situation.* What are the measures that can create this no win? These and many other logical questions would be answered in our last and final chapter.

Section 5 - Insurgency-Counterinsurgency and Peace

As we come to the end of our study, it would be appropriate to draw some conclusions from the analysis done so far. Else it would be a sterile exercise that merely narrates events and analyses them, contributing nothing to the growth of knowledge.

Unlike conventional warfare, counter-insurgency is a highly regulated affair, with rules and boundaries. The use of unbridled force is not an option. In this sense the comparison between the two forms is akin to comparison between sports like soccer and golf. Soccer has rules, so also conventional warfare, but there is less restriction on brute power. Counter-insurgency is more akin to sports like golf, where skill and subtlety count for more than brute force.

As mentioned in the introductory chapters, the very nature of the problem of insurgency precludes any kind of formulation of rules or laws. The case studies of Naga, Mizo, Kashmiri, Sri Lankan, Naxal and South African insurgencies show clearly that there is no possibility of formulation of any template that can be of universal application say in Afghanistan, Thailand, Philippines or Iraq. But the various correlations that these studies unearthed and certain commonalities encountered can lead us to formulate principles of counter-insurgency. These principles are on the same lines as the principles of war that most armies have and are concepts that were originated by German military thinker Clauswitz. These principles are nebulous and general, not specific to *how* kind of formulations.

Creation of a Perception of a 'no-win Situation'

It has become a popular *cliché* to describe insurgency and counter-insurgency as a struggle for hearts and minds of the people. In the earlier section it has been mentioned that it is also a struggle *between* hearts and minds, a conflict between lofty goals and realistic expectations. Thus instead of this nebulous catch-all concept, the author prefers a more precise aim-creation of the perception of no win.

The selection and maintenance of an aim is a crucial first principle of war. But in case of counterinsurgency, there is no enemy and victory is not the aim. While the insurgents aim at *regime change*, the counterinsurgents aim at behavioural change. Counter insurgency operations are fought primarily to win over the population to one's own point of view. Aims like destruction of the enemy or the enemy's resources or capture of territory are not applicable. In fact, there is no enemy, only misguided elements. But for the insurgents, total destruction of the regime is the aim and thus there is an inbuilt asymmetry at the level of application of force. Yet it is wrong to call this an 'asymmetrical warfare' as many do. Essentially, both the insurgents and counterinsurgents envisage and accept the use of force. A truly asymmetrical conflict would be the Gandhian 'Non Violent protest', where one side completely abjures the use of force.

Insurgents and counterinsurgents both aim to create a no-win situation for the other. The counterinsurgents thereby hope that the insurgents would give up violence and change their behaviour. On the other hand insurgents hope that if the adversary reaches there first, it would lead to the collapse of the system, rebellion in the military and eventual victory of the insurgents.

The creation of a no-win perception in the minds of leaders as well as followers and soldiers is a major concern even in conventional warfare. 'Morale' is a major target in all forms of warfare and Napoleon is quoted as having said that it is three times more important than the physical. But in case of insurgency and counterinsurgency, it is even more critical since physical destruction of the adversary is not the aim.

While the creation of a 'perception' of a no-win situation is a psychological concept, it has both physical and psychological dimensions. Here, skilful management of perception is as important as physical factors. The 'no win' situation has several dimensions.

The first and the foremost facet of the 'no-win' situation is obviously the military one. The results of an insurgency depend on this psychological battle. If the insurgents believe that they are in a no-win situation, then sooner rather than later the counterinsurgents will succeed. But if on the other hand, as in the case of the South African Apartheid regime, counterinsurgents come to this conclusion, then the insurgents win and effect a regime change. When the no-win is mutual, a compromise is possible through negotiations that would involve give-and-take and partial attainment of objectives for both the sides. If negotiations take place when a clear no-win situation has not been created, often these are mere tactical ploys to gain time. The history of numerous failed negotiations in insurgency situations is a pointer in this direction.

Strictly from this point of view, the American strategy of 'shock and awe' in the second Iraq war was a correct formulation, theoretically. The problem is that once insurgents embark on a *Guerrilla War*, the definition of victory changes. The occupation of territory or display of superior fire-power produces neither shock nor awe. The guerrillas retreat into the population, survive the assault and continue to fight.

Since almost by definition, insurgents take recourse to tactics of *guerrilla war*, a massive use of force for a short duration, can seldom produce the military no-win situation. Insurgency and counterinsurgency are like a long-drawn-out slogging match, where endurance and resolve to stay on the course, matter more than sophisticated arsenal. Shock and awe in a traditional sense is not an option in counterinsurgency, as there are severe restrictions on the kind of force that can be used. Technically, when insurgents hide in an urban populated areas, termed concrete jungles or in actual jungles, the counterinsurgents have the option to blast the entire locality at least in urban areas, in forests even that option is not available. But the issue of human rights of the innocents precludes this in urban complexes. Massive force, disproportionate to the task at hand also violates the principle of *legitimacy*. This may appear contradictory but so are the principles of war on the use of force, when one talks of concentration of force and economy of force in the same breath. Since the aim of use of force is to affect behavioural change, this cardinal difference has to be clearly understood, as from this flows the strategy and the tactics that severely circumscribe the use of 'blunt' instruments and weapons of mass destruction. This also automatically gives primacy to psychological and not physical effect of force. The counter insurgents have to be extremely careful that in exercising force and coercion, they do not reach a psychological 'point of no return', after which force, instead of changing behaviour in the desired direction, produces desperation. This suggests that the use of force must alternate with periods of peace. Thus in order to achieve the psychological goal of convincing the insurgents that they are in a no-win situation, the force used has to be neither minimum (as in a situation of civic unrest) nor maximum as in case of an all-out war between two states, but *adequate*. The adequacy of force is in terms of quality, quantity and duration and it has to be *legitimate*.

If one looks at the history of counterinsurgency and counter guerrilla wars of the last several decades, one can clearly discern an inflexion or 'tipping point'- an event or an occurrence that changed the ultimate outcome in favour of one or the other side as the result of a perception of no-win by one side. In some cases, the inflexion point was the beginning of the perception that it was a lost cause. Looking at the cases where the insurgents or the guerrillas came up trumps in Vietnam, Afghanistan and South Africa, one can clearly see the impact of these turning points. In the case of the two-decade-long Vietnam war, that point was the *Tet Offensive* in January 1968. Coinciding with the Vietnamese New Year, during which generally both sides observed cease fire, the Vietnamese guerrillas launched a successful attack on all the provincial capitals in South Vietnam as well as Saigon and Hue, the biggest cities in South Vietnam. The attack shook the Americans by its scope and breadth. The earlier optimism of Americans gave way to pessimism and domestic opposition to the war mounted. Militarily, the Vietnamese guerrillas suffered huge casualties and American forces quickly regained the cities, but the perception that they could not win this war took root, both in the military and general public in the US. After this it was a matter of time before Americans withdrew from Vietnam. The 'Tet' offensive succeeded in creating the perception of no-win in the minds of the Americans. The end however came only in 1975 when the Vietnamese forces finally captured Saigon on 29th April 1975, seven years after the

'Tet' offensive. The end was hastened when South Vietnamese regular forces defected or surrendered en-masse to the North Vietnamese and Vietcong guerrillas. The Vietnam War was lost not in the paddy fields of the Mekong delta but in American living rooms. The unprecedented television coverage brought the horrors of war right into American homes, and it is the drying of public support for the war that ultimately led to the military disengagement. The 'Tet' offensive created a situation of no-win in the minds of the general American public.

In the first Afghan War between the *Mujahideen guerrillas* and the Soviet Union, the victory came to the guerrillas only in April 1992, nearly three years after the withdrawal of the Soviet forces. The war that began in December 1979 with the arrival of Soviet forces did not end in February 1989 with the withdrawal of the Soviet forces. The Mujahideen forces, a bunch of Islamist warriors from all over the world (though the bulk were Pashtuns from Afghanistan and Pakistan) were supported by the Americans, funded by Saudi Arabia and trained and sheltered by neighbouring Pakistan. But the fall of Afghan regime only came about in 1992 when a powerful warlord, Abdul Rashid Dostum, defected to the other side. The defection of Dostum was the end result while in all fairness the withdrawal of Soviet forces in 1989 began the process of the end of the Soviet-backed regime. The Vietnam and Afghanistan examples teach a lesson in that ultimately the guerrilla forces can only win if the adversary conventional forces, desert or defect. The survival of the Najibullah regime in Afghanistan is a pointer in the direction of the power of modern conventional forces.[1]

South African 'no-win' situation came about essentially due to the loss of international political support. But even in this case, the military dimension cannot be ignored. The defensive victory of the ANC-supported forces in the battle of Cuito Cuanavale in Oct 1987 and the simultaneous loss of air superiority ushered in the perception that the South African apartheid regime

---

[1] The Najibullah regime survived for two years after the Soviet withdrawal and the end of the regime came only when the major part of force under war lord Rashid Dostum defected to the other side. Even the fall of Saigon to Vietcong and North Vietnamese forces was possible only when the South Vietnam army en-masse defected. Guerrilla fighters on their own could not achieve this .

was on a losing streak. Many South Africans continue to assert that the battle was actually won by the Apartheid regime. But Nelson Mandela could not disagree more: "Cuito Cuanavale", he asserted, "was the turning point for the liberation of our continent—and of my people—from the scourge of apartheid".[2]

This coincided with the drying-up of political support of Western nations, as the Cold War was winding up and the South African Apartheid regime was no longer an asset but a liability in the rest of Africa. Many military analysts ignore the psychological effect of a battle on a war. In the case of the *'Tet' offensive* of Vietnam War, the battle of Dien Bien Phu lost by the French and the battle of Cuito Cuanavale in Angola, the insurgents believed that they had won. Battles and wars are after all won or lost in the minds of the adversaries.

The no-win inflexion point in the case of successful counterinsurgencies in North East India was the liberation of Bangladesh in December 1971 that led to the loss of bases and military support that the erstwhile East Pakistan had provided. In the case of the Tamil insurgency in Sri Lanka, the assassination of Indian leader and former Prime Minister Rajiv Gandhi in May 1991, saw a similar loss of support to the Tamil cause. The ultimate defeat of the LTTE came about almost a decade later, but it can be safely asserted that the loss of Indian support was crucial. The 'Easter Agreement' of May 1998 that brought to an end the Irish insurgency can be similarly attributed to the lead taken by the U.S. The Irish insurgency in Northern Ireland had sustained itself largely due to the support, overt and covert by the Irish community in the US. The Easter Agreement heralded in a change in American attitude and led the IRA (Irish Republican Army) to believe that an armed resistance was no longer feasible. It is true that the economic and political integration throughout the European Union had made the parochial conflict largely redundant. That it spluttered on for such a long time, showed the longevity of historical animosities.

Secessionist insurgency movements like the ones in Kashmir, Northern

---

[2] Mail & Guardian on line, 11 July 2007, article on the occasion of 20th anniversary of the battle.

Sri Lanka, the Indian North East, Chechnya, Tibet or Northern Ireland face a major problem. It is not enough that the insurgents have popular support in their own areas, but in order to succeed they have to also win the hearts and minds of the rest of the country and create a perception of a no-win situation. Until this is not achieved, a secessionist insurgency is not likely to succeed.

The no-win situation has an economic dimension as well. In a long-drawn-out conflict, the people in the conflict zone suffer untold hardships. Over a period of time, conflict weariness settles in and a yearning for peace is palpable. The mundane chores of raising a family and leading a normal life begin to loom large in people's consciousness. In the case of South Africa for instance, economic sanctions began to bite and there was flight of capital from the country. The growth rate began to stagnate at less than 1% and big capital and industrialists switched sides and brought pressure on the Apartheid regime to give up its policy of racial discrimination. An economic no-win may produce the desired results, depending on who suffers more deprivations. A bleak economic future can bring to senses even the most ardent revolutionaries. In conversation with this author in May 1988, Mr Ton Luia (then a minister in Mizoram government and erstwhile Chief of the Mizo National Army) told of the economic privations undergone by rebels while staying in the jungles of Myanmar (the Chittagong Hill Tract or CHT for short). Talking of the long-drawn-out negotiations with the Indian Government, he mentioned that for an insurgent, a pair of clean trousers was more important than some Articles of the Constitution. The counterinsurgents have to follow a *multi-pronged approach,* with economic measures as a major part of it.

A note of caution is warranted here while dealing with insurgency that has religious motivation. No amount of force or fear of death, destruction or deprivation can bring about a no-win perception if the conflict is seen as one between God (and his *true* followers) and mere mortals. The only way out in these situations is to get the God or religion on one's side.

Battle for Legitimacy

As mentioned earlier, in a situation where a group is using violence against the State, it is, ipso facto, also challenging the legitimacy of the use of force by the other side. Here we come across a major problem when faced with *ideological conflicts*. When insurgents fight for a religion, identity or such like non-material causes, the use of force has no effect on insurgents' morale as their ideology convinces them that *ultimate victory* is theirs. The Islamist insurgents in Afghanistan/Pakistan are convinced that they are fighting *God's War (Jihad)* and death and destruction is God's will. A somewhat similar sentiment exists in the Middle East conflict between Arabs and Israelis. Unfortunately the counterinsurgents have steadfastly refused to pick up this ideological gauntlet.

In order to achieve a no-win situation and legitimacy, there is no short-cut to confront the ideology of the insurgents. The current farce of *Good Jihadists* and *Bad Jihadists* or sympathy for the Communist/ Maoists because they claim to be fighting for the poor and dispossessed, is a recipe for disaster and defeat. The three-step approach to ideological conflicts is to *contain, neutralise* and *reform*. In this important aspect of the battle, media and communication (both verbal and non-verbal) play a major role.

The social and political front of counterinsurgency lays great emphasis on the *rule of law* as the main differential between an insurgent and counter-insurgent. In an ideological conflict of this nature, economic aid or carrots, plays a minor role. In fact it is more likely to strengthen the insurgent as he can present the economic gain as consequence of his successful actions. Instead of a reduction, economic aid may actually fuel further violence. India has seen this happen in Kashmir, Nagaland and the Naxal-hit areas where economic well-being is taken for granted as their *due* and endemic violence continues. Examples of this are the Friday stone-peltings in Srinagar or frequent attacks on police forces and Government servants by the Maoists. The NATO forces led by the US are falling into precisely the same trap in Af-Pak.

There are many dimensions that enable a force to be considered legitimate. The first is ideological. A state founded on universal principles and a system that grants every citizen fundamental rights without discrimination, automatically enjoys a legitimacy that is not available to racist, theocratic or ideology-based dictatorships. The core values of the state have to be such as to appeal to not only the majority but also to the smallest minority groups. Universal Humanism has to be the basis of these core values. For instance if India was to be a *Hindu State* on the lines of Islamic States, or like Sri Lanka a Buddhist State, then in confronting a religion-based separatist movement in Kashmir, it would lack legitimacy. The problem confronting the UK in Northern Ireland is similar. With UK ideology, based on their loyalty to the Queen as the *defender of faith,* the Irish Catholics have every reason to reject it. After the demise of the Soviet Union and ushering in of the *Nation State* of Russia, the Russian Federation faces a similar dilemma in the Muslim-majority Caucasus where the Chechen rebels have been battling the state for over one and a half decades. Essentially, a multi-ethnic state has to adhere to universal values and norms in order to be legitimate. One of the most successful counterinsurgency operations ever was by India in Mizoram. During the 20-year conflict, India gained unmatched legitimacy in 1978. In that year a trenchant critic of the Armed Forces and Government, Brigadier T Sailo (Retd) led his People's Party in the elections to the local Assembly and was successful. This proved a point to the Mizo people that India meant to not just preach but also practice democracy. From this point on, the ideological foundations of the MNF were weakened beyond repair, with the insurgents finally giving up in 1986.

Legitimacy of a state is not the function of a de-jure Constitution and core values alone. The legitimacy must also be based on the 'reality' of how the state behaves and what its administrative practices are. This is different from rhetoric and is an issue of management and checks and balances. Che Guevara had stated,

"If a government has come to power through some form of popular vote, whether fraudulent or not, and if that government maintains at least an appearance of constitutional law, a guerrilla uprising cannot be brought about until all possible avenues of legal procedure have been exhausted."[3]

Mao, in his manual on guerrilla, emphasised the aspect of discipline and probity in the behaviour by the guerrilla. What is true of an insurgent is

---

[3] Griffith Brigadier General Samuel B. (Trans.), 'Guerrilla Warfare By Mao Tse Tung and Che Guevara', Cassel & Co. Ltd, London, 1962. p.132.

equally applicable to the counter insurgent as well. The common perception of *Murgi chor (Chicken stealing)* soldiers or policemen, do greater damage to the legitimacy of counterinsurgency than any amount of adverse propaganda. The British, faced with one of the longest-running insurgencies in Northern Ireland, realised that in order to be effective, the police force must have both the credibility and support of the general population. In a divided society like that of Northern Ireland, public perception of the local police as a partisan force was strongly held by the Catholic community. The secret operations to deal with the IRA underground and brutal methods of elimination of the insurgents added fuel to fire. But once the peace process was initiated and violence came under some control, establishing normal law and order became a priority. It is to this end that the British created the institution of 'Independent Commission for Police Complaints'[4.] This was also called civilian oversight over police function, in short an attempt to answer the question, "Who will police the police?" The independent body has no authority to initiate proceedings and is purely recommendatory, yet through the use of media it can generate moral pressure and its findings are taken seriously by the superior Governmental authority. In conditions where there is long tradition of obedience to law, it is possibly a workable model, but given the pressures in the counter-insurgency situation and the charged atmosphere, it may not always work. Possibly this model is more suited when the violence has been brought under control. There is no gainsaying the fact that checks and balances on the use of force are needed, both to deal with individual aberrations or institutional biases. In this regard, a combination of internal organisation along the lines of a discipline and vigilance department, with a village-level informal organisation on complaints, is the best alternative. But in order to preserve the legitimacy and avoid excesses, internal checks of reward and punishment work the best.

The quantum and quality of force being used is also important in deciding its legitimacy or otherwise. In order to have legitimacy, force cannot be excessive and has also to be discriminate. This forces the counterinsurgents

---

[4] British High Commission, New Delhi, 'Northern Ireland Peace Process', 1993. The British government established an independent commission of police complaints to ensure that citizens have a forum to vent their grievances.

to fight the conflict on the terms dictated by the guerrillas. A way out of this dilemma is to create special weapons or forces harnessing technology that can carry out precision attacks. The American-armed drones 'Predators' are an example of this innovation.

Legitimacy is also a function of the conduct of the security forces. Respect for human rights is an integral part of counter insurgency operations. This gives rise to a dilemma, since the insurgents deliberately use tactics such as hiding behind people in a populated area, where any retaliation or action in self-defence can cause collateral damage. This is unavoidable and can best be countered through media and propaganda that puts the blame squarely on the insurgents. But insurgency is also a war, a guerrilla war. In the heat of the battle there is a temptation to target the sympathisers for acts of violence by the armed insurgents. Here the need to educate troops and commanders at all levels is paramount. It must be understood that retaliation against sympathisers would only help insurgents recruit the kin of the victim, thus defeating the purpose of counter insurgency. To curb these abuses it would be best to create internal organisation within the security forces rather than have an external agency. Self-correction is better than external censure and is far more effective.

As a matter of interest, in fighting the tribal insurgency in India, the relationship between the insurgents and the soldiers never verged on total enmity. Soldiers as they came in close contact with tribal society were amazed and impressed at the village level cohesion and democratic functioning. Both sides observed an unwritten code of conduct that ensured that the women and children were never targeted, neither were the army's medical personnel, who often knowingly treated the insurgents. Over a period of time, personal relationships developed between the foes, the classic example of this was when the sister of the supreme leader of the Naga rebels married an Indian army officer.[5]

---

[5] Sharma, S. K. & Sharma, Usha, 'Documents on North Eastern India, Vol. 9 Nagaland', Mittal Publications, New Delhi, 2006. p. 380.

Adequate Force[6]

In most states based on the rule of law, there is a well-defined doctrine of using force against unarmed but violent mobs. The principle is to use 'minimum force'. This is defined as a short-term antidote to bring the mob to its senses. In the case of war or open conflict, the doctrine of 'concentration' or maximum force is in operation. In the case of insurgency, as the aim is not destruction but persuasion, the counter insurgents are expected to use 'adequate force' i.e. adequate to defend themselves and overcome the insurgent while ensuring minimum collateral damage or casualties. The other consideration is that the force used must be 'qualitatively' superior, due to it being used under a strict legal regime or by the use of superior precision technology. The overall aim is to achieve psychological domination over the insurgents. Learning from the American experience in Vietnam where the Americans ended up in a quagmire, the South African Armed Forces deliberately chose a model of creating high-tech, hard-hitting helicopter-borne teams to hit at the guerrilla bases and headquarters in lightening raids. These forces never held ground and avoided prolonged engagements. The tactics were akin to the ones followed by the Israelis. But the South Africans never even attempted to win the hearts and minds of the people (neither do Israelis). The end result was that while the Apartheid regime was militarily strong right till the end, it lost all legitimacy and international support. A balance has to be struck between what is militarily desirable and politically acceptable. Successful use of force has to be accompanied by political, social and economic measures. The stark ideological illegitimacy of the Apartheid cause was the ultimate undoing of the South African regime, and not the resistance by the ANC.

It is due to the fear of censure over wanton destruction that counter insurgency has no room for use of area covering heavy weapons like artillery or air power. Adequate force is not an easy concept to define, especially when the opponent may well take recourse to heavy weapons. Matching

---

[6] Insurgency is an armed conflict and the doctrine of *minimum force* is not applicable, though for the sake of appearances, the term is often used rhetorically by the counterinsurgent leadership. Various legal provisions for use of force in India are at Appendix A. A study of adequate force and its correlation with the success is complex and is explained in Appendix B.

the insurgents would be entirely justified in such situations. This is of particular relevance when the insurgents act as 'proxy' for some other nation. The counterinsurgents in order to create a psychology of no-win in the opponents, have to create qualitative or quantitative superiority. During the Vietnam counter guerrilla operations, many American analysts came to the conclusion that 1:30 superiority in numbers is necessary for countering guerrillas and achieving success. But adequacy of force depends on many factors other than mere numbers and includes the tactical efficiency and the state of morale etc. It is a complex question that military commanders are confronted with. In the appendix there is a statistical model of Mizo counterinsurgency that co-relates the operational success with force levels. (Appendix B)

Accurate intelligence or the lack of it plays a crucial role in both counter-insurgency and counter guerrilla operations. Most of the time, the armed forces are tactically *blind* and act more like a bull in a china shop. One solution that has been practiced by what is called *lazy General ship,* is to induct a large number of troops in the area and hope that by their sheer presence, chance encounters will take place and armed forces with superior skills, better weaponry and unlimited supply of ammunition will get the better of the guerrilla or insurgents. To some extent this did work in Kashmir in the early 1990s as well as in Iraq during the so-called 'surge' phase. However the same strategy failed miserably in Sri Lanka when the Indian Peace Keeping Force tried it, as well as in Afghanistan, since 2010. Difficult terrain and skilled guerrilla fighters were possible reasons for this apparent failure, though the jury is still out as far as Afghanistan is concerned. But even more importantly, the political leadership that lays down the deadline for withdrawal or completion of operations is responsible for forces to get de-motivated, to give their lives for a lost cause. This degrades the force employed in terms of *quality* and *effectiveness*. One has already seen earlier that the adequate force concept is related to both the quantity and quality.

Over the last several decades, the world has not seen a large-scale conflict like the two World Wars of the 20th century and hence most of the political leadership has very little or no experience of war. There is a tendency to treat a soldier like a robot. As an infantry soldier with some experience of

181

live fighting under his belt, the author wishes to debunk this notion. At a crucial stage during a fire fight, a soldier is lonely and advances only if he is convinced of the righteousness of his conduct and the influence of his immediate leadership. Else, most patrols and ambushes, bread-and-butter operations in a counterinsurgency, are carried out only on paper! The morale aspect is crucial when we consider whether a force is adequate.

Multi Pronged Approach

In the art of war, selection and maintenance of aim, concentration of force and flexibility are some important principles. In the insurgency warfare however, a multi- pronged approach is not just desirable but necessary since it is a multi-dimensional conflict. The multi-pronged approach automatically gives a degree of flexibility to switch the effort from one objective to another, or switch the emphasis from one field to another.

It has been already mentioned earlier that an insurgency may well have its roots in social, economic, political or psychological problems. Many times a revolt may start due to economic distress, as in the case of Mizoram in 1966, but later becomes a struggle for identity. It is well nigh impossible to accurately assess the root cause of trouble. Thus peace-enforcing and peace-making by addressing the root problem cannot be treated sequentially but must run parallel. This is akin to a 'broad front' strategy of conventional war. Any attempt to concentrate excessively on the military aspect, as was the case in Vietnam can only lead to assured failure.

At any given time, in a long drawn out insurgency, the dominant cause may well be entirely different than what it was in the initial stage and a counter insurgent has to be mindful of these subtle shifts. Accordingly, the emphasis has to shift from economic to political or psychological as the case may be. It is this dynamic relationship between cause and effect that makes insurgency a much more difficult proposition than a conventional conflict where the military element predominates.

Another dimension of the broad front approach is multi-agency operations. In all endeavours, whether military or civil, multiple agencies or departments have to work towards a common goal. For instance, intelligence agencies and their work are integral to any military operation. But in case of counterinsurgency this has an added reason and that is, that often the State has to simultaneously pursue contradictory policies or strategies. For instance, while the armed forces may well be engaged in military action against the insurgents, the intelligence agencies may be in contact with the same organisation and carrying on secret negotiations. This has been particularly true in North East India where the SIB (Subsidiary Intelligence Bureau) was in constant touch with the rebels while military operations were in full swing. Similarly, while political talks were going on at a Government level, economic and other developmental work was sought to be delinked from success or failure of the negotiations. Multiplicity of agencies is thus a norm in counterinsurgency and a certain degree of autonomy is granted to each. This permits the counterinsurgents to carry on contradictory strategies and lends them flexibility.

There is a major debate as to which agency/organisation must be used and for what task. There is a marked reluctance on the part of the Armed Forces to get involved in a domestic quarrel, where there is no clear external element. The Paramilitary forces are expected to carry the major burden of fighting such wars. But there is a major problem here. At the level of section or platoon, where the guerrilla war is fought, these operations are in no way different than similar operations in conventional wars. Paramilitary forces are neither trained nor equipped to fight a *war* and are often found wanting. The principle of *adequate force* also means that the armed forces cannot use their full range of equipment, a sort of *fighting with one hand tied behind one's back.* A way out of this dilemma is a middle path wherein the armed forces act *in support* of the police or the Paramilitary Forces. For instance, searches and neutralisation may be carried out by the Police, while the Armed Forces lay the outer cordon to prevent escapes. South Africa faced a similar problem when they faced ANC-led sabotage and subversion operations inside the country, while a full-blown guerrilla war was going on in South West Africa and Angola.

This worked since the ANC was unable to launch a guerrilla war inside South Africa proper. But the South Africans created special police units to do this task, which were organised and trained on the lines of the Special

Forces of the army. South Africa also consciously took a decision to not occupy territory and instead organised mobile, high-tech small task force groups to hit at the rebel bases and keep them unbalanced. This was a lesson learnt from the Vietnam War where the Americans entered the swamps and fought the guerrillas on their own terms. It is very difficult to make any definitive judgement on this issue but suffice it to say that counter insurgency must be fought as a multi agency operation and with a suitable mix of military, police, intelligence and high tech Special Forces.

Readers may have noticed the oft used *cliché* 'winning the hearts and minds of people'. This phrase conjures up the image of insurgents and counter insurgents as two lovers vying for one maiden! Yes, it is true that both the parties to the conflict do try to win over the people to their side, but the process at least for counter-insurgents is also a *struggle between heart and mind*. Since insurgents paint a picture of a romantic utopia of paradise on earth, it is futile for the counterinsurgents to compete with them on this. What the counter insurgents can achieve is to convince the *mind* of the general people that the goal of insurgents is unattainable and that the alternative that is available, is not bad. When privations brought upon by long period of fighting begin to bite, while the heart may still be swayed by the romantic notions propagated by the insurgents, the mind overcomes the heart and accepts the reasonable compromise. The insurgency counter-insurgency duel is thus not like the competition between two lovers but also a struggle between romanticism and realism. In most cases where the counter insurgency has succeeded it has been a triumph of realism over idealism.

External Influence and Sanctuaries

All insurgencies anywhere in the world have an element of foreign support; the degree may differ from case to case. It was less in the case of revolts in the North East, while it is a dominant factor in Kashmir. Without Pakistani backing, the Kashmir insurgency would not survive. The initial steady support by the Soviet Union to ANC did much to sustain it through difficult times. This external support can be military, diplomatic, economic or merely moral. In Kashmir, besides the Pakistani support, the US consistently gave its moral backing to the Islamists right up to 2001. At a particularly important stage in the 1990s, when insurgent morale was low after the surrender at the Hajratbal shrine, the US Secretary of State Ms Albright came out in support of the separatists. In a frequent occurrence in Kashmir valley, separatists would demonstrate shouting slogans praising the then American President Bill Clinton. Under such circumstances, it is impossible to achieve a no-win situation. Loss of external support can quickly lead to the collapse of insurgency, as witnessed in Nagaland and Mizoram after the 1971 war that destroyed East Pakistan.

It is axiomatic that for any remedial measures to be successful, violence has to be brought down to an acceptable level. This becomes a virtual impossibility if the inimical external power continues to pump in arms and also to offer sanctuary. As the aim of counter insurgency is to bring about a behavioural change and not destruction, rebel morale is of critical importance. In order to achieve the aim, counter insurgency has to ensure that the external support is cut off from the rebels. Even in the Irish insurgency, it was the ultimate denial of continued support by the Irish Republic to the Irish Republican Army (IRA), that paved the way for the truce in early 1998. The proactive role of the US during that period also closed the tap of support from American Irish community. The relative peace in Northern Ireland would have been impossible without these two measures.

Ending external support is also important to create a psychological no-win situation. For so long as external support exists and the state that gives support is perceived as strong, no amount of counter measures can weaken morale. The psychological dimension of external support to insurgents is as important as the supply of arms, ammunitions and finances. Interestingly, one of the reasons for the collapse (or should one say near-collapse) of insurgency in North East of India was the 1971 Indo-Pak war that saw the emergence of Bangladesh. The Mizo as well as Naga insurgents never recovered from this blow. Within a few years, the major Naga groups gave up the struggle and signed the Shillong Accord of 11 November 1975. The Mizos began serious negotiations in 1979 and finally signed the Mizo Accord in 1986. After the loss of East Pakistan support, the insurgents did turn to China. But the Chinese, while willing to give help in arms and equipment, were not ready to openly champion the rebels' cause. Thus the slide in morale of insurgents could not be checked. On the other hand, the open Pakistani support to the insurgency in Kashmir has ensured that despite successful operations against the insurgents, their morale remains high and insurgency continues. In case of South Africa, the universal support to the anti-Apartheid movement played a major role in bringing home the fact that the Racist regime in South Africa was on the losing side. In addition, steadfast military support by the Soviet Union and many other countries like India to the ANC, also played a role. It bears repetition that for counter insurgency to succeed and to create a no-win mind set, external influence has to be ended.

In areas of insurgency adjoining national borders, external support also provides sanctuaries. Sanctuaries across the border or within a state, perform the role of strategic depth. When under pressure, the insurgents can retreat to these sanctuaries for rest, refit and rejuvenation. For successful counterinsurgency, neutralisation of sanctuaries, whether within or outside, is a must.

Domination of Information Spectrum

Since the aim of insurgents and counter insurgents is to bring about a change of thinking/behaviour, information dissemination and propaganda play a major role. Perceptions are as important as facts. At the level of basic human understanding, David Hume as well as Immanuel Kant subsumes all learning under the process of perception. We sense the reality of the external world through our audio, visual, nasal and touch senses. There is no reality, only the perception of reality. Sensation, once it reaches the brain, is recorded and decoded or interpreted in reference to existing images. All reality is thus an image and previously existing images form a very important part of the process of perception. A tribal who sees an aircraft for the first time, naturally enough, relates it to the image of a bird that he knows and the aircraft is perceived as a huge bird. When no prior image exists to explain or compare the transmitted image, the human reaction is 'irrational'. Thus it is not uncommon to see a tiny toddler play with a cobra! Fear, is in a fundamental sense, an 'acquired' attribute, so is fearlessness or bravery.

The human thinking process is understood as primarily an image comparison exercise. It is akin to an analogue computer. Thus the sharper image has the tendency to be evoked more often. In turn this makes it even sharper and we have the formation of stereotypes, mindsets and fixed notions. Since these are universal and affect thinking, perception and ultimately behaviour, they cannot be ignored. This also brings in the importance of context, cultural, racial, geographical and psychological, that must be considered in any information policy.

Public media thus plays a very important role in the ultimate outcome of the struggle between insurgents and counter insurgents. Communists understand this extremely well and have special propaganda units along with the guerrilla units. Counter insurgents face a dilemma as the freedom of media is a sacrosanct principle but the media itself is keen on circulation and profits. Thus an insurgent enjoys an advantage since the media values 'exclusive' stories such as meeting an insurgent clandestinely! Media management and control of information flow can be thus critical for the success of counterinsurgency. It is rightly said that the Americans lost the Vietnam War first in the American living rooms and on television screens rather than on the battlefield. It has been mentioned right at the outset that the aim of use of force in insurgency situations, is not breaking heads, but changing the thinking inside the head. This further underscores the importance of information management. Even a liberal democracy like Britain had imposed limited censorship in 1988 to ban public airing of IRA views. In 2006, a similar law has been passed in UK to prevent the 'glorification of terrorism'. While distasteful, some form of control over information flow may well become necessary in an area of insurgency. But it is a double-edged weapon, because in such a scenario, rumour thrives and the adversary may well make use of this tool. The decision on limited censorship can be avoided if the media accepts self-restraint.

Information policy in an insurgency situation has several objectives. It is meant to raise the morale of one's own forces and lower that of the adversary. Information management also aims at winning over the sympathy and support of the general population in the conflict zone and outside it, so as to avoid the situation that the Americans faced during the Vietnam War where domestic support evaporated. With greater resources, counter insurgents can use electronic media- both the radio and television, to great effect. Specially if packaged as entertainment, it is difficult to counter. Masses facing coercive threats need an ideological prop to survive.

In addition, in counter insurgency there is no clear-cut division between tactical, strategic and policy levels. The conflict process is diffused, with crucial decision-making often devolving to the lower echelons of command. Both these factors make it desirable or even mandatory that there is 'understanding' at all levels of the chain of government. A well-informed subordinate is less likely to take actions that may well end up having adverse strategic or policy implications. Thus even the lowest-level functionary must be aware of the general situation and the basic objectives. This is unlike the principle followed by all militaries of the *need to know* as basis for information sharing. In counterinsurgency, virtually everyone needs to know everything.

Review and Conclusion

Counterinsurgency is a complex phenomenon that needs a complex answer. Any attempt at reductionism can be an invitation to disaster. It is very much a form of warfare, and can fit into the description given by Jomini as '*wars of opinion'* or Clausewitzian wars of resistance. However, these are inadequate definitions and it is better to treat insurgency as armed politics and a distinct form of warfare that needs a separate set of principles of war, summarised below,

- The aim of insurgency is regime change while that of counterinsurgency is behaviour change, from conflict to co-operation and co-existence. Thus peace process is an inherent part of counter insurgency and not a separate act.

- The aim of insurgents or counter insurgents is to create a no- win situation using military force, economic pressure or psychological domination.

- The force used by the counterinsurgents must be adequate and legitimate. Legitimacy is concerned with both the means and the ends.

- A multi-pronged and multi-agency approach by the counter insurgents has greater chance of success.

- External support, influence and sanctuaries for the insurgents must be neutralised.

- Information management is the key to ultimate success in any counterinsurgency.

The case studies referred to in the work can be divided into two clear categories, the ones that have come to a conclusion and others that await closure. The South African insurgency against Apartheid and the Mizo insurgency fall in the first category. The Sri Lankan case is ambiguous, as the LTTE has indeed been defeated militarily but it would be hazardous to assume that the Tamil revolt has ended since the grievances that led to it in first place, are yet to be addressed. In case of Nagaland, tragically, while the insurgency has indeed ended, peace remains illusive as a vested interest has developed around maintaining low-level violence. Proud Nagas are still in search of an honourable end, similar to what the Mizos got when an accord was signed with fanfare. A little imaginative effort by the Indian government to concede 'victory' to the Nagas would end it, but imaginative policies are not a strong point of most governments. The two other conflicts, i.e. Kashmir and the Naxalite revolt are ongoing and there appears to be no easy end to either.

In the case of Kashmir, ever since the failure of the armed uprising, the domestic elements as well as Pakistan seem to have embarked upon a strategy of making Kashmir Valley ungovernable. Despite sporadic attempts, India appears to have failed in creating a perception of no-win in the minds of citizens of Kashmir Valley and (certainly) their supporters in Pakistan. Many recent surveys have shown that Kashmiris have no desire to merge with Pakistan, their goal is an independent state of Jammu & Kashmir. Judging from Kashmiri separatist literature and propaganda, there seems to be no clear vision or acknowledgement of the problems of the viability of a land-locked state and the difficulties of gaining independence from two countries – a problem shared by many other ethnic groups such as the Kurds, Chechens and Baluchis. The demand for autonomy also ignores the economic price that Kashmir may have to pay for distancing from India, where the markets for Kashmir's products are and which provide revenue through tourist inflows. There appears to be no effective leadership in Kashmir that can see this and convince the people. It appears that like Germany chose Nazism and suffered, Kashmiris are doomed to a life of misery as they choose an Islamic model and independence that would certainly see the take-over of the state by *Taliban*-like extremism.

The Naxal revolt seems to be passing through a violent phase at the moment and the state is yet to drive home the truth that force will not win any concessions. At the same time, welfare measures including economic development and grant of forest rights to tribals is still work in progress. But the twin strategies of development and dominating force will, in times to come, may produce results. The new Forest Rights Act of 2006 had rectified past injustices to an extent. The Scheduled Tribes and Other Traditional Forest Dwellers (Recognition of Forest Rights) Act, 2006 came into force when the President of India signed the Bill on 29 December 2006.

But the real problem for the tribals is the fear of modernisation. While contact with the outside world has given rise to aspirations for modern goods and comforts, the tribals who are just coming out of the phase of *hunter gatherer civilisation* lack skills to compete in the modern world. The Naxals are skilfully exploiting these emotions. Inept media management has led to lack of trust between the government and the forest dwellers. The geographical fact that the Naxal-affected areas do not share an international border (unlike Kashmir) means that external influence will be absent. In the end that may well prove to be decisive. But is seems that like a Greek tragedy, unless the tribals find enlightened leadership soon, they may well continue on the violent path and bring on untold misery upon themselves.

The terrorism threat faced by the world community could well be classed as an insurgency against global order. Terrorist violence is its manifestation and a tactic. The roots of this threat lie in ethno-religious ideology that has a global aim. Conflicts and revolts from Central Asia, Chechnya, Iraq, the Middle East, Afghanistan, Kashmir, Southern Thailand, Philippines and

Indonesia have a common element, if not a degree of coordination and cooperation, amongst the insurgents. If the world is to succeed in this war against terrorism it has no choice but to face up to this insurgency. It is in this respect that the comparative study of insurgency can be of great help in understanding the process, the cause-effect chain and the successes and failures of policies, strategies and tactics.

Counter insurgency studies are often dominated by a 'reductionist' thinking and approach. But insurgencies are not simple military problems yielding to 'yes-no' logic and solutions. It is a long existing controversy whether warfare is science or an art; insurgencies certainly are closer to being an art than science. It is a long-held belief that guerrillas without popular support are like fish without water. A logical answer to insurgency therefore is to drain the water and let the fish die. Yet the concentration is usually on the catching the fish! There is also an almost religious belief on using carrots for the general population (the supporters/sympathisers) and sticks for the armed fighters. This approach negates the complexity of the situation and seldom works. What succeeds is a dexterous use of both carrot and stick against the *water* as well as the *fish*. Counterinsurgency is therefore akin to delicate brain surgery in conception and implementation.

It is hoped that this work will promote 'understanding' of insurgency at the level of policy makers and implementers in order to help the evolution of policy, doctrines, strategy and tactics. *Amen.*

Appendix A

Legal Framework for use of Force in India

Responsibility

The Indian Constitution vide article 355 has made the central govt responsible for protection of every province against external aggression and internal disturbance.

Dealing with Civil Disturbances

Criminal Procedure Code (CrPC) lays down the method of employment of Armed Forces in quelling riots.

Section 130 empowers executive magistrates to call assistance of the armed forces to disperse unlawful assembly. An officer of the Armed Forces is bound to obey this order. But the actual execution of this task is left to the discretion of the Armed Forces officer in terms of methods and quantum of force to be used. In metropolitan cities, the powers of executive magistrates are conferred on the Police Commissioner.

Section 131 gives the authority to a Commissioned officer of the armed forces authority to act in a manner similar to one described in section 130 even when a magistrate is not present, provided he is satisfied that public order is in manifest danger. He has to, however, at the earliest, seek written permission from a magistrate.

Section 132 protects an Armed Forces person against prosecution for acting under Section 130 and 131, provided the actions have been taken in "good faith" as defined in Section 52 of the Indian Penal Code (IPC).

Section 52 of the IPC defines acts done in good faith as those actions that are taken with due attention and care. In further elaboration, the person having acted under Section 130 and 131 of CrPc.

The conditions that must be fulfilled are, Necessity- each act justified,no reprisals, action not with the aim to create impact elsewhere and action must be preventive and not punitive. In addition, minimum force and impartiality have to be demonstrated too.

(THESE PROVISIONS ARE NOT APPLICABLE TO THE STATE OF JAMMU AND KASHMIR AND TRIBAL AREAS WITHOUT THE EXPRESS PERMISSION OF THE LOCAL LEGISLATURE OR THE TRIBAL COUNCIL)

Dealing with Revolts and Insurgency

The provincial govt under the provision of the Disturbed Areas Act can declare the whole province or part thereof, as disturbed. In the disturbed area, a magistrate or a police officer of the rank of not less than that of a Sub Inspector can order opening of fire, destruction of ammunition dumps, camps or fortifications. Section 6 of the above Act bars prosecution without the permission of the provincial govt.

Armed Forces Special Powers Act 1958, 1983 and 1990

This Act of Parliament extends to the entire country. Section 3 gives the authority to declare any area as DISTURBED to the provincial governor and the central govt. Section 4 defines the powers to the armed forces. These powers are,

(a) Use of force even to the extent of causing death against any person who is breaking any law, prohibiting movement or public assembly, carrying weapons, ammunition or explosive substances.

(b) Destroy any arms dumps, shelters, fortifications, training camps or hide-outs.

(c) Arrest without warrant any person who has committed or is suspected to have committed a cognizable offence or is likely to commit one. Necessary force can be used to affect this arrest.

(d) Search any premise without warrant if suspicion exists of any arms, ammunition storage there or it being used as a premise to hold hostages or as a hiding place by person who have committed a cognizable offence.

(e) All the above powers can be used by a person of the armed forces not below the rank of a non commissioned officer.

Under the provision of Section 6 of the Act, no prosecution can be launched against a person acting under this Act without the prior sanction of the central govt.

Appendix B
Mizoram Counterinsurgency: A Profile

Table 1

Year	Battalions	Operations	Own Casualties	Surrender/-Capture	Insurgent casualties
1965	2	0	0	0	0
1966	8	29	128	947	435
1967	8	107	185	2090	1225
1968	9	68	121	994	1914
1969	9	36	4	284	363
1970	14	46	23	218	46
1971	8	4	0	46	193
1972	8	0	0	98	227
1973	13	24	0	55	55
1974	13	34	3	132	0
1975	19	52	8	342	107
1976	19	12	4	169	70
1977	19	0	0	147	50
1978	12	0	3	20	150
1979	18	11	7	247	234
1980	12	9	49	128	0
1981	18	2	9	1	0
1982	18	115	9	190	73
1983	16	26	11	72	0
1984	16	13	4	85	0
1985	19	0	1	64	0
1986	19	0	0	43	0
1987	10	0	0	0	0
1988	11	0	0	0	0
1989	11	0	0	0	0

Figure 1

Mizoram Counter-Insurgency

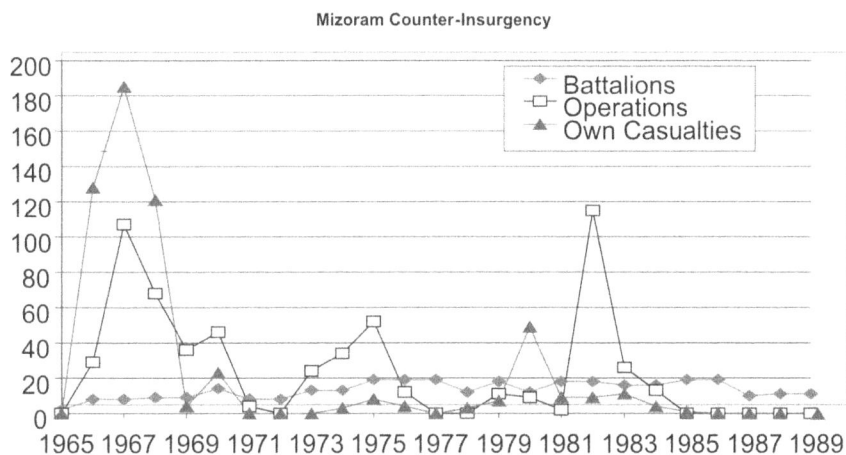

Figure 2

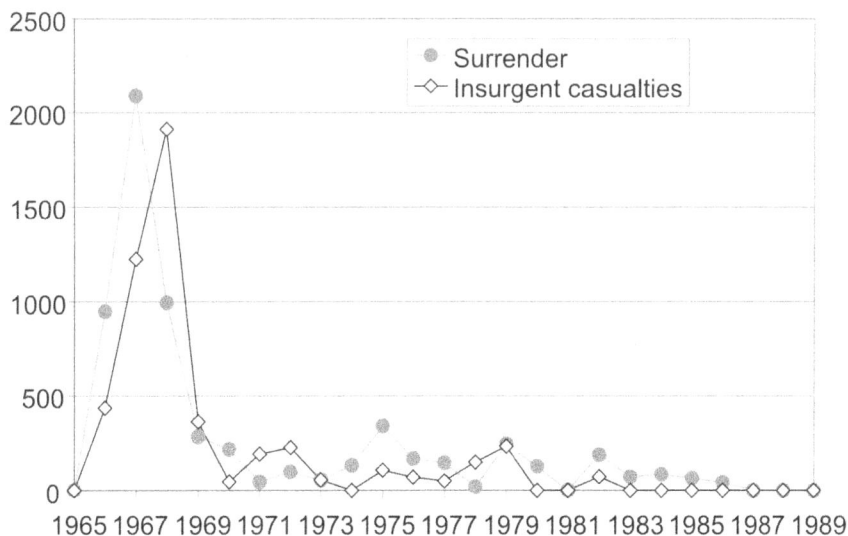

Figure 3

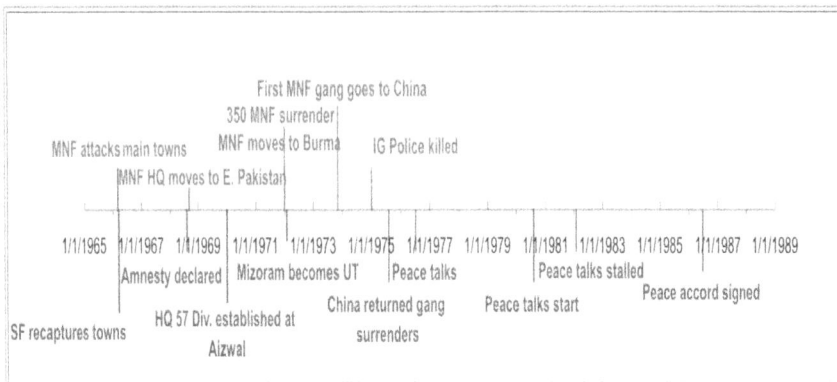

Figure 4

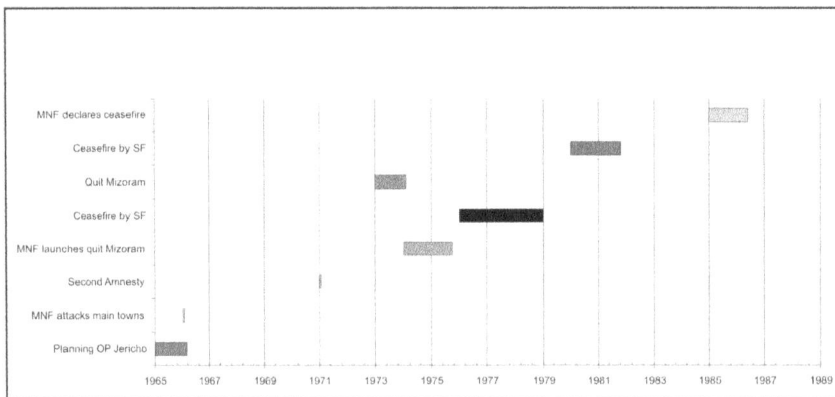

Source- Indian Army records and govt. of India archival material in ministry of Defence.

198

Counter insurgency aims to achieve military no -win situation for insurgents and use of force forms a major plank of this strategy. The data given above deals with insurgency and counter insurgency in the Indian state of Mizoram. The data covers the entire period of insurgency- from 1965 to 1989 when peace returned. Mizoram is an interesting statistical study as it is possibly one of the few very clear 'open and shut' cases of successful counterinsurgency.

Success in counterinsurgency operations is often measured in terms of insurgent casualties and capture/surrender. If taken as the criterion of success, it may appear that force level has no co-relation to success. The high rate of losses as well as successes from the year 1966 to 1969 must be seen in the backdrop of the fact that the insurgents had adopted the tactics of open confrontation. Presence of large number of ex-soldiers in the ranks was a major influence, as was the false hope of easy success. However once the insurgents switched to tactics of guerrilla warfare and the increase in force levels to 19 battalions, (more than double of the initial 8) the success ratio faithfully reflected the increased 'success' that is related both to force levels and number of operations carried out.

The success achieved also can be understood in the backdrop of frequent cease fires and amnesty schemes. In fact, Mizoram saw the insurgency cover the full gamut of open confrontation, guerrilla war, cease fire, talks, failure of talks, re-start of operations and even terror campaign (the Quit Mizoram movement that led to murders of school teachers).

The data should form a basis for an intelligent reader to work out a statistical model and *formulae* for success.

Bibliography and Notes

General - Theory

1. Aspey Robert B., 'War in the Shadows', Macdonald and Jane's, London, 1975.

2. Barash David P. 'Socio-biology and Behaviour', Elsevier, New York, 1982.

3. Basham A. L., 'The Wonder that was India,' Rupa & Co., Calcutta et al 1967. Paret

4. Bottome Edgar, 'The Balance of Terror: Nuclear Weapons and Illusion of Security' 1945-1985,' Beacon Press, Boston,1986.

5. Coser Lewis A. 'The Functions of a Social Conflict,' The Free Press, Glencoe, Ill,1956.

6. Dahl Robert S. 'Modern Political Analysis,' Prentice Hall Pub. New Delhi, July 1978.

7. Dutt Dev (Ed), 'Mao Tse Tung, On War', The English Book Depot, Dehradun, 1966.

8. Engles Frederick, 'The Role of Force in History,' Anamika Prakashan, NOIDA,1987.

9. Foreign Policy Research Institute, Spring 2001, Kurth James, 'Religion and Ethnic Conflict in Theory', p. 281-294.

10. Gallagher CSM James J, 'Low Intensity Conflicts: A guide for tactics, techniques and procedures', Lancer Publications, New Delhi 1994.

11. Griffith Brigadier General Samuel B. (Trans.), 'Guerrilla Warfare By Mao Tse Tung and Che Guevara', Cassel & Co. Ltd, London, 1962.

12. Haas Michael & Kariel Henry S. (Ed.), 'Approaches to Political Science', Chandler Pub. Co. Scranton, Penn. USA, 1970.

13. Hobbes Thomas, 'Leviathan', E. P. Dutton & Co. New York, 1950.

14. Howard Michael, 'Studies in War and Peace', Maurice Temple Smith, London, 1970. Chapter titled 'Clauswitz and Jomini'.

15. Kaplan A. 'The Conduct of Enquiry', Sachin Pub. Jaipur India, 1980.

16. Kautilya (Trans. By R. Samasastry), 'Arthasastra', Wesleyan Press, Mysore, India, 1923.

17. Kuhn Thomas S. 'Theory of Scientific Revolution', University of Chicago Press, Chicago, 1970.

18. Lenin Vladimir S. 'Imperialism: the Highest form of Capitalism,' Foreign Language Pub. House, Moscow, 1950.

19. Marx Karl, 'The Poverty of Philosophy', The American Journal of Sociology, XIII, 1908.

20. Mitchell Lt. Col. William A. 'Out Lines of World Military History,' National Service Pub. Washington DC, 1931. pp. 243-282

21. Morton Louis (Ed.), 'The American Way of War,' MacMillan Pub. New York & London, 1973.

22. New Perspective Quarterly, Summer 1994, Rushkoff Douglas & Boorstin Daniel, 'Beyond the Spectacle'. Role and importance of media, specially the new media in shaping perception and reality itself.

23. Peter (Ed), 'Makers of Modern Strategy', Princeton University Press, 1986.

24. Pruit Dean & Snyder R. C. 'Theory and Research in Causes of War.' Prentice Hall, N.J. 1969.

25. Rappaport Anatol 'Fights, Games & Debates', University of Michigan Press, Ann Arbor, 1960.

26. Schelling Thomas C., 'Strategy of Conflict',(Harvard University Press, Cambrirdge Mass. & London, 1981.

27. Toynbee, Dr AJ, 'A Study of History', Vol. VII, Armature: II

Toynbee used Jung's description of four human faculties- thinking, feeling, sensation and intuition – to indicate the predominant faculty in each of these religions. According to Toynbee, Islam and Christianity have extrovert attitudes, with sensation dominating the former, and feeling, the latter. If the statement 'God is Love' expresses Christianity's inner nature, Islam believes that 'God is Power'. Buddhism and Hinduism have introvert attitudes; the former relies on the faculty of intuition while the thinking faculty dominates the Hindu religion, which stresses direct knowledge of a non-dual reality as pathway to human liberation. Dr Toynbee's interpretation may appear to some an over-simplification of the character of each of these religions, but he does sum up each religion's core value in an unmistakable fashion.

28. Vas Lt. Gen. E. A., 'Violence in Society: The Formative years,' Natraj Pub. Dehradun, 1983

Vietnam, Afghanistan & Other Counter Guerrilla Wars

29. American Heritage Nov-Dec 2001, Ambrose Stephen E, 'Can History Help?'p.22-31. Quoting Ms Nasra Hassan. Author's conversation with Nasra at Salzburg workshop, Sep 2007. Nasra Hassan maintains that there is no divide between 'moderates' and extremists in Islam as far as ultimate goal is concerned. Both accept that Islamisation of the whole world is the goal ordained in Quran.

30. Blaufarb D. S., 'The Counterinsurgency Era: US Doctrine and Performance', New York, 1977.

31. British High Commission, New Delhi 1995, 'Northern Ireland Peace Process'.

32. Caldwell Colonel C. E., 'Small Wars', General Staff, War Office, London 1906.

33. Campbell Arthur, 'Jungle Green', Allen Unwin, London 1953.

34. Clutterbuck R. L. 'The Long Long War: Counterinsurgency in Malaya & Vietnam.' Frederick A. Praeger, New York,1966.

35. George K. Tanham, vice President Rand Corp, interview with in July 1991 at Washington DC.

36. Hassan Nasra, 'Suicide Terrorism' in 'Roots of Terrorism', Routledge, New York 2006, p. 30-42.

37. Novosti (Russian Information Agency), 'Chechnya: The White Paper', Moscow 2000.

38. The New Yorker Nov 12, 2001. 'Islam in Revolt', articles by Bernard Lewis and Nasra Hassan.

39. Washington Quarterly Winter 2002, Delpech Terese, 'The Imbalance of Terror', p.31-40.

North East India

40. Anand V. K. 'Conflict in Nagaland', Chanakya Pub. New Delhi, 1980.

Born in 1944, he joined the underground when he was 19 years old. The prime cause was anger aroused by the strong army action of 1966.

41. Directorate of Art & Culture Govt of Nagaland, 'Folk Tales from Nagaland', first published 1971, Reprint 1989, Govt Printing Press, Kohima.

42. Govt. of India archival material of Ministry of Defence.

43. Gundevia Y. D. 'War and Peace in Nagaland', Palit and Palit, Dehradun (India) 1975.

44. Hazarika Sanjoy, 'Strangers of the Mist,' Penguin Books, New Delhi et al 1995.

45. Hutton J H, 'The Sema Nagas', first published MacMillan & Co, London 1921, Reprinted by Govt of Nagaland & Oxford University Press 2007.

46. Hutton J H., 'The Angami Nagas,' first published MacMillan & Co, London 1921. Reprinted by Govt of Nagaland, 2003.

In case of Manipur, he mentioned that Mr Nehru as PM arbitrarily ceded the Kobe Valley to Burma (Myanmar) in 1949 despite the historical facts that it was ruled by Manipur. This fuelled the first unrest in Manipur.

Kukreti Major General PL, IG Assam Rifles, interview 28 March 1988. He accepted that the insurgents were always one up on the security forces since they were better in physical fitness, more adaptive, knew the language, had better intelligence, were expert in weapon use and had knowledge of flora, fauna and terrain.

He mentioned that at no time the strength of active armed insurgents was more than 1,000.

He opined that external instigation and support were the main cause of insurgency and not economic backwardness. He pointed out that the British controlled the entire North East with just 4 battalions of Assam Rifles. Their tactics were to mount punitive expeditions that were then followed by the doctor and a Padre (Christian preacher).

He was posted in Shillong from 1963-68.

His view was that rather than general search operations, it was the army's operations that were based on specific information and led to loss of cadres that were more effective.

47. Blank.

48. Lal Denga, interview on 26 March 1988.

49. Mills JP, 'The Ao Nagas', first published MacMillan & Co, London 1926, Reprinted by Govt of Nagaland, 2003.

50. Mills JP, 'The Lotha Nagas', first published MacMillan & Co, London 1922, Reprinted by Govt of Nagaland 1980.

51. Mills JP, 'The Rengma Nagas', first published MacMillan & Co, London 1937, Reprinted by Govt of Nagaland 1982.

Mr Twan Luia was the commander in chief of the Mizo National Army and at the time of interview was minister for agriculture. He was a minister from 1998 to 2008 in MNF government of Zoramthanga.

On the Naga issue, he mentioned that the Nagas had been trying assert their own identity since 1930 and this was not visualised by the Government of India and instead the Naga problem was left to the Assam Government to handle. The situation deteriorated after death of Mr Bardloi, since the next Assamese leader BR Medhi was rigid and had very little influence over the Nagas.

P. 145. Details of betrayal by Rev. Scott and breakdown of peace mission.

P. 176. Train explosion at Lumding killing 40 people while peace talks were going on in Delhi.

P. 58 Naga leaders and PM Nehru interactions. How it all began, Sir Akbar Hyderi's 9 point plan.

P.193. Break up between pro and anti-China factions of rebels. 17 June 1968 Beijing radio broadcast supporting Naga and Mizo rebels. March 1969, Mowu Angami group who had returned from China captured.

P.290. "Naga movement was a political one with suspicion and fears as a superstructure and unworthy feeling of racial separation and superiority as the basis."

52. Rao General KVK, 'Insurgency in the North East', part I &II, USI Journal, Jan-Mar and Apr-Jun 1998.

53. Research Papers available with Counter Insurgency and Jungle Warfare School (CIJW), Wirengte, Mizoram.

54. Stracey P. D. 'Nagaland Nightmare', Allied Publishers, Bombay 1968. Mr Stracy was a forest officer from 1930 to 1964.

55. Subramanium KS, 'Manipur: A History of Strife', Citizens Fact Finding Mission, Nov 23, 2009. New Delhi.

56. Thanga L.B. interview on 24 March 1988. Formerly of Indian frontier administrative service (IFAS) and chief advisor to the state govt.

57. Thanga Lal Biak, 'The Mizos,' United Pub. ,Gauhati, 1978.

58. Twan Luia, interview on 24 March 1988.

59. Zoheto, interview April 1988. Mr Zoheto Sema, an erstwhile rebel was the main negotiator in Shillong Accord in 1975-76. On rehabilitation, he along with other surrendered rebels were formed into a 111 BSF (Border Security Force) battalion and deployed on Indo-Burma border.

Zoram Thanga was the Vice President of the MNF and Finance Minister in 1988. Subsequently he was the Chief Minister of the state from 1998 to 2008.

60. Zoram Thanga, interview on 23 March 1988.

Kashmir

61. "Kashmir Papers: Reports of the UN Commission on India and Pakistan June 1948 to December 1949", (New Delhi, Min of External Affairs,1950)

62. Bains J.S., 'India's International Disputes: A Legal Study,' (Asia Publishing House, Bombay et. al. 1962)

63. Bhutto Z.A., 'The Myth of Independence,' (Oxford University Press, London,1969)

64. Bombay Chronicle, "Kashmir: Basic Facts", Bombay ,1953.

65. Brecher M. "Nehru: A Political Biography", (London, Oxford University Press, 1959).

66. Brines Russell,"The Indo-Pakistan Conflict", (London, Pall Mall Press,1968).

67. Choudhari Mohammed Ali, "The Emergence of Pakistan ", (New York, Columbia University Press, 1967).

68. Donehue J.J. and Esposito John L. (Ed),'Islam in Transition,' (Oxford University Press, Oxford, 1982)

69. Donhue J.J. & Esposito John L. (Ed.),'Islam in Transition,'(Oxford University Press, London et. al.,1982)

70. Govt of India, "Kashmir- M. C. Chagla's Speeches in the UN Security Council". (New Delhi , 1964)

71. Govt. of India, Publications Division, 'Jammu and Kashmir-Statistical Profile,' New Delhi, 1996.

72. Gul Hasan Khan, 'Memoirs: of Lt. Gen. Gul Hasan Khan', (Oxford University Press, Karachi et. al, 1993)

73. Hasan Mohibbul, "Kashmir Under Sultans", (Calcutta, Iran Society,

74. Havell E. B., 'The History of Aryan Rule in India', (G.G. Harper & Co, London)

75. Muzumdar A. K. , 'Early Hindu India', Cosmos Publications, New Delhi , 1981

76. Hodgson Marshal G. S., 'Venture of Islam Vol. III,'(Chicago university press, Chicago,1961)

77. Irvine William , " Later Mughals", Vol I, (First pub 1912), Taj Pub , DELHI, 1989.

78. Johnson Campbell & Hale Robert, "Mission with Mountbatten", (London, MacMillan,1951)

79. Kak Ram Chandra, "Ancient Monuments of Kashmir", (London, India Society,1933).

80. Karan Singh Dr., "Sadar i Riyasat", (New Delhi, Oxford,1985).

81. Kaumudi, "Kashmir , the Cultural Heritage", (Bombay ,Asia Pub. House , 1952)

82. Khushwant Singh (Ed & Trans) , "Flames of Chinar: An Autobiography of Sheikh Abdullah", (New Delhi, Viking Pub, 1992)

83. Korbel Joseph, 'Danger in Kashmir,' (Princeton University Press, Princeton, 1954).

84. Menon V. P. "The Story of Integration of Indian States", (New Delhi , Orient Longmans, 1956)

85. Mohammad Shah (Ed), "The Aligarh Movement: Basic Documents 1864-1898", Vol. III , (New Delhi, New Delhi Prakashan, 1978).

86. Mujumdar R.C."A History and Culture of Indian People: The Vedic Age", (Bombay , Bhartiya Vidya Bhavan,1965)

87. Nehru Jawahar Lal, "Selected Works of Jawaharlal Nehru Vol. 15," (New Delhi, Orient Longmans,1982)

88. Pakistan Govt. Pub., 'Struggle for Independence ,' (Karachi, 1958)

89. Pannikar K. M. , "Gulab Singh 1792-1858, Founder of Kashmir", (London, Martin Hopkins, 1930)

90. Peterson P. (Ed & Trans), Kalhana's "Rajatarangini", Vol I-III, (Bombay, Central Book Depot,1896).

91. Philip C. H. (Ed),'Historians of India and Pakistan,'(Oxford University Press, London,1961)

92. Prasad Rajendra, "India Divided", (Bombay, Allied Pub. 1946)

93. Prasad S.N. & Dharam Pal (Ed), "History of Operations in Jammu and Kashmir 1947-48", (New Delhi, Govt. of India Pub, 1987)

94. Raina N. N., "Kashmir Politics :Imperialist Manoeuvres 1846-1980", (New Delhi, Patriot Pub.,1988)

95. Rajaram N.S. 'A Hindu View of the World,' (Voice of India , New Delhi, 1998)

96. Basham A. L.'Wonder that was India' (Rupa Pub Calcutta, 1981) p. 165-166

97. Sayeed B. Khalid, 'The political System in Pakistan,'(Houghton Mifflin Co., Boston, 1967)

98. Sen Brigadier L.P., "Slender was the Thread", (New Delhi, Orient Longmans,1969)

99. Shankar V., "My Reminiscences of Sardar Patel",(New Delhi, Macmillan,1974).

100.Younghusband Sir Francis & Major E. Molyneux, "Kashmir", (London A. & C. Black Ltd, 1917)

101.   Zakaria Rafiq, "The Rise of Muslims in Indian Politics:1885-1906, (Bombay,Somaiya Pub. 1970)

Sri Lanka

102. Ariyarathane Chandra, 'History of Sri Lanka for Children', Samudra Book Publications, Kurunegala (Sri Lanka) April 2008.

103. Blaze L E, 'The Story of Sri Lanka: Outlines of history for Ceylon from the earliest times to the coming of Portuguese', Asian Educational Service, New Delhi-Chennai 2009.

104. Davis Anthony, in Asia Week, " Tiger International' dealing with the external support base of LTTE.

105. Deraniyagala S. V. 'The Pre History of Sri Lanka', Vol. I and II, Department of Archaeological Survey , Sri Lanka, 1992.

106. Dissanayake SB (translated from original Sinhalese by Christopher Neil) , 'The Bandaranaike Trio And their Unholy Duo,' Suraksha Publications, Colombo 2009.

107. Dissanayake SB (translated from original Sinhalese by Christopher Neil), 'On War Peace and Devolution of Power', Suraksha Publications, Colombo 2009.

108. Gunaratna Rohan, 'War and peace in Sri Lanka', (Institute of Fundamental Studies, Sri Lanka,Kandy,1987)

109. Hoole SRH (Ed.), ' The Broken Palmyra, Vol I Historical Background,' (Harvey Mudd College Press, Claremont, California, 1988)

110. Interview with Foreign Minister of Sri Lanka conducted in 1996

111. Interviews with rebel leaders of LTTE, conducted in 1989 at Jaffna and Trincomalee

112. Ludowyk E. F. C., 'The Story of Ceylon,' Faber & Faber, London , 1962

113. Seneviratne Maureen, 'Journal of the End Time: Extracts from a diary'

Wimal Enterprises, Colombo, 2004.

114. Tennent J. E.,' Modern History of Ceylon,' London, 1859.

115. Vitachi Tagie, 'Emergency 1958', Andre Deutsch, London ,1958.

South Africa

116. Cooper Carole et al, 'Race Relations Survey 1988-89', South African Institute Of   Race Relations, Johannesburg 1989

117. Goldenhuys DJ Prof, interview with. Aug 2008

He agreed that the economic, travel and sports sanctions were effective in psychologically denting the resolve of Apartheid regime. He opined that the military sanctions were ineffective and actually boosted the indigenous production of new weapons in collaboration with Israel. In the pre-internet era, travel sanctions impacted humanities and sciences.

He asserted that unlike Zimbabwe and Kenya, the Afrikaners had no links with mother country. Sanctions also bottled up migration, which was a major source of population growth for Whites. In the period of the 1980s, the development and progress of Afrikaans language was affected and the number of schools with that medium declined from 3000 to barely 800.

118. Heitman Helmoed-Romer, 'South African Armed Forces' Buffalo Publications, Cape Town, March 1990.

pp. 142-199 Insurgency and counter insurgency in South West Africa.

pp. 200-226 Intervention in Angola.

pp. 227-234 Blunting the 'Spear of the Nation (MK)'.

119. Heitman Helmoed-Romer, A former intelligence officer and defence analyst based in Cape Town, Interview with in Aug 2008. Mentions that the ANC was thoroughly infiltrated and the government generally had a prior warning of most of the agitation programmes. He also asserted that the battlefield success claim of the ANC was false and even the battle of Cuito Cuanvale in Angola was a defeat for the ANC.

120. Henwood Ronald, Asst. Professor University of Pretoria, Department of Political Science, interview with on 5th August 2008.

121. Interview with Mr. Mabhongo, Chief Director UN, Foreign Ministry, Pretoria, on 4 August 2008. Mr. Mabhongo mentioned that clandestine talks between ANC and the Apartheid government were carried out by younger elements like Mr Mebecki and Mr Zuma (presently President of Republic of South Africa) who was chief the intelligence wing of the ANC. He opined that the 1985 flight of American capital led to change of guard in National Party and moderate elements came to power. The aim of ANC military actions was not military victory, but to make South Africa ungovernable. He felt that the end of the regime came due to lowering of morale of the security forces, the international pariah status of South Africa and the loss of Angola to rebels.

122. Interview with Prof Sandy Africa, Professor Political Science, University of Pretoria 3 August 2008 at Pretoria. Sandy was a student activist in University of Natal and began her political career as a member of the Black Consciousness movement in 1970s. She joined UDF and was Asst. Secretary in Kwazulu Natal. She mentioned that the anti-Apartheid movement was mainly urban-based and was more political than militant. In urban areas the Apartheid regime's divide and rule policy did not succeed. She felt that due to urbanisation, the bane of rest of Africa- tribalism, was absent in South Africa. She admitted that the ANC had far less support in rural areas and border controls made infiltration of ANC cadres difficult. She also asserted that over time, economic class has emerged as more important divide than race. She agreed that the turning point in anti Apartheid struggle was the collapse of Berlin Wall on 9th Nov 1989 as that had the effect of de-linking the South African struggle from the Cold War. The economic sanctions began to bite by 1982-84 and there was flight of capital from South Africa. Militarily she felt that the 1976 attacks on camps was a low point while the battle of Cuito Cuanavale in 1986 made ANC sense victory.

123. Jeffery Anthea, 'People's War: New Light on Struggle for South Africa', Jonathan Ball Publishers, Johannesburg & Cape Town, 209. pp. 634.

   p. 13-16 Domestic pressures.

   p. xxxii-xxxiv & 17 -23. Soweto revolt.

   p.200 Effect of Angolan settlement.

   p.25-39 Lessons from Vietnam.

   p.7-9 Initial failures of ANC.

124. Mayibuye, Journal of the ANC, Vol. I , No. 3, 1990, Nayanda Siphiwe, commander of MK ' Operation Vula'.

125. Mayibuye, Nov 1992, Mncube Mthenthekli, 'Umonknonto Soldiers, I did what any soldier would have done'.

126. Mayibuye,July-Aug 1990, editorial, 'Bantustans: eroding pillars of Apartheid'.

127. Maynier David, MP, leader of democratic alliance and shadow defence minister. Interview with on 12 August 2008, Cape Town. He mentioned that the role of external element in the ending of Apartheid has been overlooked or underplayed. President Reagan and Gorbachev (of erstwhile USSR) played a major role in pressuring both the Apartheid regime and ANC to compromise. Mrs Margaret Thatcher, the then British PM played a direct role and warned the regime that the West's support would not be available. The winding-down of Cuban operations in Angola in 1987 also played a role. The anti-communist rationale used by the regime lost its relevance. South Africa increasingly felt like being under siege and over-stretched.

128. Pingla Ms Udita, interview with. 3 August 2008 at Pretoria. Deputy coordinator of the National Intelligence Co-ordination Committee. Ms Pingla mentioned that as the economic sanctions and strikes of 1985 began to bite, a delegation of South African businessmen established contact with the ANC in Dakar. This was to pave way for the release

of Mr Nelson Mandela and start direct talks with the government. She also mentioned that in 1993 Chris Arnie, head of the ANC armed wing was gunned down in his house, causing the accord to almost unravel. But here Mr. Mandela stepped in and appealed to the nation to maintain calm, a call that was heeded by all.

129. South African communist party, 'Path to Power', Johannesburg Sep 1990.

According to the analysis of the party, guerrilla warfare/armed insurgency could not succeed in South Africa since the Blacks were traditionally deprived of military knowledge and arms. Over 80% of the land was owned and cultivated by Whites, there being virtually no Black peasants. No safe rear bases were available outside and the South African open terrain gave no protection to a guerrilla. The South African Defence Forces retained high mobility and efficiency till the end. Therefore the ANC & CPSA took a conscious decision to limit themselves to a campaign of sabotage and subversion. The aim was to make South Africa *ungovernable*. The ANC enjoyed certain advantages, that is,

- Being urban oriented all targets were well within reach.

- International isolation.

- Numerical and moral superiority

130. Steward Dave, Executive director FW De Clerk Foundation Cape Town. Interview with author August 2008. Mr. Steward was the chief of staff to FW De Clerk when he was the President. He mentioned that De Clerk was a compromise candidate and known for his soft position on Apartheid. His appointment signalled the changes that the ruling party wanted. He reinforced the earlier findings that it was international isolation that ultimately led to end of Apartheid. He also agreed that shared religion played a major role in the non-violent outcome.

131. Suttner Raymond, 'The ANC: UNDERGROUND in South Africa,' Jacana Media, Auckland park South Africa, 2008. Interview with in

Johannesburg, 8 August 2008.

- The 6 million strong Black workers had potential to give strategic blows to the system using the weapon of strikes.

- The Apartheid regime increasingly relied on Black community recruits in army and police to carry out anti-Black operations.

The booklet contains the programme of the South African Communist Party adopted in 7th Congress in 1989. The party described the Apartheid regime policy as 'homelessness, joblessness, slave labour and gutter education'.

132. Vale Peter, first Nelson Mandela Chair Professor, Rhodes University, South Africa, Interview with. Most ANC leaders believed in 1970s that it would take 50 years for them to achieve their goal. 1980-83 was the darkest period for them as there was a leadership vacuum and the Zulu factor was being exploited to the hilt to split the Blacks along tribal lines. Inter-marriages amongst tribes are frequent and this helped ANC fight the Apartheid strategy of divide and rule. The Church was divided between conservatives and supporters of liberation theology. The high level of politicisation of African society made the reform process fail. The strict censorship kept the truth hidden from most Whites. Christianity made sure that the conflict was mainly racial and not religious. Church played a role on both sides of the racial divide, persons like Alan Busak, Frank Chicano, need a mention. The Church of England consistently opposed racialism.

133. WIP 73, Mar-Apr 1991, Cargill Jenny, "Creating a culture of debate'.

134. Work In Progress 61, 1989, 'The Last White Hope: Elections 1989'.

Naxalism

135. A team led by the author visited Naxal-affected areas from 13th Sep to 28th Sep 2005. The team had six members. The group was divided into three teams and visited 34 places in Bastar-Dantewada, Rajnandgaon-Kanker and Sarguja regions. A total of 204 persons were

interviewed that included government officials, subject experts, teachers, social workers, Naxal sympathisers, journalists and members of political parties. The group also interacted with a large number of common citizens.

136. Interview of Mr. Mahendra Karma, Opposition Leader, Chhattisgarh assembly. Extracts of interview with Mr Mandeep Singh, a Naxalite leader undergoing life imprisonment in jail in Sarguja district. **Your name does not indicate that you are a local person.** A: I am from Jharkhand.**Q. All the Naxalite leaders are outsiders. If this movement is for adivasis then, why is the adivasi leadership lacking here?** A: It is not correct to say that this movement is for Adivasis. We are working with the adivasis only because we want to build an army for the final fight. Ram also built his army of adivasis, and won Lanka! **Q: What is your final fight?** A: To break the structure of our own system. To win Delhi is our final aim. Only then would the problems of the lower strata of society, including the Adivasis, be solved. **Q. When did you come in contact with the Naxalites?** A: While studying in Jharkhand. **Q. What is your educational qualification?**A. I have passed HSC. After that I entered the Naxalite organisation. **Q. Do you regret taking up arms for your struggle?** A. Not at all. What is violence? Corrupt government officers loot poor adivasis. Is that not violence? In the play *"MeeNathuram Godse Boltoy"*, played out in your own Maharashtra, a person who killed Mahatma Gandhi has been highly praised. Is that not violence? Our violence has an ideological base. But the Government, with its policies, is making life difficult for the adivasis and other tribals. What ideological base do they have for their violence? **Q. Naxalism in Bihar and Jharkhand aggravated as a reaction to the private landowner's Ranveer Sena. But there is no such Sena in Chhattisgarh.** A. Ranveer Sena is a group of thugs. They harassed people who had no land. We are fighting against them. Here there is no such Sena. But the government and its administration is doing the same thing. We are fighting against them. **Q. Still, how fair is it to kill people? After coming into the jail do you regret………..** A. In your Mumbai

Arun Gawli was also killing people. He has become a leader now. We did the same but I was sentenced to life imprisonment and sent to jail. Gawli picked up the weapon for himself. He made his own group. We picked up the weapon for some philosophy, built up an organisation. But in this current system Gawli(a gangster from Mumbai who is a member of state legislature) becomes a leader and we get punished. So is it not necessary to break this system? **Q. We have heard some incidents of the Naxilites' justice system. Sometimes a person comes to you with some personal grievance against somebody. Without inquiring anything you kill that so called criminal…………..**A. It might have happened some time. **Q. You have filed an appeal in the high court against your life imprisonment. What will you do if you are released?** A. The same that I was doing before. **Q. You mentioned Gawli earlier. Gawli takes care of his people. If somebody gets killed or punished then he takes care of his family. Are your leaders taking care of your family now, when you are in prison?** A. I do not expect them to. I came in the organisation owing allegiance to an ideology and not to earn my living.

137. Interview with Dr. Raman Sinh, Chief Minister, Chhattisgarh.

138. **Laws related to Forests in India: A historical perspective**. 76,520 sq km of India's land is covered by forests. This is 23.28 per cent of the total area of India. The life of Adivasis is mainly connected with these jungles on a day to day basis. It is necessary to study forest related laws while studying the problem of Naxalism in these forests. Indian Forest Act, 1927, would have to be mentioned, if one is to look at the administration of forests in India. The Forest Department was established by the British in 1864, following which, the first Indian Forest Act 1865 was implemented. The Indian Forest Act 1927 is the amended format of this same law of 1865. Wild Animal Protection Act was enacted in 1972. Biological Diversity Act is the developed format of this Act. All living creatures, animals, tribal people are protected under this Act. The Forest Protection Act, 1980 was specially designed to

control human encroachment on forest land. Before that the right to legally regulate different encroachments which comes only under the state government was included in the list of combined rights of Centre and the State. State government then started regulating the encroachment with nominal fine, to get some advantages under the political pressure. It would start causing the loss of forests prosperity. To control this, the central rights were involved along with the state government. In 1988 the National Forest Policy was created considering forest conservation, wild life and the problems of tribes. Conservation of bio-diversity, production of useful forest products, and control of nature's balance through the participation of tribal people and specifically tribal women, is the aim of this policy. It includes management of the forests that comes under the state government, participation of centre in the same, conservation of wild animals, management of tribal people, to get control over forest enemies, forest related business etc. (Ref: National Forestry Action Programme, India by Ministry of Environment & Forests Government India).**British Policy:** Jungles were divided into two groups by the Indian Forest Act 1927. Reserved Forest and Protected Forest. Every activity is prohibited in the reserved forest. But various rights have been offered for the tribals in the protected forests. Wood from the forest can be used for the purpose of house building. Use of small jungle products in houses are permitted, but business of the same is restricted. British reserved the forests to fulfil their need of valuable wood for business. The number of tribals and their needs of forest products were very limited. But by this law British government restricted all the activities of tribals in the forests. Shifting cultivation was adivasis main mode of farming. So every year they would change the farming places. Such farming was prohibited by this law. Though these prohibitions were only applicable for reserved forests, it badly affected the tribals life. More than 100 revolts happened in next 125 years.   59.8 per cent of forest area comes under the tribal's districts, which means that most of the tribe's habitat comes under the rule of Indian Forest Department, where all the rights of these original localities have been removed. The same thing is being followed in the National Forest Policy 1952 and on the same basis in 1988.

139.   Three years table of Naxal activities in Chhatisgarh.

Type of Activity	2003	2004	Up to Oct 2005	Total
Killing	46	70	89	205
Attempted killings	101	175	187	463
Dacoity	62	60	112	234
Robbery	12	02	19	33
Arson	27	50	40	117
Beatings	10	08	03	21
Kidnappings	04	08	03	15
Others	45	50	53	148
	307	423	506	1236

Index

www.ingramcontent.com/pod-product-compliance
Lightning Source LLC
Chambersburg PA
CBHW070809300326
41914CB00078B/1919/J